Paradise Lost : BooksIX &

MIL

Paradise Lost

BOOKS IX AND X

MILTON

Paradise Lost

BOOKS IX AND X

EDITED BY

R. E. C. HOUGHTON

Emeritus Fellow and Tutor of St. Peter's College, Oxford

OXFORD UNIVERSITY PRESS

Oxford University Press, Walton Street, Oxford OX2 6DP

OXFORD NEW YORK TORONTO
DELHI BOMBAY CALCUTTA MADRAS KARACHI
PETALING JAYA SINGAPORE HONG KONG TOKYO
NAIROBI DAR ES SALAAM CAPE TOWN
MELBOURNE AUCKLAND

and associated companies in
BERLIN IBADAN

Oxford is a trade mark of Oxford University Press

First published 1969
Reprinted 1974, 1976, 1978, 1979, 1986, 1990

AN 5882
11/97
LIT

PRINTED IN HONG KONG

PREFACE

THE present edition of the crucial books of our greatest epic is the fruit of long devotion to Milton, and was prompted by dissatisfaction with some aspects of the only recent edition of these books known to the writer. The excellent edition of Verity at the turn of the century provides stiff fare for students less familiar with the Bible and the classics than were those of an earlier generation. The present work attempts to combine a fuller explanation of the language than has hitherto been offered (for which purpose it makes extensive use of the resources of the *Oxford English Dictionary*, not available to Verity), with such discussion of the subject-matter and of the poetic art as may assist a proper appreciation of a poet who has come to appear more remote and more difficult with the passage of time.

The arrangement follows the pattern set by the *New Clarendon Shakespeare* in the separation of glossarial footnotes (many of which are consciously designed for comparative beginners in Milton) from more general comment, and in the provision of a substantial selection of criticism. In the latter full account has been taken of the recent activity in Miltonic studies. This has been particularly evident in America; but the editor is proud to belong to the English Faculty which has produced within five years three books as good as those by Professor H. Gardner, C. Ricks, and D. Burden. The very valuable work of J. M. Evans on the background appeared after my edition was completed; but I am glad to have been able to incorporate a few additions suggested by it.

I should like to record my warm thanks to three colleagues—Dame Helen Gardner, the Rev. G. Midgley, and Mr. D. Burden—and also to Professor B. A. Wright (formerly of Southampton), for reading parts of my manuscript and making valuable suggestions.

R. E. C. HOUGHTON

CONTENTS

CONTENTS

INTRODUCTION

I. The Central Books of the Epic

'Milton's thought, when purged of its theology, does not exist'
(C. S. Lewis)

No one can understand *Paradise Lost*, or criticize it fairly, who does not know Books IX and X as well as he knows Books I and II, or III and IV. In fact for grasping the poem as a whole the former books are more important than the latter; and, if the earlier books are more brilliant, IX and X are more dramatic and more human. The ninth book is the pivotal book of Milton's epic. It occupies the place of the catastrophe which usually occurs in the third act of a tragedy—indeed Act III of the third draft for the proposed drama is entitled 'Lucifer contriving Adam's ruin'—and there is much in it to remind us of the dramatic form in which the author first intended to write. 'There is not an incident, hardly a line of the poem but leads backward or forward to those central lines in the Ninth Book:

> So saying, her rash hand in evil hour
> Forth reaching to the Fruit, she pluck'd, she eat:
> Earth felt the wound, and Nature from her seat
> Sighing through all her works gave signs of woe,
> That all was lost.'

So wrote Raleigh in 1900, and his interest in the epic was by no means theological; while his opinion has been echoed and developed by his latest successor in the Merton Professorship of English Literature at Oxford: 'Everything points to the Fall, leads to it and from it' (H. Gardner).

Even Tillyard, who tried somewhat perversely to transfer the crisis to Eve's speech at the end of Book X, admitted that at least you had to take the whole great area of IX and X for a watershed.

The structure of *Paradise Lost* can be viewed in several ways. If we consider the *location* of the action the movement is from Hell to Heaven (whence God sees Satan flying through Chaos), and then to Earth, where Satan lands at the end of Book III, and where, save for a brief return to Heaven and Hell in Book X, the rest of the action takes place. But between Satan's arrival in Eden for his first temptation of the sleeping Eve and the real temptation in Book IX there intervenes nearly one third of the poem, most of which is occupied by the discourse between Adam and Raphael, which relates events prior to the opening of the epic (V, 563 to the end of VIII). The purpose of Raphael's visit is both to relate the fall of the rebel angels and to teach Adam 'by terrible example the reward of disobedience'. Milton, like Homer and Virgil before him, chose to plunge *in medias res*, and turn back later to a retrospective narrative. The *chronological* arrangement of events in *Paradise Lost* therefore works out thus:

The 'Begetting' [i.e. Exaltation] of the Son and the Revolt of Satan (Book V).
The War in Heaven (Book VI).
The Creation of the World and of Man (Books VII–VIII).
The Council of the Devils in Hell (Books I–II).
The Council in Heaven and Satan's Journey to Earth (Books III–IV).
The Temptation and Fall of Man (Books IX–X).
The Future of the World (Books XI–XII).

Put more shortly the scheme is that of two Falls or Revolts, that of Satan and that of Man, the former prefiguring and partly causing the latter; or, put more optimistically, the pattern might be described as Fall, Creation, Fall, Atonement—the poem opening pessimistically in Hell but ending with modified hope.

The structure thus set out leaves in no doubt the main theme of the poem. It is announced in the opening lines. Just as the first line of the *Iliad* mentions the wrath of Achilles, and the first line of the *Aeneid* the exploits of Aeneas, so Milton proclaims his subject to be 'Mans First Disobedience' and its results, including the restorative work of Christ; but it is noticeable that here no name is mentioned, since it is the representative character of Adam's act (Adam in Hebrew means 'man') that gives universal interest to the theme ('Higher Argument', IX, 42). The idea that Satan is in any sense the hero of *Paradise Lost* seldom survives a reading of the *whole* poem; at least it cannot plausibly be maintained that the structure of the poem supports the notion that the author intended either our interest or our admiration to centre upon Satan. Indeed it may well have been to forestall the question that Milton put on his title page 'A Poem', and not, what his own nephew called *Paradise Lost*, 'An Heroic Poem'. Milton would not have disagreed with Dryden when he claimed that 'an Heroic Poem is certainly the greatest work of human nature', at least as far as literature was under consideration; so that to this 'kind', the epic, he was ready to devote his maturest powers, even if the chosen subject did not admit of a 'hero' of the old epic type. Nevertheless the title of the final draft in the Trinity MS. is '*Adam Unparadiz'd*', which is indicative of the author's view of his subject during the years of gestation; and in so far as the final form modifies the scheme of the drafts it is only in the direction of widening the theme to that of the cycles of the Miracle Plays, from the Creation of man to the Last Judgement.

THE MYTH OF THE FALL

The emphasis that has been here laid on the theme of *Paradise Lost* and the place of our books in its structure may well prompt the questions: Is the story true?, and, Did Milton believe it? Neither question admits of a simple answer. Few people today, and fewer still among qualified theologians, take the story of the Fall in Genesis as any more *literally* true than the account of Creation in seven days that precedes, or that of Noah's ark that follows it. Those who accept the Bible as the supreme authority in spiritual matters regard the first chapter of Genesis as an affirmation that God is the Creator of all things, and the third as an affirmation that man has grievously failed to fulfil the Divine intention for him, or his own highest possibilities, but that on the contrary he has brought upon himself many of the evils from which he suffers. ('Each of us has been the Adam of his own soul', as an Apocalyptic book, the Syrian Baruch, puts it.) Such people would regard the Fall story as a 'myth' enshrining a profound truth. The word does not by its origin (Greek *mythos* = 'word' or 'speech') suggest that the story is either true or false; so that it could conveniently be used by Plato for the stories concluding some of his dialogues to convey his beliefs and those of his master, Socrates, about the ultimate things. The word is also used for the traditional tales of all nations which cannot be traced to historical foundations; but the importance of the Platonic use is that, although the tale may have no historical basis, it is being employed to express an unshakeable conviction about things not capable of proof or disproof by the methods of natural science, such as the immortality of the soul. Similarly for the statement that Satan spoke to Eve in the form of a Serpent no one can produce the kind of evidence that can be used to substantiate the Norman Conquest, or the execution of Charles I; and few Christians any longer hold that this sort of truth is to be looked for in Genesis, any more than in the myths of Plato. Yet Plato's myths were not related for amusement, like fairy stories, but, like the parables of Jesus, in order to convey spiritual truth. To quote a distinguished modern theologian, writing in a different context:

'It was when Plato had to speak of things that could not be expressed in conceptual terms, things of which we cannot have knowledge in the exact sense, matters of temporal beginnings and ends, creation and final judgement, that he had recourse to myths. And without in anyway Platonizing, without forgetting for a moment that Christianity is an historical faith, which must take time seriously, must we not hold that the true theological use of myth is of that nature? I believe, for example, that Christianity can quite soundly speak of the myth of Creation and the myth of the Fall. The Creation and the Fall do not belong to history in the proper sense, and yet they are not purely timeless realities, out of all relation to time and history. And a Christian myth is a symbolical way of stating something which is neither history nor timeless reality, and which therefore cannot be stated either in purely historical or in purely conceptual terms' (D. M. Baillie).

It has been pointed out that Milton made considerable use of the most famous of Plato's myths—that of Er at the end of *The Republic*—in describing limbo and Satan's journey to Earth in Book III. It is not, however, being suggested here that the poet himself would have applied the word 'myth' to the story of *Paradise Lost* but that he may well have regarded it in the same light as myths were regarded by the only secular author whose volumes Milton ever called 'divine', that Plato whom Coleridge could dub 'Milton's darling'.

MILTON'S BELIEFS

To the question whether Milton himself believed literally in the story he embellished, it is impossible to give a conclusive answer. He was a man of immense learning and of the highest intelligence, but he was a man of his own times, a century hardly yet touched by the breath of Higher Criticism of the Bible. And we will put first one piece of evidence in favour of his having taken the Bible literally. A certain John Wilkins, brother-in-law of Oliver Cromwell, and later to be one of the founders of the Royal Society as well as Bishop of Chester, published before the middle of the seventeenth century two works on astronomy which showed that he did not regard himself as bound to accept the authority of the Bible in such matters. In the dialogue on astronomy which Milton puts into the mouths of Raphael and Adam he shows an acquaintance with the arguments of Wilkins, but prefers to follow his opponent, one Alexander Ross, in deprecating novel theories or further inquiries into what had not been revealed to man. But this is hardly enough to prove that Milton interpreted the Bible literally in matters that concerned man more intimately. He makes Raphael preface his account of the Fall with these words:

> what surmounts the reach
> Of human sense, I shall delineate so,
> By lik'ning spiritual to corporeal forms,
> As may express them best (V, 571-4).

It is true that he goes on to say that things in heaven may
be more like things on earth than we suppose, but it would
be very hard to believe that Milton conceived of a literal
war in heaven between God and the rebel angels, (any more
than did the writer of *A Treatise on Angels* in 1613, who
calls the fight 'spiritual'). He had to satisfy the epic tradition
by including warfare, and he could do so by expanding in
the most literal way a sentence in the book of Revelation:
'Now there was war in heaven'. Nor again is it credible
than an intelligent man could have understood literally the
bridge which he describes Sin and Death as building from
Hell to Earth (X, 293, etc.). This is surely a poetic embodi-
ment of the closer association between man and evil after
the Fall, just as the Spenser-like picture of Sin and her
brood (II, 765, etc.) is a poetic rendering of the biblical
words 'Sin, when it is finished, bringeth forth death'
(Jas. 1:15). When Milton is stating his beliefs in prose he
has little to say about Satan and his revolt (cf. *De Doctrina
Christiana*, I, 2); but he does there speak of God condes-
cending to accommodate himself to the capacities of man,
and such an idea could well cover those parts of the Bible
which simpler souls then, and even now, might take more
literally than he himself took them. This conception of
'accommodation' goes back to the early Fathers of the
Church. Origen, for example, says that when St. Paul
speaks of powers in heaven as 'bowing the knee to the
Father', we are not to suppose therefore that angels have
knees; and, nearer Milton's day, a divine whom he
respected more highly than patristic authorities, John

Calvin, made considerable use of the principle, as for example in explaining the 'last trump' (the trumpet which according to St. Paul was to herald the end of the world), or when he says of the damned: 'It is not a question of real fire . . . their anguish and torment are figuratively represented to us under corporal images'. So Milton certainly believed in God and the Devil; but we must not infer that he believed that either appeared in bodily form to Adam. There is at least one passage in *Paradise Lost* where God is *not* spoken of anthropomorphically:

> Boundless the Deep, because I am who fill
> Infinitude. (VII, 168–9)

A man who considered the Spirit in man a more certain guide than Scripture, and who was once bold enough to write that no Scripture could bind to the hurt of man, and yet who made the solemn asseveration that his matter was divinely inspired (as in the Prologue to Book IX) might perhaps, if pressed as to the truth of the story of the Fall, have replied somewhat as Wordsworth defended his introduction of pre-existence in his Immortality Ode: 'I took hold of the notion of pre-existence as having sufficient foundation in humanity for authorizing me to make for my purpose the best use of it I could as a poet.'

Paradise Lost is, more nearly than any other poem, the universal Christian epic. Milton 'has presented a total view of life that existed as a catholic faith in the Christendom of his day; and he presented it through a fable that grew up with that faith and expressed it exactly. The grand scheme of the poem is to tell the Christian story of God's purpose towards man' (B. A. Wright). The word 'catholic' is, of course, here used in its proper sense of 'universal', and not as a shortened form of Roman Catholic; and it is worth while insisting that to the ordinary reader Milton's beliefs will always have seemed those of orthodox Christianity, in fact just 'Christian'.

There are indeed a few points on which Milton's views were unorthodox, such as 'Mortalism' (see the Commentary at X, 792), and some tendency to Arianism and Calvinism; but these heresies are only likely to strike the more theologically minded. The common Christian will be more troubled by the general impression given of God. 'There are many of us', confessed William Temple once, in his presidential address to the English Association, 'for whom the verbal art of Milton is ruined by his bad theology.' In the only Christian poem of comparable stature we may regret the insistence on the tortures of the damned, especially when they include the poet's own enemies; but Dante, withdrawing the Almighty from sight, keeps Him the centre of Light and Love. Milton's God, like that of many Puritan writers, seems to have more of the traits of the Old Testament Jehovah than of 'the God and Father of our Lord, Jesus Christ'. Part of this impression is due to the necessity of a semi-dramatic presentation of Father and Son as separate characters, part to Milton's own stern temper (did he not live always in a 'stern taskmaster's eye'?), part to an explanation of the Atonement common at that time. Perhaps our age has learned more fully (at least in theory) the meaning of 'God is love'. At least we realize that a sound theology can never separate the Son from the Father, or God's justice from His mercy.

But many of those who feel that in the earlier books Milton is great in spite of his subject have carried over their uneasiness to the books dealing with the 'mortal sin original'—so slight a cause for so terrible a sequel? Earlier times seem to have perceived clearly enough that the sin of Adam and Eve consisted in that essence of all sin—disobedience to the known will of God. But obedience is an unpopular word in our day, and attempts have been made to show that Eve's sin consisted in curiosity, vanity, or mere gluttony. Calvin long ago pronounced it 'a childish opinion' to regard the original sin as intemperance. A recent critic, E. M. Tillyard, proposed 'mental triviality' as the sin of Eve, but later withdrew his suggestion (as T. S. Eliot withdrew most of *his* strictures on Milton's style), and confessed that he 'had made too little of the disobedience' in his *Milton*. Others have found the traditional (not biblical) apple a cause of mirth. But it may be pointed out that something simple, concrete, and unambiguous must be presented as a test case of man's duty towards God, and the prohibition to touch the fruit of a tree is something that any child can grasp; while at the same time a tree has deep and mysterious associations in folklore, which could enable it, as the tree of life or of knowledge, to symbolize man's self-sufficiency, his claim to be the sole judge of his own actions. 'The uneaten apple is the pledge and sign of man's obedience to God, the token that all is His. . . . The command that is transgressed must be an irrational one in order that it may be purely religious' (H. Gardner). Milton himself explains this in his prose treatise: 'The tree of the knowledge of good and evil . . . was a pledge, as it were the memorial of obedience. It was called the tree of the knowledge of good and evil from the event; for since Adam tasted it we not only know evil, but we know good only by means of evil' (cf. IX, 752). Satan tempts Eve with the thought that she and Adam should be 'as Gods , and in so doing makes the cause of their fall the same as his own. Pride, not Lust, was always accounted the chief of the

seven deadly sins, because in the final analysis it is Pride
that prevents man admitting that there is any authority
outside himself, any other criterion of good and evil, right
or wrong than his own will. So, for Donne, 'Pride includes
all sins'.

A recent critic of Milton's God complains that God could
have, and therefore should have, prevented the Fall: 'God
cheats his own troops to make certain that the Fall occurs',
by not letting them capture Satan at the end of Book IV.
The only answer to this is that without temptation and the
possibility of failure no freedom would exist, and that God
wanted his creatures to serve Him freely, and that not as a
taskmaster (in spite of the sonnet), but in the glad obedience
expressed by Abdiel:

> freely we serve
> Because we freely love, as in our will
> To love or not; in this we stand or fall. (V, 538)

But, however this may be, *Paradise Lost* does not end with
the Fall. It is almost as much concerned with the triumph
of grace as with man's sin and guilt; and, just as the earlier
books set the scene for the climax, so the last books give
the sequel, and are a necessary part of the whole fate of
mankind. When the poet first announced his subject, he
did not end at

> that Forbidden Tree, whose mortal taste
> Brought Death into the World, and all our woe,

but continued

> With loss of *Eden*, till one greater Man
> Restore us, and regain the blissful Seat;

and, although Milton was yet to write a 'short epic' in
which Christ would overcome the Tempter who had

defeated Adam, and to call it *Paradise Regained*, he had already brought into his longer epic the essential parts of the Christian scheme of salvation. It must be admitted that the young Milton had shown by that frigid fragment *The Passion*, as contrasted with the *Nativity Ode*, how much less congenial to him was the central theme of the Gospels than that with which three of them open; but in *Paradise Lost* he does at least recognize in the Son that supremacy of love which his treatment of the Father almost obscures:

> In him all his Father shon
> Substantially exprest, and in his face
> Divine compassion visibly appeerd,
> Love without end, and without measure Grace;

and he celebrates that love in language which is, for Milton, almost ecstatic:

> O unexampl'd love,
> Love nowhere to be found less than Divine!
> Hail Son of God, Saviour of Men, thy Name
> Shall be the copious matter of my Song
> Henceforth, and never shall my Harp thy praise
> Forget, nor from thy Fathers praise disjoin.
>
> (III, 139–42 and 411–15)

There is a painting by Giovanni di Paolo in the National Gallery of Washington which well illustrates the connection of thought in the later books of the epic. The subject is The Annunciation, which occupies the centre of the picture, while on its left Adam and Eve are shown being cast out of Paradise by an angel. It was not within the scope of Milton's epic, even had it been within his power, to display this love of God, heralded in the Annunciation and fulfilled in the Incarnation, with the tenderness of a Herbert or the ardour of a Crashaw. In his own *Nativity*

Ode Mercy was set between Justice and Truth, but in *Paradise Lost* it is difficult to avoid feeling the opposition of Mercy and Justice. The poet may not have intended to give the impression of a merciful Christ propitiating an angry Almighty, or of the suffering Son reconciling his Father to man, rather than man to God; but the interpretation of the Cross current in both Roman and Protestant theology at that time was too legalistic to satisfy later generations. This it is, more than anything else, that has alienated Christian readers in modern times. But it is the purpose of Books XI and XII to give repentant Adam hope for his descendants in the light of the future Messiah; and thus they are a necessary part of a total Christian epic. 'Man, damned for imputed sin, is saved, *if he will*, by imputed virtue' was the view of Milton and most Protestants of his time. In the second paragraph of Book XI the Son presents the Father with the fruits of Adam and Eve's penitence, and pleads his own merit for the reconciliation of God and man:

> Accept me, and in mee from these receive
> The smell of peace toward Mankinde, let him live
> Before thee reconcil'd, . . . till Death . . .
> To better life shall yield him, where with me
> All my redeem'd may dwell in joy and bliss,
> Made one with me as I with thee am one.

Paradise Lost is indeed 'a poem with no relish of damnation in it' (Frye).

Milton again recurs to the work of Christ in his sketch of the future history of the world in the middle of the last book of the poem. By 'suffering death', the penalty due to Adam's transgressions,

> The Law of God exact he shall fulfil
> Both by obedience and by love, though love

> Alone fulfil the Law . . . thy punishment
> He shall endure by coming in the Flesh
> To a reproachful life and cursed death,
> Proclaiming Life to all who shall believe
> In his redemption. (XII, 402–8)

After a long passage on the redemption wrought by Christ, Adam hails the display of love as great enough to make him doubt whether he should even repent of a sin

> That all this good of evil shall produce
> And evil turn to good.

We have here a favourite theme of medieval theology, concisely expressed in the term *Felix Culpa*, the Fortunate Fall, and popularly in the carol 'Adam lay y-bounden' ('Blesséd be the time That apple taken was'). A great English archbishop of modern times could write: 'I should not hesitate to say that a sinful world redeemed by such a sacrifice as the Crucifixion of Christ is better than a world that had never sinned' (W. Temple). But even if Milton himself believed in a 'Fortunate Fall', as he appears to do in his *Christian Doctrine* (I, 14), though leaving the question open in the poem (XII, 575–87), that was by no means the same thing as regarding the Fall as a negligible matter. For, in the end, the Fall is the representation in a myth of a reality acknowledged by Christian and Pagan alike:

> Video meliora proboque,
> Deteriora sequor (Ovid),

'The good that I would I do not: but the evil that I would not that I do' (Rom. 8:19). St. Paul's words are almost echoed in Epictetus, while Seneca is even sterner: *Tollite excusationes; nemo peccat invitus*, away with excuses! No man sins except by his own consent.

Paradise Lost is no monument to dead ideas, but topical enough for our day. Men look round at the state into which civilization has fallen and its imminent risk of greater dissolution, and ask 'why?'. Milton has dramatized the answer of orthodox Christianity—(here entirely at one with Dante's emphasis)—that the cause is man's rebellion against God, to which most of the evils and dangers surrounding us are directly due, since God does not prevent the results of man's abuse of his free will. In Adam all fell, because, like Adam, we so constantly disobey the Divine will. The apple may be mythology, but the Fall is fact; for its essence is disobedience. So Adam ends the dramatic epic with a confession near akin to the familiar doctrine of Aeschylean tragedy that learning comes by suffering:

> Henceforth I learn that to obey is best
> And love with fear the only God. (XII, 560–1)

Obedience and Love are, in Milton's view, the source of all human good.

MILTON THE POET

'I am persuaded', wrote Luther in a letter of 1523, 'that without skill in literature genuine theology cannot stand.' It is just because of Milton's skill in literature that so much of this introduction has been concerned with his theology. For the reaction against the position universally conceded to Milton down to the end of the nineteenth century is at least as much due to dislike of the poet's handling of ultimate questions as to anything else—as is illustrated by such vague objections as 'Milton is unsatisfactory', or he is 'a bad man'. It therefore seemed important in introducing these two books to approach them from a point of view ignored in previous editions, and to try and show that the myth adopted embodies an experience and a conviction shared by many men; so that even those to whom they are alien may at least understand the background and intention of the epic. But the beliefs of the author should not in any case prevent the appreciation of his poetry. It is not usually objected to Homer or Virgil that their theology is untenable; and perhaps we only object to Milton's because it touches us more nearly. A greater obstacle to the appreciation of Milton today would seem to lie in the need for careful and repeated reading, not once for the sound and once for the sense, but many times for the combined effect. The justification of a commentary as full as that here provided can only lie in increasing the enjoyment that fuller understanding brings. We may well apply to *Paradise Lost* what the old Scottish poet Gavin Douglas said of the Virgil he was translating into English: 'Well at ane blenk slee poetry not ta'en is' (good poetry is not grasped at one look). Milton is one of the greatest artists in the world, perhaps only equalled in his combination of architectural power and poetic style by Virgil and Dante. *Paradise Lost* has recently been described by a far from traditional critic as 'perhaps the richest and most intricately beautiful poem in the world' (Kermode); and this very richness and intricacy has provoked some of the strictures passed in this century upon Milton's style. It is the less necessary to reply to them here because this has been so well done recently by C. Ricks in *Milton's Grand Style*, and also because these two books are largely composed in a more direct and concrete style than much of the poem. It will suffice to note briefly special features of the books we are introducing.

During the years when Milton was intending to write a

drama on the Fall he made no less than four drafts, which
are preserved for us in the Trinity Manuscript. The centre
of the play's action would have been the substance of
Books IX and X. But in the end we have, instead of what
might have been the least dramatic of dramas, the most
dramatic of epics. The whole of *Paradise Lost* has a larger
proportion of speeches and soliloquies than other epics, but
the speeches interchanged between Satan and Eve and
between Adam and Eve are shorter and more numerous
than other speeches, such as Raphael's, and they are also
far more charged with emotion, and therefore more
dramatic. Even Satan's long soliloquy (IX, 99–178) finds
its closest parallels in the prologues to some plays of
Milton's favourite Greek dramatist, Euripides (e.g. that
spoken by Dionysus in the *Bacchae*), and in Shakespeare
(e.g. Richard III and Macbeth soliloquizing); while another
of Satan's soliloquies, his address to the Sun (IV, 32–69) was
actually said by Milton's nephew, Phillips, to have been
intended to open a drama. Again, Adam is faced with a
tragic dilemma not unlike that of Antigone in the play of
Sophocles, when he has to choose between loyalty to God
or his wife. And, finally, the quiet ending of Book X, like
that of the whole poem later, resembles the end of Greek
tragedies, and of his own imitation, yet to be written, with
its 'calm of mind, all passion spent'.

The 'grand style' which has been especially associated
with Milton since Arnold used the term, is varied in these
books more than elsewhere in two directions: by simpler
vocabulary and by looser syntax. The former takes us
back to *Comus*, the latter points forward to *Samson
Agonistes*. The following lines smack of the stage:

> Of these the vigilance
> I dread, and to elude, thus wrapt in mist

> Of midnight vapor glide obscure, and prie
> In every Bush and Brake, where hap may finde
> The Serpent sleeping, in whose mazie folds
> To hide me and the dark intent I bring (IX, 157–62);

while the longer passage from 479 to 493 of the same book, as Satan prepares to approach Eve, reproduces the grammar of a man thinking aloud. Further remarks on variations of style will be found in the Commentary from time to time. Style is necessarily more difficult to pin down than subject matter; for it is more a case of individual impression, and the power to discriminate only comes from experience. But it is, in the end, the power and charm of style which will keep *Paradise Lost* alive for all lovers of poetry. 'His art', as G. M. Hopkins wrote, 'is incomparable.' It is this that most differentiates Milton from that one of his predecessors to whose matter he is nearest in these books, Sylvester, whose translation of Du Bartas with the title *The Divine Works and Days* had appeared at the beginning of the century (see Appendix II). For when we speak of style in the fullest sense we do not mean only vocabulary or syntax or the various figures of speech to which rhetoricians have assigned names, but something going beyond all these, namely the writer's power to convey to us his own mind: 'The style is the man.' T. S. Eliot admitted antipathy to the man, and Middleton Murry dubbed him 'a bad man of a very particular kind'. Others, without denying an occasional bitterness and harshness in Milton, might prefer to echo Coleridge: 'He was, as every great poet has ever been, a good man', and to find in these two books strong proof of Milton's own 'plain, heroic, magnitude of mind'.

PARADISE LOST

BOOK IX

THE ARGUMENT

SATAN *having compast the Earth, with meditated guile returns as a mist by Night into Paradise, enters into the Serpent sleeping. Adam and Eve in the Morning go forth to thir labours, which Eve proposes to divide in several places, each labouring apart: Adam consents not, alledging the danger, lest that Enemy, of whom they were forewarnd, should attempt her found alone: Eve loath to be thought not circumspect or firm enough, urges her going apart, the rather desirous to make trial of her strength; Adam at last yields: The Serpent finds her alone; his suttle approach, first gazing, then speaking, with much flattery extolling Eve above all other Creatures. Eve wondring to hear the Serpent speak, asks how he attaind to human speech and such understanding not till now; the Serpent answers, that by tasting of a certain Tree in the Garden he attaind both to Speech and Reason, till then void of both: Eve requires him to bring her to that Tree, and finds it to be the Tree of Knowledge forbidd'n: The Serpent now grown bolder, with many wiles and arguments induces her at length to eat; she pleas'd with the taste deliberates a while whether to impart thereof to Adam or not, at last brings him of the Fruit, relates what perswaded her to eat thereof: Adam at first amaz'd, but perceiving her lost, resolves through vehemence of love to perish with her; and extenuating the trespass, eats also of the Fruit; The Effects thereof in them both; they seek to cover thir nakedness; then fall to variance and accusation of one another.*

No more of talk where God or Angel Guest
With Man, as with his Friend, familiar us'd
To sit indulgent, and with him partake
Rural repast, permitting him the while
Venial discourse unblam'd: I now must change   5
Those Notes to Tragic; foul distrust, and breach
Disloyal on the part of Man, revolt,
And disobedience: On the part of Heav'n
Now alienated, distance and distaste,
Anger and just rebuke, and judgement giv'n,   10
That brought into this World a world of woe,
Sin and her shadow Death, and Miserie
Deaths Harbinger: Sad task, yet argument
Not less but more Heroic then the wrauth
Of stern *Achilles* on his Foe persu'd   15
Thrice Fugitive about *Troy* Wall; or rage
Of *Turnus* for *Lavinia* disespous'd,
Or *Neptun*'s ire or *Juno*'s, that so long

N.B. Words used in a sense still usual, to be found in one-volume dictionaries (e.g. the *Concise Oxford*), are not normally glossed in these footnotes.

1 *No more*, there can be, or will be, no more.   *where*, in which.

2 *familiar* can be taken *both* adjectivally with the preceding words *and* adverbially with the following words.

3 *indulgent*, doing a favour, gracious to man.

5 *Venial*, pardonable (because) permitted.

6 *Those Notes*, i.e. the tone implied by such familiarity.   *Tragic notes*, to which the following words are in apposition.   *breach*, breaking of trust and obedience.

10 *giv'n*, pronounced.

12 *her shadow*, because Death always accompanies Sin.   *Miserie*, pain and sickness.

13 *Harbinger*, herald, preceder.   *Sad task*, to relate which will be a sad task.   *argument*, subject (Lat. *argumentum*); cf. 28.

15 *his Foe*, i.e. Hector.

17 *disespous'd*, taken away from marriage with himself.

Perplexd the *Greek* and *Cytherea*'s Son;
If answerable stile I can obtaine   20
Of my Celestial Patroness, who deignes
Her nightly visitation unimplor'd,
And dictates to me slumbring, or inspires
Easie my unpremeditated Verse:
Since first this Subject for Heroic Song   25
Pleas'd me long choosing, and beginning late;
Not sedulous by Nature to indite
Warrs, hitherto the onely Argument
Heroic deemd, chief maistrie to dissect
With long and tedious havoc fabl'd Knights   30
In Battels feignd; the better fortitude
Of Patience and Heroic Martyrdom
Unsung; or to describe Races and Games,
Or tilting Furniture, emblazond Shields,
Impreses quaint, Caparisons and Steeds;   35

19 *Perplexd*, tormented (not only in mind).   *the Greek*, i.e. Odysseus
Cytherea's son, i.e. Aeneas; scan Cÿthĕrēă.

20 *answerable*, appropriate, corresponding to the dignity of the subject.

21 *my Celestial Patroness*, Urania, the 'heavenly Muse' of I, 6, III, 19,
and VII, 1-12. (Urania was the classical muse of astronomy—Gk. *ouranos* =
heaven—but Milton invokes 'the meaning not the name', VII, 5.)

24 *Easie*, without any effort on my part.

25 *Since*, ever since (syntactically 5-41 form one sentence).

27 *sedulous*, careful, i.e. (here) anxious.   *indite*, compose, write
poetry about.

29 *chief maistrie to dissect*, it being considered the highest skill in poetry to
describe in detail (mastery = the skill of a master of an art).

30 *With . . . havoc*, with all the confusion involved.   *fabl'd*, told in
fables, so *both* famous *and* fictitious.

31-3 *the better . . . Unsung* the nobler endurance . . . being left unsung;
the words are a parenthesis in a construction resembling the Latin ablative
absolute.

34 *tilting Furniture*, the apparatus of jousts.   *emblazond*, adorned with
heraldic devices.

35 *Impreses* (accent on first *or* second syllable), crests or devices on
shields, etc. Cf. 'Raz'd out my impress, leaving me no sign' (*Richard II*,
III, i, 25).   *quaint*, elaborate.   *Caparisons*, horses' trappings.

Bases and tinsel Trappings, gorgious Knights
At Joust and Torneament; then marshald Feast
Serv'd up in Hall with Sewers, and Seneshals;
The skill of Artifice or Office mean,
Not that which justly gives Heroic name   40
To Person or to Poem. Mee of these
Nor skilld nor studious, higher Argument
Remaines, sufficient of it self to raise
That name, unless an age too late, or cold
Climat, or Years damp my intended wing   45
Deprest; and much they may, if all be mine,
Not Hers who brings it nightly to my Ear.

　　The Sun was sunk, and after him the Starr
Of *Hesperus*, whose Office is to bring
Twilight upon the Earth, short Arbiter   50
Twixt Day and Night, and now from end to end
Nights Hemisphere had veild th' Horizon round:
When *Satan* who late fled before the threats

36 *Bases*, skirts or kilts that could be mailed (a word used by Sidney and Spenser).　　*tinsel Trappings*, bright equipment (the phrase is in *F.Q.* III, i, 15).　　*gorgious*, magnificent (the spelling is due to derivation from Old French).

37 *marshald*, arranged by marshals.

38 *Sewers*, attendants who set the tables and the guests.　　*Seneshals*, household stewards.

39 'all of which are matters of petty skill and menial tasks', in apposition to 33–8.

41–3 *Mee ... Remaines*, a nobler subject awaits me who am not learned in nor concerned with chivalry ('studious of' is a Latinism).

43–4 *raise That name*, lift up, create the name 'heroic' for my poem.

44 *too late*, i.e. in the world's history.

45–6 *damp ... Deprest*, i.e. damp, and so keep down to earth a poetic flight intended to soar ('above th'Aonian mount', I, 15).

50 *Arbiter*, perhaps here 'bridging the gap'; Sidney had called the sun at the equinox 'indifferent arbiter between the night and day', though this preserved the sense of 'judge' more than Milton does here.

52 *Nights*, Night's; so 'Mans' in 56, etc.

Of *Gabriel* out of *Eden*, now improv'd
In meditated fraud and malice, bent   55
On Mans destruction, maugre what might hap
Of heavier on himself, fearless returnd.
By Night he fled, and at Midnight returnd
From compassing the Earth, cautious of day,
Since *Uriel* Regent of the Sun descri'd   60
His entrance, and forewarnd the Cherubim
That kept thir watch; thence full of anguish driv'n,
The space of sev'n continu'd Nights he rode
With darkness, thrice the Equinoctial Line
He circl'd, four times crossd the Carr of Night   65
From Pole to Pole, traversing each Colure;
On th' eighth returnd, and on the Coast averse
From entrance or Cherubic Watch, by stealth
Found unsuspected way. There was a place,
Now not, though Sin, not Time, first wraught the
     change,   70

54-5 Satan had overheard Adam and Eve speaking about the forbidden
Tree (IV, 411-39), and could lay his plans accordingly.   *fraud*, deceit.

56 *maugre*, in spite of (Fr. *malgré*).   *hap*, fall.

56-7 *what . . . Of heavier*, whatever heavier punishment. (This 'partitive
genitive' is a direct imitation of Gr. and Lat. use; e.g. *aliquid amari*=
something of bitter=some bitterness.)

59 *compassing*, encircling; the word used by Sylvester too in para-
phrasing Job 1:7.   *cautious of day*, taking precautions against (showing
himself by) daylight.

60-2 See IV, 549, etc.

61 *Cherubim* is plural.

62 *driv'n*, into headlong motion by his anguish.

63-6 i.e. Satan spent three nights going round the world at the Equator
from East to West, and four going round from North to South.   *Col-
ures* were imaginary lines connecting the two poles.   *the Carr of Night*,
the chariot of Night (personified) which went from West to East, as the
Sun in his chariot went from East to West.

67 *averse*, turned away from, opposite to.

70 *Now not*, now no longer existing.

Where *Tigris* at the foot of Paradise
Into a Gulf shot under ground, till part
Rose up a Fountain by the Tree of Life;
In with the River sunk, and with it rose
Satan involv'd in rising Mist, then sought   75
Where to lie hid; Sea he had searcht and Land
From *Eden* over *Pontus*, and the Poole
Mæotis, up beyond the River *Ob*;
Downward as farr Antartic; and in length
West from *Orontes* to the Ocean barrd   80
At *Darien*, thence to the Land where flowes
Ganges and *Indus:* thus the Orb he roamd
With narrow search; and with inspection deep
Considerd every Creature, which of all
Most opportune might serve his Wiles, and found   85
The Serpent suttl'st Beast of all the Field.
Him after long debate, irresolute
Of thoughts revolv'd, his final sentence chose
Fit Vessel, fittest Imp of fraud, in whom

71 *Tigris*, the great river that with the Euphrates enclosed Mesopotamia. It was taken to be the river which 'went out of Eden' (Gen. 2:10), to spring up in four streams in Paradise.

74 *sunk*, sank (verb, not participle only, as now).

79 *Antartic*, to the South.

80–1 *barrd at Darien*, blocked by the isthmus of Panama.

82 *Orb*, world (Lat. *orbis terrarum*).

83 *narrow*, close.

84 *which*, to see which.

85 *Most opportune*, being most suitable; at the same time the adjective may be taken adverbially, as with 'familiar' (2).

86 *suttl'st*, to be the subtlest (see Gen. 3:1).

87–8 'His final decision, after turning over in his mind various considerations and being uncertain, settled upon the serpent as an appropriate instrument for his purpose.'

89 *Imp*, child, offspring (especially a child of the devil, but often applied humorously).

To enter, and his dark suggestions hide   90
From sharpest sight: for in the wilie Snake,
Whatever sleights none would suspicious mark,
As from his wit and native suttletie
Proceeding, which in other Beasts observ'd
Doubt might beget of Diabolic pow'r   95
Active within beyond the sense of brute.
Thus he resolv'd, but first from inward griefe
His bursting passion into plaints thus pourd.

    O Earth, how like to Heav'n, if not preferrd
More justly, Seat worthier of Gods, as built   100
With second thoughts, reforming what was old!
For what God after better worse would build?
Terrestrial Heav'n, danc't round by other Heav'ns
That shine, yet bear thir bright officious Lamps,
Light above Light, for thee alone, as seems,   105
In thee concentring all thir precious beams
Of sacred influence: as God in Heav'n
Is Center, yet extends to all, so thou
Centring receav'st from all those Orbs; in thee,
Not in themselves, all thir known vertue appeers   110
Productive in Herb, Plant, and nobler birth

90 *suggestions*, temptations.
92 'Whatever sleights were seen, no one would note them as suspicious.'
94–5 i.e. which, if observed in other beasts, might suggest devilish power.
99–100 *if not . . . justly*, if it does not deserve to be preferred to heaven.
100 *Gods* probably means angels here, as in 164, but might include God.
103 *Terrestrial Heav'n*, a heaven on earth (in loose apposition to 'Earth'. 99). *Heav'ns* here apparently = heavenly bodies, stars.
104 *officious*, serviceable (as in VIII, 99).
106 *in thee concentring*, directing upon thee ('Earth') as centre.
107 *sacred*, since 'God is Light' (III, 1).
109 *Centring*, remaining in the centre.
110 *vertue*, influence, power; the last syllable is elided metrically.

Of Creatures animate with gradual life
Of Growth, Sense, Reason, all summd up in Man.
With what delight could I have walkt thee round,
If I could joy in aught, sweet interchange   115
Of Hill and Vallie, Rivers, Woods and Plaines,
Now Land, now Sea, and Shores with Forrest crownd,
Rocks, Dens, and Caves; but I in none of these
Find place or refuge; and the more I see
Pleasures about me, so much more I feel   120
Torment within me, as from the hateful siege
Of contraries; all good to mee becomes
Bane, and in Heav'n much worse would be my state.
But neither here seek I, no nor in Heav'n
To dwell, unless by maistring Heav'ns Supreame;   125
Nor hope to be my self less miserable
By what I seek, but others to make such
As I, though thereby worse to me redound:
For onely in destroying I finde ease
To my relentless thoughts; and him destroyd,   130
Or won to what may work his utter loss,
For whom all this was made, all this will soon

112 *gradual life*, life in its various degrees (of vegetable, animal, rational).

113 *Sense*, feeling.   *Reason*, understanding; cf. 11.1130.

114 *thee round*, round thee (an order which would have thrown too much emphasis on 'thee'.)

115 *sweet interchange* (in loose apposition to 'thee') a walk which would have yielded a sweet variety.

119 *place*, a suitable place to stay.

121-2 *from the hateful siege Of contraries*, because I am besieged by contrary feelings; *or* (if 'siege' is taken in the archaic sense of 'seat') as being the hateful seat of conflicting emotions.

123 *bane*, evil, a curse (that which causes ruin or woe).

125 *Heav'ns Supreame*, God.

128 *to me redound*, come back upon me.

130 *him destroyd*, when he (man) has been destroyed. For construction cf. 31-3.

Follow, as to him linkt in weal or woe:
In wo then; that destruction wide may range:
To mee shall be the glorie sole among   135
Th' infernal Powers, in one day to have marrd
What hee *Almightie* stil'd, six Nights and Days
Continu'd making, and who knows how long
Before had bin contriving, though perhaps
Not longer then since I in one Night freed   140
From servitude inglorious welnigh half
Th' Angelic Name, and thinner left the throng
Of his adorers: hee to be aveng'd,
And to repaire his numbers thus impaird,
Whether such vertue spent of old now faild   145
More Angels to Create, if they at least
Are his Created, or to spite us more,
Determind to advance into our room
A Creature formd of Earth, and him endow,
Exalted from so base original,   150
With Heav'nly spoils, our spoils: What he decreed
He effected; Man he made, and for him built
Magnificent this World, and Earth his seat,
Him Lord pronounc'd, and, O indignitie!
Subjected to his service Angel wings,   155

133 *Follow*, to destruction; see 782–4 and X, 651 etc.
134 *In wo then*, let it be in woe.   *wide*, widely (but cf. 'familiar', 2).
137 *hee Almightie stil'd*, he who is called the Almighty.
140 *then since*, than from the day when.
142 *th' Angelic Name*, the race of angels (see *O.E.D.* 'name' II, 4b).
145 *vertue*, power.
150 *base original*, lowly origin.
151 *our spoils*, the rank of which he had despoiled us.
152 The first foot is 'He effect' slurred.
153 *Magnificent*, gains additional force by its predicative position, as well as by coming first in the line.
155 *Angel wings*, the wings of angels, i.e. winged angels.

And flaming Ministers to watch and tend
Thir earthie Charge: Of these the vigilance
I dread, and to elude, thus wrapt in mist
Of midnight vapor glide obscure, and prie
In every Bush and Brake, where hap may finde   160
The Serpent sleeping, in whose mazie foulds
To hide me, and the dark intent I bring.
O foul descent! that I who erst contended
With Gods to sit the highest, am now constraind
Into a Beast, and mixt with bestial slime,   165
This essence to incarnate and imbrute,
That to the highth of Deitie aspir'd;
But what will not Ambition and Revenge
Descend to? who aspires must down as low
As high he soard, obnoxious first or last   170
To basest things. Revenge, at first though sweet,
Bitter ere long back on it self recoiles;
Let it; I reck not, so it light well aimd,
Since higher I fall short, on him who next
Provokes my envie, this new Favorite   175
Of Heav'n, this Man of Clay, Son of despite,

156 *flaming Ministers*, radiant servants, particularly the 'Flaming Cherubim' (VI, 102); cf.' Who maketh his angels spirits and his ministers a flame of fire' (Heb. 1:7).

157 *earthie*, earthly, and also humble; cf. 149.

160 *hap*, chance.

161–2 Cf. 83–6.

164–6 *constraind* has the double sense of (1) 'compressed' literally, and (2) forced, with 'to incarnate'.

166 'to turn my spiritual being into the fleshly substance of man and beast' (Lat. *caro* flesh, and verb *incarnare*).

169 *down*, descend (sc. 'go'; *O.E.D.* 'down', VI).

170 *obnoxious*, liable to, at the mercy of (Latinism).

174 *higher*, aiming higher.   *next*, to God.

176 *Son of despite*, born from God's scorn of us (but the idiom is a Hebraism; e.g. 'sons of folly'=fools).

Whom us the more to spite his Maker rais'd
From dust: spite then with spite is best repaid.
    So saying, through each Thicket Danck or Drie,
Like a black mist low creeping, he held on   180
His midnight search, where soonest he might finde
The Serpent: him fast sleeping soon he found
In Labyrinth of many a round self-rowld,
His head the midst, well stor'd with suttle wiles:
Not yet in horrid Shade or dismal Den,   185
Nor nocent yet, but on the grassie Herbe
Fearless unfeard he slept: in at his Mouth
The Devil enterd, and his brutal sense,
In heart or head, possessing soon inspir'd
With act intelligential; but his sleep   190
Disturbd not, waiting close th' approach of Morn.
Now whenas sacred Light began to dawne
In *Eden* on the humid Flours, that breath'd
Thir morning Incense, when all things that breathe,
From th' Earths great Altar send up silent praise   195
To the Creator, and his Nostrils fill
With grateful Smell, forth came the human pair

179 *Danck*, dank, wet (a word of variable spelling and uncertain derivation).

181 *where*, looking to see where (implied by 'search').

184 *the midst*, in the middle (of his coils).

186 *Nor* Ed. 2: *Not* Ed. 1.   *nocent*, harmful (Lat. *noceo*), i.e. poisonous.   *grassie Herbe* is Virgil's *graminis herbam* = herb consisting of grass.

187 *Fearless* of man.   *unfeard*, by man or other animals.

188 *brutal*, brutish, of a brute or animal.

190 *act intelligential*, mental activity; the third or rational stage of 113.

191 *close*, in hiding, and perhaps also 'attentively' as in 'close reading' (a sense found as early as 1662).

192 *sacred*, cf. 107.

193 *breath'd*, breathed out, exhaled (one use of Lat. *spirare*; already found in Spenser).

197 *grateful*, pleasing.

And joind thir vocal Worship to the Quire
Of Creatures wanting voice; that done, partake
The season, prime for sweetest Sents and Aires;   200
Then commune how that day they best may ply
Thir growing work: for much thir work outgrew
The hands dispatch of two Gardning so wide.
And *Eve* first to her Husband thus began.

    Adam, well may we labour still to dress   205
This Garden, still to tend Plant, Herb and Flour,
Our pleasant task enjoind, but till more hands
Aid us, the work under our labour grows,
Luxurious by restraint; what we by day
Lop overgrown, or prune, or prop, or bind,   210
One night or two with wanton growth derides,
Tending to wilde. Thou therefore now advise
Or hear what to my mind first thoughts present:
Let us divide our labours, thou where choice
Leads thee, or where most needs, whether to wind   215
The Woodbine round this Arbour, or direct

198 *Quire*, the usual spelling till the end of the seventeenth century in spite of the derivation from Lat. *chorus* and Gk. *choros*.

199 *wanting*, lacking.   *that done*, an absolute construction (*eo facto*). *partake*, share in enjoying.

200 *The season*, the time of day (cf. *O.E.D.* s.v. 12 'a particular time'); *or* just the time of year, i.e. spring, since it was always spring in Paradise (IV, 268).   *prime*, first, best.   *Sents*, scents; Milton retains the older spelling which showed the derivation from Lat. *sentire*.

201 *commune*, talk over.

203 *wide*, widely, over so large an area (Milton never uses 'widely').

205 *still*, continually (as often in Shakespeare).   *dress*, cultivate (Gen. 2:15).   207 *enjoind*, laid upon us (by God).

208-9 i.e. our pruning only serves to strengthen the growth.   *Luxurious*, luxuriant; the word, like 'wanton' (211), is here innocent, but has suggestive overtones (see I, 498, etc.).

212 *wilde*, wildness; adjective used as noun, as in Lat. and Gr. in neuter.

215 *most needs*, there is most need. (This use would appear to be that of *O.E.D.* under *need* vb. II, 4 (archaic).)

The clasping Ivie where to climb, while I
In yonder Spring of Roses intermixt
With Myrtle, find what to redress till Noon:
For while so near each other thus all day   220
Our task we choose, what wonder if so near
Looks intervene and smiles, or object new
Casual discourse draw on, which intermits
Our dayes work brought to little, though begun
Early, and th' hour of Supper comes unearnd.   225
　　To whom mild answer *Adam* thus returnd.
Sole *Eve*, Associat sole, to me beyond
Compare above all living Creatures deare,
Well hast thou motiond, well thy thoughts imployd
How we might best fulfill the work which here   230
God hath assign'd us, nor of me shalt pass
Unprais'd: for nothing lovelier can be found
In Woman, then to studie houshold good,
And good works in her Husband to promote.
Yet not so strictly hath our Lord impos'd   235
Labour, as to debarr us when we need
Refreshment, whether food, or talk between,
Food of the mind, or this sweet intercourse
Of looks and smiles, for smiles from Reason flow,

218 *Spring*, 'a copse, grove or wood consisting of young trees springing
up naturally . . . now dialectical [but] frequent in 16th and 17th centuries'
(*O.E.D.*).
219 *redress*, prop up, set right.
220 *so near*, when we are so near one another (compressed syntax).
223 *intermits*, interrupts.
224 *brought to little*, i.e. by this interruption.
227 *Sole Eve*, the one and only woman.
228 *Compare*, comparison (but originally from 'compeer' = equal).
229 *motiond*, proposed (as the noun is still used).
237 *between*, in intervals of work.
239 *Reason*, i.e. the great prerogative of man, intelligence (cf. 113).
Animals can scarcely be said to smile!

To brute deni'd, and are of Love the food,   240
Love not the lowest end of human life.
For not to irksom toile, but to delight
He made us, and delight to Reason joind.
These paths and Bowers doubt not but our joint hands
Will keep from Wilderness with ease, as wide   245
As we need walk, till younger hands ere long
Assist us: But if much converse perhaps
Thee satiate, to short absence I could yeild.
For solitude somtimes is best societie,
And short retirement urges sweet returne.   250
But other doubt possesses me, least harm
Befall thee severd from me; for thou knowst
What hath bin warnd us, what malicious Foe
Envying our happiness, and of his own
Despairing, seeks to work us woe and shame   255
By sly assault; and somwhere nigh at hand
Watches, no doubt, with greedy hope to find
His wish and best advantage, us asunder,
Hopeless to circumvent us joind, where each
To other speedie aide might lend at need;   260
Whether his first design be to withdraw
Our fealtie from God, or to disturb
Conjugal Love, then which perhaps no bliss
Enjoyd by us excites his envie more;
Or this, or worse, leave not the faithful side   265

245 *Wilderness*, wildness (212).
248 *satiate*, exhaust.   *yeild*, consent, agree (cf. 902).
250 *urges*, inclines to.
251 *least*, lest.
258 *advantage*, opportunity.
259 *Hopeless to circumvent*, having no hope of getting the better of.
262 *fealtie*, loyalty.
265 *Or this*, whether this is his intention.

That gave thee being, still shades thee and protects.
The Wife, where danger or dishonour lurks,
Safest and seemliest by her Husband staies,
Who guards her, or with her the worst endures.

    To whom the Virgin Majestie of *Eve*,   270
As one who loves, and some unkindness meets,
With sweet austeer composure thus reply'd.

    Ofspring of Heav'n and Earth, and all Earths Lord,
That such an Enemie we have, who seeks
Our ruin, both by thee informd I learne,   275
And from the parting Angel over-heard
As in a shadie nook I stood behind,
Just then returnd at shut of Eevning Flours.
But that thou shouldst my firmness therfore doubt
To God or thee, because we have a foe   280
May tempt it, I expected not to hear.
His violence thou fearst not, being such,
As wee, not capable of death or paine,
Can either not receave, or can repell.
His fraud is then thy fear, which plain inferrs   285
Thy equal fear that my firm Faith and Love
Can by his fraud be shak'n or seduc't;
Thoughts, which how found they harbour in thy brest,

270 *Virgin*, innocent (of sin or shame). The corresponding adjective is used by Latin poets of mothers, and by Italian poets as meaning 'beautiful'.
  272 *austeer*, serious (Eve being hurt by Adam's mistrust).
  274-6 'I learn that we have such an enemy . . . both from your lips and from what I overheard the departing angel say.' The *Angel* was Raphael, who had left Adam with a final warning to resist temptation (VIII, 640-3).
  281 *May tempt it*, who may tempt it.
  282 *being such*, his violence being of such a nature.
  283 *capable of*, liable to.
  284 *receave*, be affected by.
  285 *fraud*, cunning (the alternative to force).   *thy fear*, what you fear. *plain*, plainly.   *inferrs*, suggests.
  288 'How did you allow such thoughts to dwell in your breast?'

Adam, missthought of her to thee so dear?
　　To whom with healing words *Adam* reply'd,   290
Daughter of God and Man, immortal *Eve*,
For such thou art, from sin and blame entire:
Not diffident of thee do I dissuade
Thy absence from my sight, but to avoid
Th' attempt it self, intended by our Foe.   295
For hee who tempts, though in vain, at least asperses
The tempted with dishonour foul, suppos'd
Not incorruptible of Faith, not prooff
Against temptation: thou thy self with scorne
And anger wouldst resent the offerd wrong,   300
Though ineffectual found: misdeem not then,
If such affront I labour to avert
From thee alone, which on us both at once
The Enemie, though bold, will hardly dare,
Or daring, first on mee th' assault shall light.   305
Nor thou his malice and false guile contemn;
Suttle he needs must be, who could seduce
Angels; nor think superfluous others aid.
I from the influence of thy looks receave

289 *missthought of her*, wrongly conceived about her, i.e. 'If I am as dear to you as you said (238), how could you think so badly of me?'

291–2 Eve, like Adam, is immortal as long as she remains free from sin, for 'the wages of sin is death' (Rom. 6:23).　　*entire* is derived from Lat. *integer*=untouched, whole.

293 *diffident of thee*, because I distrust you.　　*dissuade*, persuade (you) against.

296 *asperses*, sprinkles, covers.

297 *suppos'd* (with 'the tempted'), in that she is assumed to be.

298 *of Faith*, in respect of loyalty (to God).

300–1 *the offerd . . . found*, the insult done you in tempting you, however unsuccessful its outcome.　　*misdeem*, misunderstand, i.e. take amiss.

305 *daring*, if he should dare.

306 *contemn*, despise (Lat. *contemnere*).

Access in every Vertue, in thy sight   310
More wise, more watchful, stronger, if need were
Of outward strength; while shame, thou looking on,
Shame to be overcome or over-reacht
Would utmost vigor raise, and rais'd unite.
Why shouldst not thou like sense within thee feel   315
When I am present, and thy trial choose
With mee, best witness of thy Vertue tri'd.

   So spake domestick *Adam* in his care
And Matrimonial Love; but *Eve*, who thought
Less attributed to her Faith sincere,   320
Thus her reply with accent sweet renewd.

   If this be our condition, thus to dwell
In narrow circuit strait'nd by a Foe,
Suttle or violent, wee not endu'd
Single with like defence, wherever met,   325
How are we happie, still in fear of harm?
But harm precedes not sin: onely our Foe

310 *Access*, increase (accent on first syllable, as in 511).

311 *if need were*, if it should be needed.   313 *over-reacht*, deceived.

314 *rais'd unite*, when vigour had been raised it would unite *either* us *or* the qualities implied in 311, i.e. wisdom, etc.

315 *like sense*, sensation of strength or confidence.

317 *best . . . tri'd*, who would be the best person to see the trial of your virtue (because the best strengthener of it).

318 *domestick*, acting as the householder, or (perhaps) caring for his home, and so thoughtful for his wife. There does not seem to be any use of this epithet by Milton elsewhere or by other writers which decides its precise force here.

320 *Less*, too little, less than was due (a classical idiom).   *attributed*, accent on first and third syllables.

323 *strait'nd*, hemmed in, morally as much as physically.

324–5 *wee . . . wherever met*, we, when taken alone, not being his equal, wherever we should encounter him (i.e. even on our own ground). This 'wee' is picked up by the 'we' of 326.

326 *still*, constantly.

327 *harm . . . sin*, we cannot really be harmed if we do not sin; cf. 291–2.

Tempting affronts us with his foul esteem
Of our integritie: his foul esteeme
Sticks no dishonor on our Front, but turns   330
Foul on himself; then wherfore shunnd or feard
By us? who rather double honour gaine
From his surmise prov'd false, finde peace within,
Favour from Heav'n, our witness from th' event.
And what is Faith, Love, Vertue unassaid   335
Alone, without exterior help sustaind?
Let us not then suspect our happie State
Left so imperfet by the Maker wise,
As not secure to single or combin'd:
Fraile is our happiness, if this be so,   340
And *Eden* were no *Eden* thus expos'd.

   To whom thus *Adam* fervently repli'd.
O Woman, best are all things as the will
Of God ordaind them, his creating hand
Nothing imperfet or deficient left   345
Of all that he Created, much less Man,
Or aught that might his happie State secure,

328 *Tempting*, by the mere fact of daring to tempt us.   *esteem*, estimation, opinion.

330 *Front*, brow, forehead, i.e. on us, 'Front' being an echo of 'affront', 328.

331 *wherfor shunnd*, why should he be avoided.

333 *surmise*, suspicion, imputation of fault.

334 *our witness from th' event*, who will be witness of our having stood the trial (successfully).

335 *what is*, what are they worth.

335–6 *unassaid . . . sustaind*, unless tested when their possessor is alone and not helped by anyone else.

338 *Left*, to have been left.

339 'as not to be safe for us, whether alone or together'.

341 *were no Eden*, would be unworthy of its name (the Hebrew for 'delight').   *expos'd*, at the mercy of foes.

347 *secure*, protect; contrast the meaning of the adjective at 371.

Secure from outward force; within himself
The danger lies, yet lies within his power:
Against his will he can receave no harme. 350
But God left free the Will, for what obeyes
Reason, is free, and Reason he made right,
But bid her well beware, and still erect,
Least by some faire appeering good surpris'd
She dictate false, and missinform the Will 355
To do what God expresly hath forbid.
Not then mistrust, but tender love enjoines,
That I should mind thee oft, and mind thou mee.
Firm we subsist, yet possible to swerve,
Since Reason not impossibly may meet 360
Some specious object by the Foe subornd,
And fall into deception unaware,
Not keeping strictest watch, as she was warnd.
Seek not temptation then, which to avoide
Were better, and most likelie if from mee 365
Thou sever not: Trial will come unsought.
Wouldst thou approve thy constancie, approve
First thy obedience; th' other who can know,

349 *within his power*, i.e. to avoid or resist.

353 *beware*, take care (an old verb).   *and still erect*, and always (be) on the alert.

354 'lest taken off her guard by something apparently good.'

355 *dictate false*, give wrong orders.   *missinform*, wrongly instruct.

358 *mind thee*, remind thee.   *mind thou mee*, take good note of what I say. N.B. Three heavily accented syllables in succession twice for emphasis; cf. 375.

359 *subsist*, are, stand.   *possible to swerve*, capable of turning aside.

361 *specious*, pleasant-seeming.   *subornd* (with 'object') made his instrument (originally = 'decked out').

362 *unaware* (with 'Reason'), caught off her guard.

365 *most likelie*, to happen.

367 *approve*, make good, prove.

Not seeing thee attempted, who attest?
But if thou think, trial unsought may finde   370
Us both securer then thus warnd thou seemst,
Go; for thy stay, not free, absents thee more;
Go in thy native innocence, relie
On what thou hast of vertue, summon all,
For God towards thee hath done his part, do thine.   375
    So spake the Patriarch of Mankinde, but *Eve*
Persisted; yet submiss, though last, repli'd.

    With thy permission then, and thus forewarnd
Chiefly by what thy own last reasoning words
Touchd onely, that our trial, when least sought,   380
May finde us both perhaps farr less prepar'd,
The willinger I goe, nor much expect
A Foe so proud will first the weaker seek;
So bent, the more shall shame him his repulse.

    Thus saying, from her Husbands hand her hand   385
Soft she withdrew, and like a Wood-Nymph light
Oread or *Dryad*, or of *Delia*'s Traine,

369 *attempted*, tempted, attacked.   *attest*, bear witness (to it).

370-2 'But if you think that temptation coming upon us by surprise (some other time) may find us more careless than you seem to be now, thus prepared, then go (and face temptation); your presence under compulsion is worse than your absence.' The key to the passage is to note that ' securer' does not mean 'safer' but 'more careless', 'overconfident', which is its original sense, since Lat. *securus* is derived from *sine cura*.

375 *towards* is one syllable metrically.

377 *submiss, though last*, submissively though having the last word.

380 *Touch'd*, touched upon.   *trial*, temptation.   *least sought*, i.e. not, as now, prepared for.

384 *So bent*, if he does so intend.

386 *Soft*, primarily adjective for adverb 'softly', i.e. gently (cf. 'willinger', 382), but perhaps also adjective with 'hand'.

387 *Oread*, mountain-nymph (Gr. *oros* = mountain).   *Dryad*, tree-nymph (Gr. *drus* = oak tree.).   *Delia*, Artemis, Gr. goddess of hunting, born at Delos.

Betook her to the Groves, but *Delia*'s self
In gate surpassd and Goddess-like deport,
Though not as shee with Bow and Quiver armd,   390
But with such Gardning Tools as Art yet rude,
Guiltless of fire had formd, or Angels brought.
To *Pales*, or *Pomona*, thus adornd,
Likest she seemd, *Pomona* when she fled
Vertumnus, or to *Ceres* in her Prime,   395
Yet Virgin of *Proserpina* from *Jove*.
Her long with ardent look his Eye persu'd
Delighted, but desiring more her stay.
Oft he to her his charge of quick returne
Repeated, shee to him as oft engag'd   400
To be returnd by Noon amid the Bowre,
And all things in best order to invite
Noontide repast, or Afternoons repose.
O much deceav'd, much failing, hapless *Eve*,
Of thy presum'd return! event perverse!   405
Thou never from that houre in Paradise
Foundst either sweet repast, or sound repose;
Such ambush hid among sweet Flours and Shades
Waited with hellish rancor imminent

389 *gate*, 'gait' is the later spelling in this sense.   *deport*, deportment, bearing.

392 *Guiltless of*, having no experience of, innocent of.

393 *Pales, or Pomona*, Roman goddesses of pastoral life and of fruit respectively. Pomona was wooed by Vertumnus, a minor rustic deity.

395-6 *Ceres . . . Jove*, young Ceres before Jupiter made her the mother of Proserpina. Ceres (Gr. *Demeter*) was the goddess of corn.

402 *all things*, to have all things.

405 *Of thy presum'd return*, in respect of, as to . . . *event perverse*, How different was the issue!

408 *Shades*, trees rather than shady places, by analogy with Virgil's use of *umbrae*.

409 *imminent*, threatening, may both qualify 'rancour' and govern 'to interrupt'.

To intercept thy way, or send thee back 410
Despoild of Innocence, of Faith, of Bliss.
For now, and since first break of dawne the Fiend,
Meer Serpent in appearance, forth was come,
And on his Quest, where likeliest he might finde
The onely two of Mankinde, but in them 415
The whole included Race, his purposd prey.
In Bowre and Field he sought, where any tuft
Of Grove or Garden-Plot more pleasant lay,
Thir tendance or Plantation for delight,
By Fountain or by shadie Rivulet 420
He sought them both, but wishd his hap might find
Eve separate, he wishd, but not with hope
Of what so seldom chanc'd, when to his wish,
Beyond his hope, *Eve* separate he spies,
Veild in a Cloud of Fragrance, where she stood, 425
Half spi'd, so thick the Roses bushing round
About her glowd, oft stooping to support
Each Flour of slender stalk, whose head though gay
Carnation, Purple, Azure, or spect with Gold,
Hung drooping unsustaind, them she upstaies 430
Gently with Mirtle band, mindless the while,
Her self, though fairest unsupported Flour,
From her best prop so farr, and storm so nigh.

413 *Meer Serpent*, pure serpent, simply a serpent (as opposed to a Rabbinic tradition which made him half human).

418 *more pleasant*, i.e. than another, and so 'especially pleasant'.

419 *Thir tendance*, the object of their tending or care.

421 *his hap might find*, he might chance to find.

423 *to his wish*, agreeable to his wish, as he wished.

429 *Carnation*, red (adjective).

431 *mindless*, heedless, i.e. forgetful of her own weakness.

432–3 *Her self . . . nigh*, although she herself was so far from her best prop and storm was so nigh (the last three words in the absolute construction).

Neerer he drew, and many a walk travers'd
Of stateliest Covert, Cedar, Pine, or Palme,   435
Then voluble and bold, now hid, now seen
Among thick-woven Arborets and Flours
Imborderd on each Bank, the hand of *Eve*:
Spot more delicious then those Gardens feignd
Or of reviv'd *Adonis*, or renownd   440
Alcinous, host of old *Laertes* Son,
Or that, not Mystic, where the Sapient King
Held dalliance with his faire *Egyptian* Spouse.
Much he the Place admir'd, the Person more.
As one who long in populous City pent,   445
Where Houses thick and Sewers annoy the Aire,
Forth issuing on a Summers Morn to breathe
Among the pleasant Villages and Farmes
Adjoind, from each thing met conceaves delight,
The smell of Grain, or tedded Grass, or Kine,   450
Or Dairie, each rural sight, each rural sound;

434 *travers'd*, accent on the last syllable.

436 *voluble*, turning on himself, rolling (though 434 cannot be taken to imply any other means of progress!).

437 *Arborets*, small trees or shrubs (Lat. *arbor*).

438 *imborderd*, planted in borders.   *hand*, handiwork.

439 *feignd*, mythical, fictititious.

440 *Or . . . or*, either . . . or.   *reviv'd Adonis*, a Syrian youth beloved by Aphrodite (Venus), who revived him after he had been killed by a boar, and kept him in a garden.

441 *Alcinous* (pronounce as four syllables with accent on second, Alcĭnŏus), king of Phaeacia where Homer's Odysseus landed in his wanderings after the fall of Troy. His garden enjoyed eternal summer.

442 *not Mystic*, historical, not fabulous.   *the Sapient King*, Solomon, famous for his wisdom (Lat. *sapientia*), married the daughter of Pharaoh, king of Egypt (1 Kings 3:1); his garden is spoken of in the Song of Songs, a book of the Bible which used to be ascribed to Solomon.

446 *Sewers* in those days were not underground.   *annoy*, make noisome.

450 *tedded*, spread out to dry.

If chance with Nymphlike step fair Virgin pass,
What pleasing seemd, for her now pleases more,
Shee most, and in her look summs all Delight.
Such Pleasure took the Serpent to behold   455
This Flourie Plat, the sweet recess of *Eve*
Thus earlie, thus alone; her Heav'nly forme
Angelic, but more soft, and Feminine,
Her graceful Innocence, her every Aire
Of gesture or lest action overawd   460
His Malice, and with rapin sweet bereav'd
His fierceness of the fierce intent it brought:
That space the Evil one abstracted stood
From his own evil, and for the time remain
Stupidly good, of enmitie disarmd,   465
Of guile, of hate, of envie, of revenge;
But the hot Hell that alwayes in him burnes,
Though in mid Heav'n, soon ended his delight,
And tortures him now more, the more he sees
Of pleasure not for him ordaind: then soon   470
Fierce hate he recollects, and all his thoughts
Of mischief, gratulating, thus excites.
    Thoughts, whither have ye led me, with what sweet
Compulsion thus transported to forget

453 *for her*, because of her (presence).
454 *summs*, collects into a small compass, embraces, sums up.
456 *Plat*, a variant form of 'plot'.   *recess*, withdrawing place.
460 *lest*, least, whereas Milton spells our 'lest' as 'least'.
461 *rapin sweet*, delightful robbery (but the earliest texts spell 'rapine').
463 *That space*, for the moment.   *abstracted*, withdrawn.
465 *stupidly*, like a man in a stupor, dazed (and so the words are not quite an oxymoron).
468 *Though . . . Heav'n*, even when he was in mid-heaven.
471 *recollects*, probably 're-collects' rather than 'remembers'.
472 *gratulating*, rejoicing.   *excites*, rouses up.
474 *transported*, agreeing with 'me'.   *to forget*, after 'led me' as well as after 'transported'.

What hither brought us, hate, not love, nor hope   475
Of Paradise for Hell, hope here to taste
Of pleasure, but all pleasure to destroy,
Save what is in destroying, other joy
To mee is lost. Then let me not let pass
Occasion which now smiles: behold alone   480
The Woman, opportune to all attempts,
Her Husband, for I view farr round, not nigh,
Whose higher intellectual more I shun,
And strength, of courage hautie, and of limb
Heroic built, though of terrestrial mould,   485
Foe not informidable, exempt from wound,
I not; so much hath Hell debas't, and paine
Infeebl'd me, to what I was in Heav'n.
Shee fair, divinely fair, fit Love for Gods,
Not terrible, though terrour be in Love   490
And beautie, not approacht by stronger hate,
Hate stronger, under shew of Love well feignd,

476 *for Hell*, instead of Hell.

476–9 'I have not come here with any hope of pleasure, but rather to destroy the pleasure of others, since no other pleasure is left me.'

479 *let pass*, pass by, neglect.

480 *Occasion . . . smiles*, a favourable opportunity.

481 *opportune to all attempts*, liable to, favourably situated for, any attack.

482 *Her Husband . . . not* (being) *nigh*, absolute construction.

483 *intellectual*, intellect, mind (occasionally used as a noun before Milton).

485 *mould*, substance (cf. 149).

486–7 Cf. 283. Satan 'first knew pain' in his conflict with Michael (VI, 327).

488 *to*, compared to.

489 *Shee* (is) *fair*; but 'Shee' may rather be felt as parallel to 'Husband' (482) in construction, i.e. she being fair, or while she is fair.

490 *terrour*, awe; cf. 'awful', 537.

491 *not approacht*, when it is not approached as it is in this case.

492 'Hate which is all the stronger when disguised as love'.

The way which to her ruin now I tend.
  So spake the Enemie of Mankind, enclos'd
In Serpent, Inmate bad, and toward *Eve*   495
Addressd his way, not with indented wave,
Prone on the ground, as since, but on his reare,
Circular base of rising foulds, that tour'd
Fould above fould a surging Maze, his Head
Crested aloft, and Carbuncle his Eyes;   500
With burnisht Neck of verdant Gold, erect
Amidst his circling Spires, that on the grass
Floted redundant: pleasing was his shape,
And lovely, never since of Serpent kind
Lovelier, not those that in *Illyria* chang'd   505
Hermione and *Cadmus*, or the God
In *Epidaurus*; nor to which transformd
Ammonian Jove, or *Capitoline* was seen,
Hee with *Olympias*, this with her who bore

493 *The way*, in apposition to the idea of his approach in 491.   ***tend***,
direct.

496 *Addressd*, directed.   ***indented***, going in and out like the teeth
(Lat. *dentes*) of a saw.

498 *tour'd*, towered up.

500 *carbuncle*, red like carbuncles.

501 *verdant Gold*, i.e. mixed green and gold, green shot with gold.

502 *Spires*, coils (Lat. *spirae*).

503 *redundant*, copious and wave-like (Lat. *unda* = wave).

504-5 *lovely, never since . . . lovelier*, so lovely that there has never
been any lovelier serpent.

505 *Illyria*, roughly the modern Albania.   ***chang'd***, changed into
themselves, *or* took in exchange for themselves.

506 *Hermione and Cadmus*, a queen and king of Thebes in Greece.   ***the***
God, Aesculapius.

507 *Epidaurus*, in the NE. of the Peloponnese.

507-9 'Nor those serpents into whom Juppiter Ammon or Juppiter of
the Capitol were seen transformed, the former with Olympias, the latter
with the mother of Scipio Africanus'.

Scipio the highth of *Rome*. With tract oblique   510
At first, as one who sought access, but feard
To interrupt, side-long he works his way.
As when a Ship by skilful Stearsman wrought
Nigh Rivers mouth or Foreland, where the Wind
Veres oft, as oft so steers, and shifts her Saile;   515
So varied hee, and of his tortuous Traine
Curld many a wanton wreath in sight of *Eve*,
To lure her Eye; shee busied heard the sound
Of rusling Leaves, but minded not, as us'd
To such disport before her through the Field,   520
From every Beast, more duteous at her call
Then at *Circean* call the Herd disguis'd.
Hee boulder now, uncalld before her stood;
But as in gaze admiring: Oft he bowd
His turret Crest, and sleek enameld Neck,   525
Fawning, and licked the ground whereon she trod.
His gentle dumb expression turnd at length
The Eye of *Eve* to mark his play; hee glad
Of her attention gaind, with Serpent Tongue
Organic, or impulse of vocal Air,   530
His fraudulent temptation thus began.

510 *the highth*, the height, chief man (*O.E.D.* sub 'height', II, 11 has no
parallel to this metaphorical use.)   *tract oblique*, indirect path.

512 *side-long*, coming towards her from the side, not the front.

513 *wrought*, worked; a nautical use of 'working' a ship.

517 *wanton*, sportive.

522 'than were the herd of men changed into swine when called by
Circe.'

525 *turret*, tower-like (cf. 498).   *enameld*, smooth and variegated
(cf. 501).

529-30 'either making the serpent's tongue his own instrument or
imparting a movement to the air which produced sound', i.e. a simulated
voice (*Organic*=serving as an instrument or means).

531 *fraudulent*, deceptive (as coming from 'the father of lies').

Wonder not, sovran Mistress, if perhaps
Thou canst, who art sole Wonder, much less arm
Thy looks, the Heav'n of mildness, with disdain,
Displeas'd that I approach thee thus, and gaze   535
Insatiat, I thus single, nor have feard
Thy awful brow, more awful thus retir'd.
Fairest resemblance of thy Maker faire,
Thee all things living gaze on, all things thine
By gift, and thy Celestial Beautie adore   540
With ravishment beheld, there best beheld
Where universally admir'd; but here
In this enclosure wild, these Beasts among,
Beholders rude, and shallow to discerne
Half what in thee is fair, one man except,   545
Who sees thee? (and what is one?) who shouldst be
    seen
A Goddess among Gods, ador'd and serv'd
By Angels numberless, thy daily Train.
    So gloz'd the Tempter, and his Proem tun'd;

532 *sovran*, peerless, excelling; a word of various spelling derived from
Lat. *supremus*.

532–3 i.e. if you, an unique source of wonder to others, can yourself
feel wonder.

534 *the Heav'n of mildness*, supremely gentle.

536 *I thus single*, i.e. (presumably) and therefore not to be feared.

537 *awful*, inspiring awe or reverence.   *thus retir'd*, when you are
alone.

538–9 'All living things gaze on thee, O thou who art the fairest . . .
faire.' For God made man in his own image (Gen. 1:27).

541–2 i.e. and it would be best beheld where it could be universally
admired.

542–6 The order is again inverted: 'but who sees thee here . . .?'

544 *shallow to discerne*, too shallow to appreciate.

545 *one man except*, with the exception of one man.

548 *Train*, following (of servants and admirers).

549 *gloz'd*, spoke flatteringly. This sense, now rare, presumably came
from the first sense of 'put a gloss on', 'explain' via the second sense

Into the Heart of *Eve* his words made way,   550
Though at the voice much marveling; at length
Not unamaz'd she thus in answer spake.

    What may this mean? Language of Man pronounc't
By Tongue of Brute, and human sense exprest?
The first at lest of these I thought deni'd   555
To Beasts, whom God on thir Creation-Day
Created mute to all articulat sound;
The latter I demurr, for in thir looks
Much reason, and in thir actions oft appeers.
Thee, Serpent, suttl'st beast of all the field.   560
I knew, but not with human voice endu'd;
Redouble then this miracle, and say,
How cam'st thou speakable of mute, and how
To mee so friendly grown above the rest
Of brutal kind, that daily are in sight?   565
Say, for such wonder claims attention due.

    To whom the guileful Tempter thus reply'd.
Empress of this fair World, resplendent *Eve*,
Easie to mee it is to tell thee all
What thou commandst, and right thou shouldst be
    obeyd: 570

'extenuate'.   *Proem*, prologue (Gk. *prooimion*, a musical introduction).
tun'd, as in tuning an instrument.

    552 *Not unamaz'd*, a stronger word than now; cf. its literal use at 161
and 640.

    558 *The latter I demurr*, as to whether they have sense I am doubtful,
hesitate to affirm.

    559 *reason*, intelligence, good sense.

    560 *suttl'st beast*, to be the subtlest beast (as Raphael informed Adam at
VII, 495).

    563 *speakable of mute*, able to speak after being dumb; for 'of' used like
ex in Lat. and *ek* in Gk. cf. 'Of pure now purer air Meets his approach',
IV, 153-4.

    564 *grown*, hast thou grown.

    565 *brutal kind*, the race of animals.

I was at first as other Beasts that graze
The trodd'n Herb, of abject thoughts and low,
As was my food, nor aught but food discernd
Or Sex, and apprehended nothing high:
Till on a day roaving the field, I chanc'd   575
A goodly Tree farr distant to behold
Load'n with fruit of fairest colours mixt,
Ruddie and Gold: I nearer drew to gaze;
When from the boughes a savorie odour blown,
Grateful to appetite, more pleas'd my sense   580
Then smell of sweetest Fenel, or the Teats
Of Ewe or Goat dropping with Milk at Eevn,
Unsuckt of Lamb or Kid, that tend thir play.
To satisfie the sharp desire I had
Of tasting those fair Apples, I resolv'd   585
Not to deferr; hunger and thirst at once,
Powerful perswaders, quick'nd at the sent
Of that alluring fruit, urg'd me so keene.
About the mossie Trunk I wound me soon,
For high from ground the branches would require   590
Thy utmost reach or *Adams*: Round the Tree
All other Beasts that saw, with like desire
Longing and envying stood, but could not reach.
Amid the Tree now got, where plentie hung
Tempting so nigh, to pluck and eat my fill   595
I spar'd not, for such pleasure till that hour
At Feed or Fountain never had I found.

580 *Grateful*, pleasing, welcome.
581 *Fenel* = fennel, a fragrant herb.
583 *tend*, are intent on.
586 *deferr*, delay.   587 *sent*, scent.
588 *keene*, keenly (archaic as adverb).
595 *Tempting so nigh*, so temptingly near, tempting from its very proximity.

Sated at length, ere long I might perceave
Strange alteration in me, to degree
Of Reason in my inward powers, and Speech   600
Wanted not long, though to this shape retaind.
Thenceforth to Speculations high or deep
I turnd my thoughts, and with capacious mind
Considerd all things visible in Heav'n,
Or Earth, or Middle, all things fair and good;   605
But all that fair and good in thy Divine
Semblance, and in thy Beauties heav'nly Ray
United I beheld; no Fair to thine
Equivalent or second, which compelld
Mee thus, though importune perhaps, to come   610
And gaze, and worship thee of right declar'd
Sovran of Creatures, universal Dame.
  So talkd the spirited sly Snake; and *Eve*
Yet more amaz'd unwarie thus reply'd.
  Serpent, thy overpraising leaves in doubt   615
The vertue of that Fruit, in thee first prov'd:
But say, where grows the Tree, from hence how farr?
For many are the Trees of God that grow
In Paradise, and various, yet unknown

599–600 *to degree of Reason*, amounting to the acquisition of reason, (*not* the recent slang 'to a degree' !).

601 *Wanted not long*, was not long in coming.   *though . . . retained*, although I was still kept within the same form, viz. a serpent's. Grammatically 'retained' agrees with 'me' in 599.

605 *Middle*, the air between earth and heaven.

606 *that fair and good*, that (same) fairness and goodness; so in 608.

610 *importune* (read as i'mportúne), unseasonably.

612 *universal Dame*, mistress of all (Lat. *domina*).

613 *spirited*, possessed by an (evil) spirit.

614 *unwarie*, taken off her guard; Milton used the adjective as Lat. would use *incautus*.

616 *in thee first proved*, which you alone have tested.

619 *yet*, as yet.

To us, in such abundance lies our choice,   620
As leaves a greater store of Fruit untoucht,
Still hanging incorruptible, till men
Grow up to thir provision, and more hands
Help to disburden Nature of her Bearth.
　　To whom the wilie Adder, blithe and glad.   625
Empress, the way is readie, and not long,
Beyond a row of Myrtles, on a Flat,
Fast by a Fountain, one small Thicket past
Of blowing Myrrh and Balme; if thou accept
My conduct, I can bring thee thither soon.   630
　　Lead then, said *Eve*. Hee leading swiftly rowld
In tangles, and made intricate seem strait,
To mischief swift. Hope elevates, and joy
Bright'ns his Crest: as when a wandring Fire
Compact of unctuous vapor, which the Night   635
Condenses, and the cold invirons round,
Kindl'd through agitation to a Flame,
Which oft, they say, some evil Spirit attends,

622 *incorruptible*, not decaying through overripeness.

623 *Grow up to thir provision*, increase in numbers to the extent of what is provided for them.

624 *Bearth*, what she bears, her fruit.

625 *blithe*, gay (referring specially to outward manifestation of joy).

626 *readie*, close at hand *and/or* direct (both archaic meanings).

627 *Flat*, level place; cf. Shakespeare's 'Till of this flat a mountain you have made'.

629 *blowing*, blossoming; cf. Shakespeare's 'I know a bank where the wild thyme blows'.

631 *rowld*, rolled himself along; cf. Virgil's *rapit orbes per humum*.

632 *strait*, straight (of different derivation from strait=narrow).

634 *a wandering fire* (*ignis fatuus*), a person or thing that misleads by means of fugitive appearances, a will-o'-the-wisp or Jack-o'-lantern.

635 *Compact of*, made up of.　　*unctuous*, oily.

636 *invirons round*, environs, encircles.

Hovering and blazing with delusive Light,
Misleads th' amaz'd Night-wanderer from his way   640
To Boggs and Mires, and oft through Pond or Poole,
There swallowd up and lost, from succour farr.
So glisterd the dire Snake, and into fraud
Led *Eve* our credulous Mother, to the Tree
Of prohibition, root of all our woe;   645
Which when she saw, thus to her guide she spake.

Serpent, we might have spar'd our coming hither,
Fruitless to mee, though Fruit be here to excess,
The credit of whose vertue rest with thee,
Wondrous indeed, if cause of such effects.   650
But of this Tree we may not taste nor touch;
God so commanded, and left that Command
Sole Daughter of his voice; the rest, we live
Law to our selves, our Reason is our Law.

To whom the Tempter guilefully repli'd.   655
Indeed? hath God then said that of the Fruit
Of all these Garden Trees ye shall not eate,
Yet Lords declar'd of all in Earth or Aire?

To whom thus *Eve* yet sinless. Of the Fruit
Of each Tree in the Garden we may eate,   660
But of the Fruit of this fair Tree amidst
The Garden, God hath said, Ye shall not eate
Thereof, nor shall ye touch it, least ye die.

640 *amaz'd*, bewildered.

642 *There swallowd up*, there to be, i.e. where he is, swallowed up.

643 *fraud*, 'the state of being defrauded or deluded' (*O.E.D.* s.v. 5; this passive sense being peculiar to Milton).

644–5 *Tree of prohibition*, a Hebrew idiom for 'forbidden tree', as it is called in I, 2.

649–50 'Let belief in the power of this fruit remain with you, which is indeed wonderful, if it has the results you allege.'

653 *the rest*, as to the rest (a Latin construction).

She scarse had said, though brief, when now more
    bold
The Tempter, but with shew of Zeale and Love   665
To Man, and indignation at his wrong,
New part puts on, and as to passion mov'd,
Fluctuats disturbed, yet comely, and in act
Rais'd, as of som great matter to begin.
As when of old som Orator renound   670
In *Athens* or free *Rome*, where Eloquence
Flourishd, since mute, to som great cause addrest,
Stood in himself collected, while each part,
Motion, each act won audience ere the tongue,
Somtimes in highth began, as no delay   675
Of Preface brooking through his Zeal of Right:
So standing, moving, or to highth upgrown
The Tempter all impassiond thus began.

    O Sacred, Wise, and Wisdom-giving Plant,
Mother of Science, Now I feel thy Power   680
Within me cleere, not onely to discerne

664 *said . . . brief*, spoken briefly.

665 *shew*, pretence.

666 *his wrong*, wrong done to man.

667 *New part puts on*, takes on a new character or role (like an actor). *as*, as if.

668 *fluctuats*, sways his body (cf. 631–2).

668–9 *in act Rais'd*, with lofty deportment, or gesture. The Lat. *actus* is used by Quintilian of the action accompanying oral delivery.

669 *as of . . . begin*, as if about to speak on.

672 *to . . . addrest*, having prepared himself for.

673 *in himself collected*, with all his faculties under full control.   *each part*, i.e. of his body.

674 *Motion*, each movement, action.   *won audience*, predisposed his hearers to attention ('audience' =hearing).

675 *in highth began*, began with passionate feeling (not working up to it).

677 *to highth upgrown*, rearing himself to his full height.

680 *Science*, all knowledge (not only Natural Science).

Things in thir Causes, but to trace the wayes
Of highest Agents, deemd however wise.
Queen of this Universe, doe not believe
Those rigid threats of Death; ye shall not Die: 685
How should ye? by the Fruit? it gives you Life
To Knowledge: By the Threatner? look on mee,
Mee who have toucht and tasted, yet both live,
And life more perfet have attaind then Fate
Meant me, by ventring higher then my Lot.   690
Shall that be shut to Man, which to the Beast
Is op'n? or will God incense his ire
For such a petty Trespass, and not praise
Rather your dauntless vertue, whom the pain
Of Death denounc't, whatever thing Death be,   695
Deterrd not from atchieving what might leade
To happier life, knowledge of Good and Evil;
Of good, how just? of evil, if what is evil
Be real, why not known, since easier shunnd?
God therefore cannot hurt ye, and be just;   700

683 *highest Agents*, active beings of the highest rank (not here those who act as agents for another).   *deemd however wise*, however wise they are deemed.

685 *Those rigid threats*, see 661-3.

687 *To*, in addition to. It is the Tree of Life as well as of Knowledge. *the Threatner*, i.e. God.

689 *then*, than.

690 *ventring*, venturing (the spelling gives the required metrical value).

691 *that*, i.e. the opportunity to eat any fruit in the garden.

692 *incense his ire*, kindle his wrath.

694 *pain*, penalty (the first meaning, Lat. *poena*=punishment).

695 *denounc't*, proclaimed, i.e. threatened.

698-9 i.e. if eating the fruits should lead to knowledge of good, how can it be just for you to be punished for it; if to knowledge of evil, why shouldn't you know evil in order more easily to avoid it?

698 *evil . . . evil*, scan as one syllable 'e'il'.

700 *ye* was originally nom. and voc. only, but from sixteenth century other cases also.

Not just, not God; not feard then, nor obeid:
Your feare it self of Death removes the feare.
Why then was this forbid? Why but to awe,
Why but to keep ye low and ignorant,
His worshippers; he knows that in the day   705
Ye Eate thereof, your Eyes that seem so cleere,
Yet are but dim, shall perfetly be then
Op'nd and cleerd, and yee shall be as Gods,
Knowing both Good and Evil as they know.
That yee should be as Gods, since I as Man,   710
Internal Man, is but proportion meet,
I of brute human, yee of human Gods.
So ye shall die perhaps, by putting off
Human, to put on Gods, death to be wisht,
Though threat'nd, which no worse then this can
                                                   bring.   715
And what are Gods that Man may not become
As they, participating God-like food?
The Gods are first, and that advantage use
On our belief, that all from them proceeds;
I question it, for this fair Earth I see,   720
Warmd by the Sun, producing every kind,

701 'If He is not just, He is not God, and therefore not to be feared or obeyed.'

702 i.e. your fear of death would be fear of an unjust God—a contradiction in terms; so your fear has no ground for existing.

703 *awe*, overawe you.

711 *Internal Man*, man in my mind, not body; see 600–1.

712 *of . . . of*, from being; see 563.

713–14 *putting off Human*, shedding humanity, the human state.   *Gods*, the state of God, divinity.

715 i.e. the threatened state can be nothing worse than changing your state to that of gods.

718–19 *that advantage . . . belief*, use that advantage to make us believe.

Them nothing: If they all things, who enclos'd
Knowledge of Good and Evil in this Tree,
That whoso eats thereof, forthwith attains
Wisdom without their leave? and wherein lies   725
Th' offence, that Man should thus attain to know?
What can your knowledge hurt him, or this Tree
Impart against his will if all be his?
Or is it envie, and can envie dwell
In heav'nly brests? these, these and many more   730
Causes import your need of this fair Fruit.
Goddess humane, reach then, and freely taste.

He ended, and his words replete with guile
Into her heart too easie entrance won:
Fixt on the Fruit she gaz'd, which to behold   735
Might tempt alone, and in her ears the sound
Yet rung of his perswasive words, impregnd
With Reason, to her seeming, and with Truth;
Meanwhile the hour of Noon drew on, and wak'd
An eager appetite, rais'd by the smell   740
So savorie of that Fruit, which with desire,
Inclinable now grown to touch or taste,
Sollicited her longing eye; yet first
Pausing a while, thus to her self she mus'd.

Great are thy Vertues, doubtless, best of Fruits,   745
Though kept from Man, and worthy to be admir'd,
Whose taste, too long forborn, at first assay

722–3 *If they* (produced) *all things*, i.e. they would not have produced
this tree, endangering their supremacy.

731 *import*, carry with them, imply.

732 *humane*, human.

735–6 *which to behold . . . alone*, the mere sight of which.

737 *impregned*, impregnated, filled; 'impregns' is used as the present
tense in IV, 500.

742 *Inclinable . . . to*, inclined, leaning towards, i.e. tempting.

747 *assay*, trial.

Gave elocution to the mute, and taught
The Tongue not made for Speech to speak thy praise:
Thy praise hee also who forbids thy use,   750
Conceales not from us, naming thee the Tree
Of Knowledge, knowledge both of good and evil;
Forbids us then to taste, but his forbidding
Commends thee more, while it inferrs the good
By thee communicated, and our want: 755
For good unknown sure is not had, or had
And yet unknown, is as not had at all.
In plain then, what forbids he but to know,
Forbids us good, forbids us to be wise?
Such prohibitions binde not. But if Death   760
Bind us with after-bands, what profits then
Our inward freedom? In the day we eate
Of this fair Fruit, our doom is, we shall die.
How dies the Serpent? hee hath eat'n and lives,
And knows, and speaks, and reasons, and discernes,   765
Irrational till then. For us alone
Was death invented? or to us deni'd
This intellectual food, for beasts reserv'd?
For Beasts it seems: yet that one Beast which first
Hath tasted, envies not, but brings with joy   770
The good befall'n him, Author unsuspect,

748 *elocution*, power of speech.   *the mute*, i.e. the Serpent.

754 *while it inferrs*, at the same time as it suggests.

755 *our want*, what we miss.

756-7 'For surely we cannot be said to possess a good we do not know of; if we do possess it without knowing we do, that is no better than not possessing it.'

758 *in plain* (words); cf. 'in few', X, 157.

758-9 'In forbidding us knowledge, is he not forbidding us something good, forbidding us wisdom?'

768 *intellectual food*, food for the mind (as giving knowledge).

771 *Author unsuspect*, an informant not to be suspected.

Friendly to man, farr from deceit or guile.
What fear I then, rather what know to feare
Under this ignorance of Good and Evil,
Of God or Death, of Law or Penaltie? 775
Here grows the Cure of all, this Fruit Divine,
Fair to the Eye, inviting to the Taste,
Of vertue to make wise: what hinders then
To reach, and feed at once both Bodie and Mind?
　　So saying, her rash hand in evil hour 780
Forth reaching to the Fruit, she pluckd, she eat:
Earth felt the wound, and Nature from her seat
Sighing through all her Works gave signs of woe,
That all was lost. Back to the Thicket slunk
The guiltie Serpent, and well might, for *Eve* 785
Intent now wholly on her taste, naught else
Regarded, such delight till then, as seemd,
In Fruit she never tasted, whether true
Or fansied so, through expectation high
Of knowledg, nor was God-head from her thought. 790
Greedily she ingorg'd without restraint,
And knew not eating Death: Satiate at length,
And highth'nd as with Wine, jocond and boon,
Thus to her self she pleasingly began.

776 *Divine*, because teaching divinity.

778 *Of vertue*, possessing the power.

781 *eat*, alternative preterite to 'ate', but pronounced 'et'.

787–90 *such delight* . . . , 'for, as it seemed to her, she had never yet tasted such delightful fruit—whether the delight really lay in the taste or in her expectation of the knowledge it would bring her; nor was the thought of Godhead altogether absent from her mind.'

792 *knew not eating*, knew not that she was eating. (The participle after verbs of knowing and seeing is a Greek use, imitated also in Latin poetry.)

793 *jocond*, merry.　　*boon*, gay, jolly (a rare sense derived from the associations of 'a boon companion', originally a good companion, from Lat. *bonus*).

794 *pleasingly*, as if pleased with herself.

O Sovran, vertuous, precious of all Trees   795
In Paradise, of operation blest
To Sapience, hitherto obscur'd, infam'd,
And thy fair Fruit let hang, as to no end
Created; but henceforth my early care,
Not without Song, each Morning, and due praise   800
Shall tend thee, and the fertil burden ease
Of thy full branches offerd free to all;
Till dieted by thee I grow mature
In knowledge, as the Gods who all things know;
Though others envie what they cannot give;   805
For had the gift bin theirs, it had not here
Thus grown. Experience, next to thee I owe,
Best guide; not following thee, I had remaind
In ignorance, thou op'nst Wisdoms way,
And giv'st access, though secret she retire.   810
And I perhaps am secret; Heav'n is high,
High and remote to see from thence distinct

795 *vertuous, precious*, for most virtuous (cf. 778) and precious (as Virgil uses *sancte deorum* for *sanctissime deorum* in *Aen.* IV, 576); the idiom is made easier if we consider 'of' as 'among'.

796-7 *of operation . . . Sapience*, having the blessed effect of producing wisdom.   *obscur'd*, unknown.   *infam'd*, without fame (possibly 'of bad repute', but this is scarcely consistent with 'obscur'd').

798-9 'And having thy fair fruit allowed to hang (unpicked), as if the tree had been created purposelessly' (loose syntax).

801 *fertil*, fertile, but so spelt to take the stress off the last syllable, as with 'Femal', 822.

803 *dieted*, fed on a special food; the Gk. noun from which it is derived means first a 'way of life'.

805 see 720-2.   *others*, the gods.   *envie*, grudge.

807 *owe*, am under an obligation. Eve is congratulating herself on her daring.

808 *not following*, if I had not followed.

810 *access*, accent on last syllable.   *secret*, into hiding.

811 *secret*, hidden from God (cf. 'The Lord shall not see' Ps. 94:7).

812 *to see*, for seeing.

Each thing on Earth; and other care perhaps
May have diverted from continual watch
Our great Forbidder, safe with all his Spies   815
About him. But to *Adam* in what sort
Shall I appeer? shall I to him make known
As yet my change, and give him to partake
Full happiness with mee, or rather not,
But keep the odds of Knowledge in my power   820
Without Copartner? so to add what wants
In Femal Sex, the more to draw his Love,
And render me more equal, and perhaps,
A thing not undesireable, somtime
Superior; for inferior who is free?   825
This may be well: but what if God have seen,
And Death ensue? then I shall be no more,
And *Adam* wedded to another *Eve*,
Shall live with her enjoying, I extinct;
A death to think. Confirmd then I resolve,   830
Adam shall share with me in bliss or woe:
So dear I love him, that with him all deaths
I could endure, without him live no life.

     So saying, from the Tree her step she turnd,
But first low Reverence don, as to the power   835

815 *safe*, safely out of the way, harmless, as when Macbeth asks if
Banquo's 'safe'; and cf. *Tempest*, III. i. 19–21.

817 *appeer*, the word suggests deception.

818 *give him to*, grant to him to.

820 *odds*, balance, superiority.

821 *so . . . wants*, and by so doing add what is lacking.

824 *somtime*, occasionally.

829 *enjoying*, in joy, enjoying himself and her.   *I extinct*, a nominative
absolute, where Latin would have had the ablative, *me extincto*.

830 *Confirmd*, firmly.

835 *But . . . don*, but after making obeisance.   *as*, as if, i.e. not to the
tree as a tree.

That dwelt within, whose presence had infus'd
Into the plant sciential sap, deriv'd
From Nectar, drink of Gods. *Adam* the while
Waiting desirous her return, had wove
Of choicest Flours a Garland to adorne   840
Her Tresses, and her rural labours crown,
As Reapers oft are wont thir Harvest Queen.
Great joy he promisd to his thoughts, and new
Solace in her return, so long delayd;
Yet oft his heart, divine of somthing ill,   845
Misgave him; hee the faultring measure felt;
And forth to meet her went, the way she took
That Morn when first they parted; by the Tree
Of Knowledge he must pass; there he her met,
Scarse from the Tree returning; in her hand   850
A bough of fairest fruit that downie smil'd,
New gatherd, and ambrosial smell diffus'd.
To him she hasted, in her face excuse
Came Prologue, and Apologie to prompt,
Which with bland words at will she thus addressd. 855

Hast thou not wonderd, *Adam*, at my stay?
Thee I have misst, and thought it long, depriv'd

837 *sciential*, producing knowledge.

839 *desirous*, with longing.   *wove*, woven.

845 *divine of*, foreboding, anticipating (a Lat. construction like *sententia divina futuri* in Horace).

846 *faultring measure*, irregular heart-beat (of excitement, especially fear).

847 *the way she took*, taking the same way she had taken.

851 *downie smil'd*, looked attractive with the down still on it.

852 *ambrosial*, like ambrosia, the food of the gods.

853–4 *excuse . . . prompt* (probably), excuse was ready on her tongue, and more formal defence behind, in reserve; see Commentary.

855 'which apology, having fair-seeming words at her command, she thus expressed' (*or* 'at will' might mean 'as the words came into her head').

Thy presence, agonie of love till now
Not felt, nor shall be twice, for never more
Mean I to trie, what rash untri'd I sought,   860
The paine of absence from thy sight. But strange
Hath bin the cause, and wonderful to heare:
This Tree is not as we are told, a Tree
Of danger tasted, nor to evil unknown
Op'ning the way, but of Divine effect   865
To op'n Eyes, and make them Gods who taste;
And hath bin tasted such: the Serpent wise,
Or not restraind as wee, or not obeying,
Hath eat'n of the fruit, and is become,
Not dead, as we are threat'nd, but thenceforth   870
Endu'd with human voice and human sense,
Reasoning to admiration, and with mee
Perswasively hath so prevaild, that I
Have also tasted, and have also found
Th' effects to correspond, op'ner mine Eyes,   875
Dimm erst, dilated spirits, ampler Heart,
And growing up to Godhead; which for thee
Chiefly I sought, without thee can despise.
For bliss, as thou hast part, to mee is bliss,
Tedious, unshar'd with thee, and odious soon.   880

858 *agonie of love*, in apposition with the idea of deprivation expressed in the preceding phrase.

860 *rash*, agrees with 'I', 'untri'd' with the object 'what'.

864 *tasted*, if, or when, tasted.

865 *of Divine effect*, causing or producing divinity.

867 *hath . . . such*, has proved such when tasted.

868 *Or . . . or*, either . . . or.

872 *to admiration*, so as to win admiration.

875 *to correspond*, i.e. with his promises.

876 *Dimm erst*, that was formerly dim.   *dilated spirits*, I have found my spirits more expanded.

879 *as*, in proportion as.

Thou therfore also taste, that equal Lot
May joine us, equal Joy, as equal Love;
Least thou not tasting, different degree
Disjoine us, and I then too late renounce
Deitie for thee, when Fate will not permit.   885
    Thus *Eve* with Countnance blithe her storie told;
But in her Cheek distemper flushing glowd.
On th' other side, *Adam*, soon as he heard
The fatal Trespass don by *Eve*, amaz'd,
Astonied stood and Blank, while horror chill   890
Ran through his veins, and all his joints relaxd;
From his slack hand the Garland wreath'd for *Eve*
Down dropd, and all the faded Roses shed:
Speechless he stood and pale, till thus at length
First to himself he inward silence broke.   895
    O fairest of Creation, last and best
Of all Gods Works, Creature in whom excelld
Whatever can to sight or thought be formd,
Holy, divine, good, amiable, or sweet!
How art thou lost, how on a sudden lost,   900
Defac't, deflourd, and now to Death devote?

881 *Lot,* (good) fortune, fate.

883–4 'Lest, if you do not taste, a difference of degree (status or rank)
come between us.'

884 *renounce,* i.e. try to renounce.

886 *blithe,* see 625.

887 *distemper,* feverish excitement ('deranged or disordered condition
of the body or mind', *O.E.D.*), a term used more widely formerly than
now; cf. 'distemper'd, discontented thoughts' IV, 808.

890 *Astonied,* dazed, stunned, stupefied (a biblical word).   *blank,*
utterly disconcerted (cf. 'look blank').

899 *amiable,* lovely (Lat. *amabilis*), used of the Hesperian fruit in IV,
250; but the modern sense of pleasant disposition is also pre-Miltonic.

901 *deflourd,* robbed of your bloom or innocence, usually of beauty or
virginity.   *devote*(d), doomed, dedicated; cf. 'to destruction sacred
and devote', III, 208 (Virgil's *pesti devota futurae* of Dido).

Rather how hast thou yeelded to transgress
The strict forbiddance, how to violate
The sacred Fruit forbidd'n? som cursed fraud
Of Enemie hath beguil'd thee, yet unknown,   905
And mee with thee hath ruind, for with thee
Certain my resolution is to Die;
How can I live without thee, how forgoe
Thy sweet Converse and Love so dearly joind,
To live again in these wilde Woods forlorn?   910
Should God create another *Eve*, and I
Another Rib afford, yet loss of thee
Would never from my heart; no no, I feel
The Link of Nature draw me: Flesh of Flesh,
Bone of my Bone thou art, and from thy State   915
Mine never shall be parted, bliss or woe.

　So having said, as one from sad dismay
Recomforted, and after thoughts disturbd
Submitting to what seemd remediless,
Thus in calme mood his Words to *Eve* he turnd.   920

　Bold deed thou hast presum'd, adventrous *Eve*,
And peril great provok't, who thus hast dar'd
Had it bin only coveting to Eye

905 *Enemie*, almost a dissyllable, liquids making the slur easy.
907 *certain*, fixed, firm.
909 *Love . . . joind*, love of thee so dearly joined with me; cf. 970.
911-12 See Gen. 2:21.
914-15 *Flesh . . . Bone*. The phraseology is from Gen. 2:23-4, made still
more familiar by its repetition in the N.T. (Matt. 19:4-6, etc.).
915 *State*, situation, condition.
919 accent *remédiless*.
921 *presum'd* ventur'd upon (an old use).
922-5 i.e. it would have been daring even to eye it covetously, it was
much more daring to taste it when it lay under a curse; 'coveting' is either
a present participle, equivalent here to an adverb, or a verbal noun, i.e.
had your daring only consisted in the act of coveting.

That sacred Fruit, sacred to abstinence,
Much more to taste it under banne to touch.   925
But past who can recall, or don undoe?
Not God Omnipotent, nor Fate; yet so
Perhaps thou shalt not Die, perhaps the Fact
Is not so hainous now, foretasted Fruit,
Profan'd first by the Serpent, by him first   930
Made common and unhallowd ere our taste;
Nor yet on him found deadly, hee yet lives,
Lives, as thou saidst, and gaines to live as Man
Higher degree of Life, inducement strong
To us, as likely tasting to attaine   935
Proportional ascent, which cannot be
But to be Gods, or Angels Demi-gods.
Nor can I think that God, Creator wise,
Though threatning, will in earnest so destroy
Us his prime Creatures, dignifi'd so high,   940
Set over all his Works, which in our Fall,
For us created, needs with us must faile,
Dependent made; so God shall uncreate,

924 *sacred to*, dedicated to.

925 *banne*, ban. The sense 'prohibition' is first recorded here (*O.E.D.*, IV), but develops naturally from the earlier meaning of 'curse', 'anathema'.

926 *past*, the past.

927 *so*, even so.

928 *the Fact*, the deed (Lat. *factum*).

929 *hainous*, heinous, hateful, criminal. Milton retains the spelling of the French root.   *foretasted Fruit*, now that the fruit has been already tasted.

933 *gaines . . . Man*, attains to living like a man (in intelligence), instead of like a beast.

935 *as likely tasting*, as being likely if we taste.

937 *Angels Demi-gods*, Angels, that is Demigods; we should have inserted a comma between the nouns.

943 *Dependent made*, since they were made subservient to us.

Be frustrate, do, undo, and labour loose,
Not well conceav'd of God, who though his Power 945
Creation could repeate, yet would be loath
Us to abolish, least the Adversary
Triumph and say; Fickle their State whom God
Most Favors; who can please him long? Mee first
He ruind, now Mankind; whom will he next? 950
Matter of scorne, not to be giv'n the Foe.
However I with thee have fixt my Lot,
Certain to undergoe like doom; if Death
Consort with thee, Death is to mee as Life;
So forcible within my heart I feel 955
The Bond of Nature draw me to my owne,
My own in thee, for what thou art is mine;
Our State cannot be severd, we are one,
One Flesh; to loose thee were to loose my self.

   So *Adam*, and thus *Eve* to him repli'd. 960
O glorious trial of exceeding Love,
Illustrious evidence, example high!
Ingaging me to emulate, but short
Of thy perfection, how shall I attaine,
Adam, from whose deare side I boast me sprung, 965
And gladly of our Union heare thee speak,
One Heart, one Soul in both; whereof good prooff

---

944 *frustrate*(d).   *loose*, Milton's spelling of 'lose', waste his labour (so in 959).

945 *Not . . . God*, and that is a proceeding we cannot attribute to God; 'of God' = in the case of God.

951 i.e. God would not give Satan this opportunity to blaspheme.

953 *certain to*, resolved to (cf. Virgil's *certa mori* of Dido).

954 *Consort with thee*, keep company with you; i.e. if you die.

961 *trial* is occasionally used for 'proof' in older English; cf. 975.

962 *Illustrious evidence*, clear proof.

963 *Ingaging*, urging, inducing.   *short*, falling short as I do.

964 *attaine*, come up to (the love you show).

This day affords, declaring thee resolvd,
Rather then Death or aught then Death more dread
Shall separate us, linkt in Love so deare,   970
To undergoe with mee one Guilt, one Crime,
If any be, of tasting this fair Fruit,
Whose vertue, for of good still good proceeds,
Direct, or by occasion hath presented
This happie trial of thy Love, which else   975
So eminently never had bin known.
Were it I thought Death menac't would ensue
This my attempt, I would sustain alone
The worst, and not perswade thee, rather die
Deserted, then oblige thee with a fact   980
Pernicious to thy Peace, chiefly assur'd
Remarkably so late of thy so true,
So faithful Love unequald; but I feel
Farr otherwise th' event, not Death, but Life
Augmented, op'nd Eyes, new Hopes, new Joyes,   985
Taste so Divine, that what of sweet before
Hath toucht my sense, flat seems to this, and harsh.
On my experience, *Adam*, freely taste,
And fear of Death deliver to the Windes.

969–70 A parenthesis.   *rather then Death*, rather than that death.
971 *one*, the same.
973 *vertue*, power, effect.   *of good*, from good.   *still*, always.
974 *Direct, or by occasion*, directly or indirectly.
976 *bin*, been (so spelt to indicate light stress).
977 *Death menac't*, the death threatened (by God).   *ensue*, follow on.
980 *oblige thee with a fact*, make you guilty of a deed (Lat. *obligare*).
981 *chiefly assur'd*, chiefly because I am assured.
982 *remarkably so late*, to a remarkable degree lately.
984 *farr . . . th' event*, that the issue will be quite otherwise.
986 *sweet*, sweetness; see 56–7.
987 *to this*, compared to this.
989 *deliver to the Windes*, abandon, ignore.

   So saying, she embrac'd him, and for joy   990
Tenderly wept, much won that hee his Love
Had so enobl'd, as of choice to incurr
Divine displeasure for her sake, or Death.
In recompence (for such compliance bad
Such recompence best merits) from the bough   995
She gave him of that fair enticing Fruit
With liberal hand: he scrupl'd not to eat
Against his better knowledge, not deceav'd,
But fondly overcome with Femal charm.
Earth trembl'd from her entrails, as again   1000
In pangs, and Nature gave a second groan,
Skie lowr'd, and muttering Thunder, som sad drops
Wept at compleating of the mortal Sin
Original; while *Adam* took no thought,
Eating his fill, nor *Eve* to iterate   1005
Her former trespass feard, the more to soothe
Him with her lov'd societie, that now
As with new Wine intoxicated both
They swim in mirth, and fansie that they feel
Divinite within them breeding wings   1010
Wherewith to scorn the Earth: but that false Fruit
Farr other operation first displaid,
Carnal desire enflaming; hee on *Eve*
Began to cast lascivious Eyes, shee him

   992 *of choice*, deliberately, of his own free will, not 'deceaved' as Eve
was.
   999 *fondly*, foolishly, but not excluding the sense of 'prompted by love'.
   1000-1 Cf. 782-4.
   1002-3 'The sky looked threatening, and, uttering low rumbles, wept
some sad drops at the completion of the first and fatal sin (by mortals).
   1005 *iterate*, repeat.
   1007 *that*, so that.
   1009 Cf. 'swim in joy Erelong to swim at large', of mankind before the
Flood (XI, 621-3).

As wantonly repaid; in Lust they burne: 1015
Till *Adam* thus 'gan *Eve* to dalliance move.
   Eve, now I see thou art exact of taste,
And elegant, of Sapience no small part,
Since to each meaning savour we apply,
And Palate call judicious; I the praise   1020
Yeild thee, so well this day thou hast purveyd.
Much pleasure we have lost, while we abstain
From this delightful Fruit, nor known till now
True relish, tasting; if such pleasure be
In things to us forbidd'n, it might be wisht,   1025
For this one Tree had bin forbidd'n ten.
But come, so well refresht, now let us play,
As meet is, after such delicious Fare;
For never did thy Beautie since the day
I saw thee first and wedded thee, adornd   1030
With all perfections, so enflame my sense
With ardor to enjoy thee, fairer now
Then ever, bountie of this vertuous Tree.
   So said he, and forbore not glance or toy
Of amorous intent, well understood   1035
Of *Eve*, whose Eye darted contagious Fire.
Her hand he seis'd, and to a shadie bank,
Thick overhead with verdant roof imbowr'd

1017 *art exact of taste*, have a fine sense of taste.   *elegant*, fastidious. *sapience*, wisdom (cf. 797).

1019-20 'Since we use the word *savour* with both meanings (physical and moral), and apply the word *judicious* to the taste (as well as to mental judgements).'

1021 *purvey'd*, provided food.

1023 *known*, have we known.

1026 *For*, instead of.

1027 *play*, cf. 1042 and 1045.

1033 *bountie of*, thanks to.   *vertuous*, cf. 778 and 973.

1034 *toy*, caress, as in the verb to 'toy with'.

He led her nothing loath; Flours were the Couch,
Pansies, and Violets, and Asphodel,   1040
And Hyacinth, Earths freshest softest lap.
There they thir fill of Love and Loves disport
Took largely, of thir mutual guilt the Seale,
The solace of thir sin, till dewie sleep
Oppressd them, wearied with thir amorous play.   1045
Soon as the force of that fallacious Fruit,
That with exhilerating vapour bland
About thir spirits had plaid, and inmost powers
Made erre, was now exhal'd, and grosser sleep
Bred of unkindly fumes, with conscious dreams   1050
Encumberd, now had left them, up they rose
As from unrest, and each the other viewing,
Soon found thir Eyes how op'nd, and thir minds
How dark'nd; Innocence, that as a veile
Had shadowd them from knowing ill, was gon,   1055
Just Confidence, and native Righteousness,
And Honour from about them, naked left
To guiltie Shame: hee coverd, but his Robe
Uncoverd more. So rose the *Danite* strong
Herculean Samson from the Harlot-lap   1060
Of *Philistean Dalilah,* and wak'd

1041 *Earths . . . lap,* in apposition to the 'Flours' in general.
1043 *mutual,* common (a usage now regarded as incorrect).
1044 *dewie,* falling gently (*O.E.D.*), or, perhaps, coming with the dew.
1046 *fallacious,* deceptive.
1050 *unkindly fumes,* unnatural vapours.   *conscious,* guilty.
1053 *thir Eyes how op'nd,* how much their eyes had been opened.
1055 *knowing ill,* evil thoughts.   *was gon* is predicate both to 'innocence' and to the three nouns in 1056–7.
1056 *confidence,* self-confidence (based on innocence).
1058–9 'Shame covered them, but that covering revealed more than it concealed' (viz. their guilt).   *the Danite,* man of the tribe of Dan.
1060–1 Accent *Hercúlean, Philistéan Dálilah.*

Shorn of his strength, They destitute and bare
Of all thir vertue: silent, and in face
Confounded long they sate, as strook'n mute,
Till *Adam*, though not less then *Eve* abasht,   1065
At length gave utterance to these words constraind.

    O *Eve*, in evil hour thou dist give eare
To that false Worm, of whomsoever taught
To counterfet Mans voice, true in our Fall,
False in our promisd Rising; since our Eyes   1070
Op'nd we find indeed, and find we know
Both Good and Evil, Good lost, and Evil got,
Bad Fruit of Knowledge, if this be to know,
Which leaves us naked thus, of Honour void,
Of Innocence, of Faith, of Puritie,   1075
Our wonted Ornaments now soild and staind,
And in our Faces evident the signes
Of foul concupiscence; whence evil store;
Eev'n Shame, the last of evils; of the first
Be sure then. How shall I behold the face   1080
Henceforth of God or Angel, earst with joy
And rapture so oft beheld? those heav'nly shapes
Will dazle now this earthly, with thir blaze
Insufferably bright. O might I here
In solitude live savage, in some glade   1085

1064 *strook'n*, struck, stricken.
1068 *Worm*, serpent, used of reptiles generally down to eighteenth
century.   *of whomsoever taught*, by whomsoever he was taught.
1069 *true in our Fall*, whose words as to our fall were true.
1071 *indeed*, i.e. as foretold (Gen. 3:5).
1073 *if this be to know*, if this counts as knowledge.
1077 *And* (leaves) *in our Faces*.
1078 *whence evil store*, whence come a mass of evils.
1079 *last*, final, worst.   *first*, minor (evils).
1083 *this earthly* (shape); or 'earthly' may be used as a noun for earthly
being, as in 'My earthly', VIII, 453.

Obscur'd, where highest Woods impenetrable
To Starr or Sun-light, spread thir umbrage broad,
And brown as Eevning: Cover me ye Pines,
Ye Cedars, with innumerable boughs
Hide me, where I may never see them more.   1090
But let us now, as in bad plight, devise
What best may for the present serve to hide
The Parts of each from other, that seem most
To Shame obnoxious, and unseemliest seen,
Some Tree whose broad smooth Leaves together
     sowd,   1095
And girded on our loins, may cover round
Those middle parts, that this new commer, Shame,
There sit not, and reproach us as unclean.

    So counseld hee, and both together went
Into the thickest Wood, there soon they chose   1100
The Figtree, not that kind for Fruit renownd,
But such as at this day to *Indians* known
In *Malabar* or *Decan* spreads her Armes
Braunching so broad and long, that in the ground
The bended Twigs take root, and Daughters grow   1105
About the Mother Tree, a Pillard shade
High overarcht, and echoing Walks between;
There oft the *Indian* Herdsman shunning heate
Shelters in coole, and tends his pasturing Herds

1088 *brown*, dark.
1090 *them*, 'those heavenly shapes' (1082).
1091 *as in*, since we are in.
1093 *Parts*, private parts.   *other*, one another.
1094 *obnoxious*, liable; cf. 170.   *seen*, to be seen, or when seen.
1095 *Some Tree*, in apposition to ' What best . . .', object of 'devise'.
sowd, sewn.
1097 *new commer*, new-comer.
1103 *Malabar*, the west or south-west coast of India.   *Decan*, or
Deccan, the south or the whole of the Indian peninsula.

At Loopholes cut through thickest shade: Those
 Leaves   1110
They gatherd, broad as *Amazonian* Targe,
And with what skill they had, together sowd,
To gird thir waste, vain Covering if to hide
Thir guilt and dreaded shame; O how unlike
To that first naked Glorie. Such of late   1115
Columbus found th' *American*, so girt
With featherd Cincture, naked else and wilde,
Among the Trees on Iles and woodie Shores.
Thus fenc't, and as they thought, thir shame in part
Coverd, but not at rest or ease of Mind,   1120
They sate them down to weep, nor onely Teares
Raind at thir Eyes, but high Winds worse within
Began to rise, high Passions, Anger, Hate,
Mistrust, Suspicion, Discord, and shook sore
Thir inward State of Mind, calme Region once   1125
And full of Peace, now tost and turbulent:
For Understanding rul'd not, and the Will
Heard not her lore, both in subjection now
To sensual Appetite, who from beneath
Usurping over sovran Reason claimd   1130
Superior sway: From thus distemperd brest,
Adam, estrang'd in look and alterd stile,
Speech intermitted thus to *Eve* renewd.

1111 *Amazonian Targe*, the shield carried by the Amazons.
1113 *if* (intended) *to hide*.
1117 *Cincture*, girdle.   *else*, except for that.
1122 *worse within*, all the worse for being within them.
1128 *lore*, teaching, instruction.
1131 *thus distemperd*, disordered in the way described, i.e. ruled by passion (cf. 887).
1132 'changed in his way of looking (at Eve) and manner of speaking', with the suggestion of estrangement.
1133 *intermitted*, broke off (at 1098).

Would thou hadst heark'nd to my words, and staid
With me, as I besought thee, when that strange   1135
Desire of wandring this unhappie Morn,
I know not whence possessd thee; we had then
Remaind still happie, not as now, despoild
Of all our good, sham'd, naked, miserable.
Let none henceforth seek needless cause to approve   1140
The Faith they owe; when earnestly they seek
Such proof, conclude, they then begin to faile.

To whom soon mov'd with touch of blame thus *Eve*.
What words have past thy Lips, *Adam* severe,
Imput'st thou that to my default, or will   1145
Of wandring, as thou callst it, which who knows
But might as ill have happ'nd thou being by,
Or to thy self perhaps: hadst thou bin there,
Or here th' attempt, thou couldst not have discernd
Fraud in the Serpent, speaking as he spake;   1150
No ground of enmitie between us known,
Why hee should mean me ill, or seek to harme.
Was I to have never parted from thy side?
As good have grown there still a liveless Rib.
Being as I am, why didst not thou the Head   1155
Command me absolutely not to go,
Going into such danger as thou saidst?
Too facil then thou didst not much gainsay,
Nay, didst permit, approve, and fair dismiss.

1140 *approve*, make good, prove.
1141 *owe*, are under an obligation to pay or express.
1147 *as ill have happ'nd*, have turned out as badly.
1149 *here th' attempt*, had the temptation occurred here.
1151 *known*, being, or having been, known.
1155 *as I am*, i.e. a woman and subject to my husband.
1159 *fair dismiss*, dismiss me favourably, or with thy blessing; see
372–5.

Hadst thou bin firm and fixt in thy dissent,   1160
Neither had I transgrest, nor thou with mee.
    To whom then first incenst *Adam* repli'd.
Is this the Love, is this the recompence
Of mine to thee, ingrateful *Eve*, exprest
Immutable when thou wert lost, not I,   1165
Who might have liv'd and joyd immortal bliss,
Yet willingly chose rather Death with thee:
And am I now upbraided, as the cause
Of thy transgressing? not anough severe,
It seems, in thy restraint: what could I more?   1170
I warnd thee, I admonishd thee, foretold
The danger, and the lurking Enemie
That lay in wait; beyond this had bin force,
And force upon free Will hath here no place.
But confidence then bore thee on, secure   1175
Either to meet no danger, or to finde
Matter of glorious trial; and perhaps
I also errd in overmuch admiring
What seemd in thee so perfet, that I thought
No evil durst attempt thee, but I rue   1180
That errour now, which is become my crime.
And thou th' accuser. Thus it shall befall
Him who to worth in Woman overtrusting
Lets her Will rule; restraint she will not brook,
And left to her self, if evil thence ensue,   1185

1163–5 i.e. is your love for me equal to that which I showed for
you?   *mine*, my love.   *exprest immutable*, shown to be unchanging;
see 961–2.
    1169–70 *not . . . restraint*, was I not strict enough in restraining you?
    1173 *beyond this had bin*, to go further would have been.
    1175 *confidence*, self-confidence (cf. 1056), over-confidence.   *secure*,
safe as you thought (see 371).
    1177 *glorious trial*, a trial that would bring you glory.

Shee first his weak indulgence will accuse.
Thus they in mutual accusation spent
The fruitless hours, but neither self-condemning,
And of thir vain contest appeerd no end.

1186 *first*, i.e. before he can accuse her.
1189 *contest*, accented on the last syllable, as regularly by Milton.

PARADISE LOST

BOOK X

THE ARGUMENT

Mans transgression known, the Guardian Angels forsake Paradise, and return up to Heaven to approve thir vigilance, and are approv'd, God declaring that the entrance of Satan could not be by them prevented. He sends his Son to judge the Transgressors, who descends and gives Sentence accordingly; then in pity cloathes them both, and reascends. Sin and Death sitting till then at the Gates of Hell, by wondrous sympathie feeling the success of Satan in this new World, and the sin by Man there committed, resolve to sit no longer confin'd in Hell, but to follow Satan thir Sire up to the place of Man: To make the Way easier from Hell to this World to and fro, they pave a broad Highway or Bridge over Chaos, according to the Track that Satan first made; then preparing for Earth, they meet him proud of his success returning to Hell; thir mutual gratulation. Satan arrives at Pandemonium, in full assembly relates with boasting his success against Man; instead of applause is entertaind with a general hiss by all his audience, transformd with himself also suddenly into Serpents, according to his doom giv'n in Paradise; then deluded with a shew of the forbidd'n Tree springing up before them, they greedily reaching to take of the Fruit, chew dust and bitter ashes. The proceedings of Sin and Death; God foretells the final Victory of his Son over them, and the renewing of all things; but for the present commands his Angels to make several alterations in the Heavens and Elements. Adam more

and more perceiving his fall'n condition, heavily bewailes, rejects
the condolement of Eve; she persists and at length appeases him:
Then to evade the Curse likely to fall on thir Offspring, proposes
to Adam violent wayes, which he approves not, but conceiving
better hope, puts her in mind of the late Promise made them, that
her Seed should be reveng'd on the Serpent, and exhorts her
with him to seek Peace of the offended Deity, by repentance and
supplication.

MEANWHILE the hainous and despiteful act
Of *Satan* done in Paradise, and how
Hee in the Serpent had perverted *Eve*,
Her Husband shee, to taste the fatal fruit,
Was known in Heav'n; for what can scape the Eye   5
Of God All-seeing, or deceave his Heart
Omniscient, who in all things wise and just,
Hinderd not *Satan* to attempt the minde
Of Man, with strength entire, and free Will armd,
Complete to have discoverd and repulst   10
Whatever wiles of Foe or seeming Friend.
For still they knew, and ought to have still rememberd
The high Injunction not to taste that Fruit,
Whoever tempted; which they not obeying,
Incurrd, what could they less, the penaltie,   15

1 *hainous* (=heinous), hateful, most wicked (as in IX, 929).   *despiteful*, envious, full of spite (see IX, 175–8).
3 *in* (the form of) *the Serpent*.
7 *who in all things wise*, who, being in all things.
8 *to attempt*, from tempting, attacking.
10 *Complete*, fully able.
11 *Whatever*, any (whatsoever).
12 *they*, Adam and Eve (implied in 'Man', 9).
13 *high*, given them from on high, and also (perhaps) strong, vital.
15 *what could they less*, what less could they have incurred?

And manifold in sin, deserv'd to fall.
Up into Heav'n from Paradise in hast
Th' Angelic Guards ascended, mute and sad
For Man, for of his state by this they knew,
Much wondring how the suttle Fiend had stoln   20
Entrance unseen. Soon as th' unwelcome news
From Earth arriv'd at Heaven Gate, displeas'd
All were who heard, dim sadness did not spare
That time Celestial visages, yet mixt
With pitie, violated not thir bliss.   25
About the new-arriv'd, in multitudes
Th' ethereal People ran, to hear and know
How all befell: they towards the Throne Supream
Accountable made haste to make appear
With righteous plea, thir utmost vigilance,   30
And easily approv'd; when the most High
Eternal Father from his secret Cloud,
Amidst in Thunder utterd thus his voice.
      Assembl'd Angels, and ye Powers returnd
From unsuccessful charge, be not dismaid,   35
Nor troubl'd at these tidings from the Earth,
Which your sincerest care could not prevent,

16 *manifold in sin*, having committed many sins in one.
18 *Th' Angelic Guards*, the Cherubim of IX, 61–2, those serving under
Gabriel (IV, 561–end).
19 *by this* (time), an abbreviation also found in Shakespeare.
22 *Heaven* is here adjectival; cf., e.g., 'London Wall'.
24 *mixt with pitie*, being, or because it was, mixed with pity.
28 *they*, the angelic guards (18).
28–9 *towards*, to be taken with both 'accountable' and 'made haste',
and perhaps also with 'make appear'.   *Accountable*, liable to render an
account (with 'they').
31 *approv'd*, made good (their defence).
33 *Amidst*, in the midst, among them.
35 *charge*, mission, that with which you were charged (cf. IX, 157).

Foretold so lately what would come to pass,
When first this Tempter crossd the Gulf from Hell.
I told ye then he should prevail and speed   40
On his bad Errand, Man should be seduc't
And flatterd out of all, believing lies
Against his Maker; no Decree of mine
Concurring to necessitate his Fall,
Or touch with lightest moment of impulse   45
His free Will, to her own inclining left
In even scale. But fall'n he is, and now
What rests, but that the mortal Sentence pass
On his transgression, Death denounc't that day,
Which he presumes already vain and void,   50
Because not yet inflicted, as he feard,
By some immediat stroak; but soon shall find
Forbearance no acquittance ere day end.
Justice shall not return as bountie scornd.
But whom send I to judge them? whom but thee   55
Vicegerent Son, to thee I have transferrd

38 *Foretold*, i.e. since you were told beforehand (see III, 92-6); but the
construction is probably that of the Latin ablative absolute, like *iis praedictis*.
40 *speed*, succeed.
42 *out of all, believing*, beyond everything into believing . . . (For this
use of 'out of' see *O.E.D.* s.v. 10b.)
44 *Concurring*, co-operating (with his will).
45 *moment*, weight (Lat. *momentum*).
48 *rests*, remains (a Latinism, *restat*).   *mortal*, deathly.   *pass*, should
be passed.
49 *Death denounc'd*, the sentence of Death which was proclaimed.
that day, i.e. immediately he eat that fruit (Gen. 2:17).
52 *immediat stroak*, cf. 210.   *shall find*, man shall find.
53 *acquittance*, acquittal (as in *Hamlet*, IV. vii. 1).
54 i.e. Justice shall not returned to me scorned (in vain) like the bounty
(all my gifts to man) which did not satisfy him. Justice will pursue him to
his death.
56 *Vicegerent*, discharging the function (Lat. *gerere*) instead of (*vice*)
another; as a regent rules for an infant king.

All Judgement, whether in Heav'n, or Earth, or Hell.
Easie it may be seen that I intend
Mercie collegue with Justice, sending thee
Mans Friend, his Mediator, his design'd   60
Both Ransom and Redeemer voluntarie,
And destind Man himself to judge Man fall'n.

So spake the Father, and unfoulding bright
Toward the right hand his Glorie, on the Son
Blaz'd forth unclouded Deitie; hee full   65
Resplendent all his Father manifest
Expressd, and thus divinely answerd milde.

Father Eternal, thine is to decree,
Mine both in Heav'n and Earth to do thy will
Supream, that thou in mee thy Son belov'd   70
Mayst ever rest well pleas'd. I go to judge
On Earth those thy transgressors, but thou knowst,
Whoever judg'd, the worst on mee must light,
When time shall be, for so I undertook
Before thee; and not repenting, this obtaine   75
Of right, that I may mitigate thir doom
On mee deriv'd, yet I shall temper so

58 *Easie*, easily (cf. IX, 24).

59 *collegue* (= colleague), go along with (here probably the verb).

60 *Mediator*, i.e. between God and man.   *his design'd*, designed to be his.

62 *destind Man himself*, destined to be himself a man, i.e. at the Incarnation; we might have expected 'thyself', but the words after 'thee' make the third person possible.

65 *full*, fully.

67 *Expressd*, showed forth *or* reflected.

68 *thine is*, it is thy part, office (a classical idiom).

72 *those*: Keightley conjectured; *these*: early editions.

74 *time shall be*, the right moment comes (cf. 'when the fulness of time was come', Gal. 4:4).

77 *deriv'd*, turned aside (Lat. *derivare*, of a river).

Justice with Mercie, as may illustrat most
Them fully satisfi'd, and thee appease.
Attendance none shall need, nor Train, where none   80
Are to behold the Judgement, but the judg'd,
Those two; the third best absent is condemnd,
Convict by flight, and Rebel to all Law:
Conviction to the Serpent none belongs.

    Thus saying, from his radiant Seat he rose   85
Of high collateral glorie: him Thrones and Powers,
Princedoms, and Dominations ministrant
Accompanied to Heaven Gate, from whence
Eden and all the Coast in prospect lay.
Down he descended strait; the speed of Gods   90
Time counts not, though with swiftest minutes wingd.
Now was the Sun in Western cadence low
From Noon, and gentle Aires due at thir hour
To fan the Earth now wak'd, and usher in
The Eevning coole, when he from wrauth more coole 95
Came the mild Judge and Intercessor both
To sentence Man: the voice of God they heard
Now walking in the Garden, by soft windes
Brought to thir Ears, while day declin'd; they heard,

78 *illustrat*, show (spelling shows accent on second syllable).
79 *Them*, Justice and Mercie, or possibly Adam and Eve.
80 *Attendance . . . need*, no attendants will be necessary.
82 *best absent*, best in absence.
83 *Convict*, convicted.
84 *Conviction*, proof of guilt (as in a law court).   *belongs*, is needed,
appropriate.
86 *collateral*, as Father and Son sat side-by-side (Lat. *latus*), so their
glory was equal.
89 *Coast*, adjacent parts (biblical, but usually in plural).
90–1 i.e. time, however swift, cannot measure the speed of divine
(angelic) flight; see Commentary.
92 *cadence*, decline (Lat. *cado* = fall).
93 *Noon*, its position at midday.

And from his presence hid themselves among   100
The thickest Trees, both Man and Wife, till God
Approaching, thus to *Adam* calld aloud.

    Where art thou *Adam*, wont with joy to meet
My coming seen farr off? I miss thee here,
Not pleas'd, thus entertaind with solitude,   105
Where obvious dutie erewhile appeard unsought:
Or come I less conspicuous, or what change
Absents thee, or what chance detains? Come forth.
He came and with him *Eve* more loth, though first
To offend, discount'nanc't both, and discompos'd;   110
Love was not in thir looks, either to God
Or to each other, but apparent guilt,
And shame, and perturbation, and despaire,
Anger, and obstinacie, and hate, and guile.
Whence *Adam* faultring long, thus answerd brief.   115

    I heard thee in the Garden, and of thy voice
Affraid, being naked, hid my self. To whom
The gracious Judge without revile repli'd.

    My voice thou oft hast heard, and hast not feard,
But still rejoyc't, how is it now become   120
So dreadful to thee? that thou art naked, who

103 *wont*, who wert accustomed.

106 i.e. in a situation where you used of your own accord to do me the
courtesy of coming to meet me ('obvious' bears the sense of the Lat.
obvius, coming to meet, in the way).

107 *Or...or*, either...or, modern usage omitting the first.

108 *Absents thee*, makes thee absent.

109–10 *though . . . offend*, i.e. and who therefore should be first to
confess her sin.

110 *discount'nanc't*, out-of-countenance, shame-faced.

112 *apparent*, obvious.

115 *Whence*, in this state of mind.   *faultring long*, after much hesita-
tion.

118 *revile*, reproaching (him).

120 *still*, always.

Hath told thee? hast thou eat'n of the Tree
Whereof I gave thee charge thou shouldst not eat?

   To whom thus *Adam* sore beset repli'd.
O Heav'n! in evil strait this day I stand   125
Before my Judge, either to undergoe
My self the total Crime, or to accuse
My other self, the partner of my life;
Whose failing, while her Faith to mee remaines,
I should conceal, and not expose to blame   130
By my complaint; but strict necessitie
Subdues me, and calamitous constraint,
Least on my head both sin and punishment,
However insupportable, be all
Devolv'd; though should I hold my peace, yet thou   135
Wouldst easily detect what I conceale.
This Woman whom thou mad'st to be my help.
And gav'st me as thy perfet gift, so good,
So fit, so acceptable, so Divine,
That from her hand I could suspect no ill,   140
And what she did, whatever in it self,
Her doing seemd to justifie the deed;
Shee gave me of the Tree, and I did eate.

   To whom the sovran Presence thus repli'd.
Was shee thy God, that her thou didst obey   145
Before his voice, or was shee made thy guide,
Superior, or but equal, that to her
Thou dist resigne thy Manhood, and the Place

125 *strait*, straits, dilemma.
126 *undergoe*, take upon me.
138 *perfet*, perfect.
139 pronounce *accéptáble*.
141–2 'whatever she did, however trifling it was in itself, seemed worth doing because *she* did it'.
147 *but equal*, merely equal.

Wherein God set thee above her made of thee,
And for thee, whose perfection farr excelld   150
Hers in all real dignitie; Adornd
She was indeed, and lovely to attract
Thy Love, not thy Subjection, and her Gifts
Were such as under Government well seemd,
Unseemly to beare rule, which was thy part   155
And person, hadst thou known thy self aright.
    So having said, he thus to *Eve* in few:
Say Woman, what is this which thou hast done?
    To whom sad *Eve* with shame nigh overwhelmd,
Confessing soon, yet not before her Judge   160
Bold or loquacious, thus abasht repli'd.
    The Serpent me beguil'd and I did eate.
    Which when the Lord God heard, without delay
To Judgement he proceeded on th' accus'd
Serpent though brute, unable to transferre   165
The Guilt on him who made him instrument
Of mischief, and polluted from the end
Of his Creation; justly then accurst,
As vitiated in Nature: more to know
Concernd not Man (since he no furder knew)   170

149 *of thee*, from thee, out of thy flesh.
154 *such as . . . seem'd*, such as seemed good provided they (i.e. she)
were kept under control (by her husband).
155 *Unseemly*, unsuitable to.
156 *person*, role, character (orignally in Latin a dramatic term; cf.
'impersonate').
157 *in few*, in few words (as Lat. *pauca = pauca verba*); a Shakespearian usage.
165 *unable*, who was unable (with 'Serpent').
166 *him*, Satan.
167 *polluted*, *either* 'and who polluted him', *or* a past participle, parallel
to 'instrument'.
169 *more to know*, i.e. as to the Serpent's punishment.
170 *since he no furder knew*, i.e. or God would have given him that
knowledge.

Nor alterd his offence; yet God at last
To *Satan* first in sin his doom apply'd,
Though in mysterious terms, judg'd as then best:
And on the Serpent thus his curse let fall.

Because thou hast done this, thou art accurst   175
Above all Cattel, each Beast of the Field;
Upon thy Belly groveling thou shalt goe,
And dust shalt eat all the days of thy Life.
Between Thee and the Woman I will put
Enmitie, and between thine and her Seed;   180
Her Seed shall bruise thy head, thou bruise his heel.

So spake this Oracle, then verifi'd
When *Jesus* son of *Mary* second *Eve*,
Saw Satan fall like Lightning down from Heav'n,
Prince of the Aire; then rising from his Grave   185
Spoild Principalities and Powers, triumphed
In op'n shew, and with ascension bright
Capitivity led captive through the Aire,
The Realme it self of *Satan* long usurpt,
Whom he shall tread at last under our feet;   190
Eevn hee who now foretold his fatal bruise,
And to the Woman thus his Sentence turnd.

Thy sorrow I will greatly multiplie
By thy Conception; Childern thou shalt bring

171 *at last*, in the end.

172 *first in sin*, who was the first sinner (a parenthesis).

173 *mysterious* applies chiefly to 181 below.   *judg'd . . . best*, as at
that time he thought best.

185 *Prince of the Aire*, goes with 'Satan'.

186-7 *triumphd In op'n show*, openly made a show of them, put them to
ridicule.

188-9 *Captivity*, his prisoners.   *the Aire . . . usurpt*, the air which had
long been a sphere usurped by Satan.

191 *his*, Satan's

192 i.e. he turned to the woman to sentence her.

194 *by*, as a result of.   *Childern*, the old plural form; so in 336.

In sorrow forth, and to thy Husbands will   195
Thine shall submit, hee over thee shall rule.

On *Adam* last thus judgement he pronounc'd.
Because thou hast heark'nd to the voice of thy Wife,
And eat'n of the Tree concerning which
I charg'd thee, saying: Thou shalt not eate therefo,   200
Curst is the ground for thy sake, thou in sorrow
Shalt eate thereof all the days of thy Life;
Thorns also and Thistles it shall bring thee forth
Unbid, and thou shalt eate th' Herb of the Field,
In the sweat of thy Face shalt thou eate Bread,   205
Till thou return unto the ground, for thou
Out of the ground wast tak'n: know thy Birth,
For dust thou art, and shalt to dust returne.

So judg'd he Man, both Judge and Saviour sent,
And th' instant stroke of Death denounc't that day   210
Remov'd farr off; then pittying how they stood
Before him naked to the aire, that now
Must suffer change, disdaind not to begin
Thenceforth the forme of servant to assume,
As when he washd his servants feet, so now   215
As Father of his Familie he clad
Thir nakedness with Skins of Beasts, or slain,
Or as the Snake with youthful Coate repaid;
And thought not much to cloathe his Enemies:
Nor hee thir outward onely with the Skins   220

209 i.e. sent as both judge and saviour.

210 *denounc't that day*, see 49 above.

212–13 *now . . . change*, see 651, etc., below.

217 *or*, cf. 107.

218 i.e. skins which had been (sloughed off and) replaced, as in the case of snakes.

219 *thought* (it) *not* (too) *much* (trouble).   *his Enemies*, because man's sin put him at enmity with God.

220 *thir outward* (nakedness), object of 'arraying' (223).

Of Beasts, but inward nakedness, much more
Opprobrious, with his Robe of righteousness,
Araying coverd from his Fathers sight.
To him with swift ascent he up returnd,
Into his blissful bosom reassum'd   225
In glory as of old, to him appeas'd
All, though all-knowing, what had past with Man
Recounted, mixing intecession sweet.
Meanwhile ere thus was sinnd and judg'd on Earth,
Within the Gates of Hell sate Sin and Death,   230
In counterview within the Gates, that now
Stood op'n wide, belching outrageous flame
Farr into *Chaos*, since the Fiend passd through,
Sin op'ning, who thus now to Death began.

    O Son, why sit we here each other viewing   235
Idlely, while *Satan* our great Author thrives
In other Worlds, and happier Seat provides
For us his ofspring deare? It cannot be
But that success attends him; if mishap,
Ere this he had returnd, with fury driv'n   240
By his Avengers, since no place like this
Can fit his punishment, or their revenge.

222 *Opprobrious*, offensive.

225 *reassum'd*, taken back.

226–8 'recounted to his Father, who was now appeased, all that had
passed concerning Man, although the Father was omniscient, inter-
mingling with his narrative generous pleadings for Man.'

229 *was sinn'd and judg'd*, sin and judgement had taken place; an imita-
tion of a Latin impersonal construction like *pugnatum est*=it was fought,
i.e. a battle took place; cf. VI, 335.

231 *In counterview*, opposite one another.   *now*, i.e. since Satan's
visit to Earth; cf. II, 883–4.

234 *Sin op'ning*, on Sin opening them (an absolute construction).

236 *our . . . Author*, the author of our being.

239 *if mishap*, sc. had attended him.

241 Avengers Ed. 2: Avenger Ed. 1.   *like this*, so well as this.

Methinks I feel new strength within me rise,
Wings growing, and Dominion giv'n me large
Beyond this Deep; whatever drawes me on,   245
Or sympathie, or som connatural force
Powerful at greatest distance to unite
With secret amity things of like kinde
By secretest conveyance. Thou my Shade
Inseparable must with mee along: 250
For Death from Sin no power can separate.
But least the difficultie of passing back
Stay his return perhaps over this Gulfe
Impassable, impervious, let us try
Adventrous work, yet to thy power and mine   255
Not unagreeable, to found a path
Over this Maine from Hell to that new World
Where *Satan* now prevailes, a Monument
Of merit high to all th' infernal Host,
Easing thir passage hence, for intercourse,   260
Or transmigration, as thir lot shall lead.
Nor can I miss the way, so strongly drawn
By this new felt attraction and instinct.
    Whom thus the meager Shadow answerd soon.
Goe whither Fate and inclination strong   265

245 *this Deep*, Hell.   *whatever* (it may be that) *draws me on.*
246 *connatural*, depending on our (natural) relationship of parent and child.
249 *Shade*, shadow, inseparable companion (cf. IX, 12).
250 *along*, go along.
254 *impervious*, allowing no way (Lat. *via*) through (Lat. *per*).
256 *unagreeable*, unsuitable.   *found* lay the foundation for (Lat. *fundare*; cf. fundamental).
257 *Maine*, sea of air, the 'Chaos damp' of 283.
258 *a Monument*, i.e. the 'path' would be this.
260 *intercourse*, going to and from the earth.
261 *transmigration*, permanent removal to earth.
263 *instinct* (accent on last syllable), i.e. secret physical sympathy.
264 *meager*, thin (cf. Fr. *maigre*).

Leads thee, I shall not lag behinde, nor erre
The way, thou leading, such a sent I draw
Of carnage, prey innumerable, and taste
The savour of Death from all things there that live:
Nor shall I to the work thou enterprisest   270
Be wanting, but afford thee equal aid.
    So saying, with delight he snuffd the smell
Of mortal change on Earth. As when a flock
Of ravenous Fowl, though many a League remote,
Against the day of Battel, to a Field,   275
Where Armies lie encampt, come flying, lur'd
With sent of living Carcasses design'd
For death, the following day, in bloodie fight.
So sented the grim Feature, and upturnd
His Nostril wide into the murkie Air,   280
Sagacious of his Quarrey from so farr.
Then Both from out Hell Gates into the waste
Wide Anarchie of *Chaos* damp and dark
Flew divers, and with power (thir power was great)
Hovering upon the Waters, what they met   285
Solid or slimie, as in raging Sea
Tost up and down, together crowded drove
From each side shoaling towards the mouth of Hell.

266 *erre*, miss, stray from.
267 *sent*, scent.   *draw*, into my nostrils.
270 *enterprisest*, undertakest.
273 *mortal* probably includes both the notions of *fatal* and brought about by and affecting *man*.
274 *ravenous Fowl*, i.e. vultures.   *remote*, distant, from a distance.
277 *design'd*, destined.
279 *Feature*, a thing made, a shape (cf. manufacture, Lat. *factura*).
281 *Sagacious of*, smelling (Lat. *sagax* is specially used of dogs scenting).
284 *divers*, in different directions.
285-8 'drove together in a heap whatever they met . . . so that it formed a shoal towards the mouth of Hell'.

As when two Polar Winds blowing adverse
Upon the *Cronian* Sea, together drive   290
Mountains of Ice, that stop th' imagind way
Beyond *Petsora* Eastward, to the rich
Cathaian Coast. The aggregated Soile
Death with his Mace petrific, cold and dry,
As with a Trident smote, and fixd as firm   295
As *Delos* floating once; the rest his look
Bound with *Gorgonian* rigor not to move,
And with *Asphaltic* slime; broad as the Gate,
Deep to the Roots of Hell the gatherd beach
They fast'nd, and the Mole immense wraught on   300
Over the foaming Deep high Archt, a Bridge
Of length prodigious joining to the Wall
Immoveable of this now fenceless World
Forfeit to Death; from hence a passage broad,
Smooth, easie, inoffensive down to Hell.   305
So, if great things to small may be compar'd,
Xerxes, the Libertie of *Greece* to yoke,
From *Susa* his *Memnonian* Palace high

289 *adverse*, from opposite directions.

290 *the Cronian Sea*, the Arctic (Lat. *Cronium Mare*).

291 *imagind*, supposed to exist.

292 *Petsora*, the river, gulf and sea of Pechora, on the north coast of Russia, round longitude 55 degrees.

293 *Cathaian Coast*, the coast of Cathay, to the north of China. *aggregated*, heaped up.

294 *Mace*, sceptre.   *petrific*, petrifying, turning to stone.   *cold and dry* agree with 'Soile', not with 'Mace'.

296 *the rest* are probably the remaining elements, viz. hot and moist.

297 *Gorgonian rigor*, imposing immobility like the Gorgon's look, which was supposed to turn men to stone.

298 *Asphaltic slime*, bitumen (a form of petroleum).

300 *Mole*, causeway (Lat. *moles* = mass).   303 *fenceless*, unprotected.

304 *Forfeit to*, given over to (as payment for man's sin).   *hence* (making) *a passage*.

305 *inoffensive*, unobstructed.

Came to the Sea, and over *Hellespont*
Bridging his way, *Europe* with *Asia* joind,   310
And scourg'd with many a stroak th' indignant waves.
Now had they brought the work by wondrous Art
Pontifical, a ridge of pendent Rock
Over the vext Abyss, following the track
Of *Satan*, to the self same place where hee   315
First lighted from his Wing, and landed safe
From out of *Chaos* to the outside bare
Of this round World: with Pinns of Adamant
And Chains they made all fast, too fast they made
And durable; and now in little space   320
The Confines met of Empyrean Heav'n
And of this World, and on the left hand Hell
With long reach interpos'd; three several wayes
In sight, to each of these three places led.
And now thir way to Earth they had descri'd,   325
To Paradise first tending, when behold
Satan in likeness of an Angel bright
Betwixt the *Centaure* and the *Scorpion* stearing
His *Zenith*, while the Sun in *Aries* rose:
Disguis'd he came, but those his Childern dear   330
Thir Parent soon discernd, though in disguise.

312–13 *Art Pontifical*, the skill or technique of bridge-building (Lat. *pons* = bridge and *facio* = make); so 'Pontifice', 348.

313 *pendent*, hanging (in Chaos).

314 *vext*, with storms; cf. 286.

317–18 *to*, on to.   *the outside bare . . . World*, the outer shell of the Universe.

321 Accent *Empyréan*.

323 *With long reach*, i.e. the bridge just made.   *interpos'd*, came between the way up to heaven and that down into the universe to earth.

326 *To . . . tending*, aiming for Paradise first.   *behold*, you might have seen.

328–9 *stearing his Zenith*, directing his course upward.

Hee, after *Eve* seduc't, unminded slunk
Into the Wood fast by, and changing shape
To observe the sequel, saw his guileful act
By *Eve*, though all unweeting, seconded   335
Upon her Husband, saw thir shame that sought
Vain covertures; but when he saw descend
The Son of God to judge them, terrifi'd
He fled, not hoping to escape, but shun
The present, fearing guiltie what his wrauth   340
Might suddenly inflict; that past, returnd
By Night, and listning where the hapless Paire
Sate in thir sad discourse, and various plaint,
Thence gatherd his own doom: which understood
Not instant, but of future time, with joy   345
And tidings fraught, to Hell he now returnd,
And at the brink of *Chaos*, neer the foot
Of this new wondrous Pontifice, unhop't
Met who to meet him came, his Ofspring dear.
Great joy was at thir meeting, and at sight   350
Of that stupendious Bridge his joy encreas'd.

332 *after Eve seduc't*, after the seduction of Eve (the Lat. construction of *post Troiam captam.*)   *unminded*, unnoticed.

335 *unweeting*, unknowing (i.e. that Satan had deceived her as to the consequences of the act).   *seconded*, repeated.

337 *covertures*, coverings (IX, 1110–30).

340 *guiltie*, in his consciousness of guilt.

341 *that past*, that fear (of immediate punishment) over.

343 *plaint*, complainings, lamentations.

344–5 *which . . . time*, and when he understood that his doom referred to the future, not to that moment.

345–6 *joy and tidings*, i.e. joyful tidings.   *to Hell*, i.e. towards Hell: cf. 393–4.

347 *the foot*, the upper end (in this case).

348–9 *unhop't Met who*, met those he had not expected to find there.

351 *stupendious*, an old form of 'stupendous'.   *encreas'd*, increased Anglo-French and Middle English spelling).

Long he admiring stood, till Sin, his faire
Inchanting Daughter, thus the silence broke.
   O Parent, these are thy magnific deeds,
Thy Trophies, which thou view'st as not thine own, 355
Thou art thir Author and prime Architect:
For I no sooner in my Heart divin'd,
My Heart, which by a secret harmonie
Still moves with thine, joind in connexion sweet,
That thou on Earth hadst prosperd, which thy looks 360
Now also evidence, but straight I felt
Though distant from thee Worlds between, yet felt
That I must after thee with this thy Son;
Such fatal consequence unites us three:
Hell could no longer hold us in her bounds, 365
Nor this unvoyageable Gulf obscure
Detain from following thy illustrious track.
Thou hast atchiev'd our libertie, confin'd
Within Hell Gates till now, thou us impow'rd
To fortifie thus farr, and overlay 370
With this portentous Bridge the dark Abyss.
Thine now is all this World, thy vertue hath won
What thy hands builded not, thy Wisdom gaind
With odds what Warr hath lost, and fully aveng'd
Our foile in Heav'n; here thou shalt Monarch reign, 375
There didst not; there let him still Victor sway,
As Battel hath adjudg'd, from this new World

354 *magnific*, glorious, magnificent.
363 *after*, go after.
364 *fatal consequence*, fated connection (especially used of *logical* con-
nection).
370 *fortifie*, build (like Lat. *munire viam*).
372 *vertue*, courage.
374 *With odds*, with additions, more than.
375 *Our foile*, our being foiled, our defeat.

Retiring, by his own doom alienated,
And henceforth Monarchie with thee divide
Of all things, parted by th' Empyreal bounds,   380
His Quadrature, from thy Orbicular World,
Or trie thee now more dangerous to his Throne.
      Whom thus the Prince of Darkness answerd glad.
Fair Daughter, and thou Son and Grandchild both,
High proof ye now have giv'n to be the Race   385
Of *Satan* (for I glorie in the name,
Antagonist of Heav'ns Almightie King)
Amply have merited of mee, of all
Th' Infernal Empire, that so neer Heav'ns dore
Triumphal with triumphal act have met,   390
Mine with this glorious Work, and made one Realm
Hell and this World, one Realm, one Continent
Of easie thorough-fare. Therefore while I
Descend through Darkness, on your Rode with ease
To my associat Powers, them to acquaint   395
With these successes, and with them rejoyce,
You two this way, among those numerous Orbs
All yours, right down to Paradise descend;
There dwell and Reign in bliss, thence on the Earth

378 *doom*, judgement (on man).   *alienated*, made distant, estranged.
380 *th' Empyreal bounds*, the limits of the highest heaven.
381 *Quadrature*, square.   *Orbicular*, round.
382 *trie*, prove.
384 *thou*, Death; see Commentary on 235.
385 *to be the Race*, that you are sprung from.
386 *the name*. Satan means 'the Adversary' or 'Opposer'.
388–9 'You have deserved well of me and of all the powers of Hell'.
390 i.e. you have matched my triumph in perverting man by yours in building this bridge.
394 *your Rode*, the road you have made.
397 *those numerous Orbs*, i.e. the stars and planets which Satan had passed on his journey to and return from Earth; cf. Commentary at 314–24.

Dominion exercise and in the Aire,   400
Chiefly on Man, sole Lord of all declar'd,
Him first make sure your thrall, and lastly kill.
My Substitutes I send ye, and Create
Plenipotent on Earth, of matchless might
Issuing from mee: on your joint vigor now   405
My hold of this new Kingdom all depends,
Through Sin to Death expos'd by my exploit.
If your joint power prevaile, th' affaires of Hell
No detriment need feare: goe and be strong.

   So saying he dismissed them; they with speed   410
Thir course through thickest Constellations held
Spreading thir bane; the blasted Starrs lookd wan,
And Planets, Planet-strook, real Eclips
Then sufferd. Th' other way Satan went down
The Causey to Hell Gate; on either side   415
Disparted Chaos over built exclaimd,
And with rebounding surge the barrs assaild,
That scornd his indignation: through the Gate,
Wide op'n and unguarded, Satan passd,
And all about found desolate; for those   420
Appointed to sit there, had left thir charge,
Flown to the upper World; the rest were all
Farr to th' in-land retir'd, about the walls

402 *make sure your thrall*, make sure of him as the slave of sin (and death).
404 (scan) *Plenipotent*, with full authority.
406 *all*, entirely (as in the modern use, e.g. 'it all depends on me').
409 *detriment*, harm.
413 *Planet-strook*, sick or ailing, as if stricken by (other) planets.
Eclips, loss of light.
415 *Causey*, cause(y)way (Fr. *chaussée*).
416 *over built*, built over.   *exclaimd*, protested.
417 *the barrs*, i.e. of the bridge.
418 *his*, Chaos being personified, as in II, 895, etc.
423 *th' in-land*, scan as one foot, 'th' inland'.

Of *Pandæmonium*, Citie and proud seate
Of *Lucifer*, so by allusion calld,   425
Of that bright Starr to *Satan* paragond.
There kept thir Watch the Legions, while the Grand
In Council sate, sollicitous what chance
Might intercept thir Emperour sent, so hee
Departing gave command, and they observ'd.   430
As when the *Tartar* from his *Russian* Foe
By *Astracan* over the Snowie Plaines
Retires, or *Bactrian* Sophi from the hornes
Of *Turkish* Crescent, leaves all waste beyond
The Realme of *Aladule*, in his retreate   435
To *Tauris* or *Casbeen*: So these the late
Heav'n-banisht Host, left desert utmost Hell
Many a dark League, reduc't in careful Watch
Round thir Metropolis, and now expecting
Each hour thir great adventurer from the search   440
Of Forren Worlds: hee through the midst unmarkt,
In shew plebeian Angel militant
Of lowest order, passd; and from the dore
Of that *Plutonian* Hall, invisible

424 *Pandæmonium*, the place of all the devils (Gk. *pan* + *daimon*).

426 *Of that bright Star . . . paragon'd* to that bright star (viz. Lucifer) equated with Satan.

427 *the Grand*, the grandees, chief lords.

428 *sollicitous*, anxious as to.

429 *sent*, i.e. on a mission to Earth.

433 *Sophi*, Shah.

434–5 *hornes of Turkish Crescent*, i.e. the Turkish armies, whose flag showed a half-moon.

436–7 *these . . . Host*, these devils who had lately been expelled from Heaven.   *utmost*, the outer parts of (cf. 'in-land', 423).

442 *shew*, appearance.   *plebeian*, common, ordinary.

444 *Plutonian*, Pluto was the ruler of the underworld in classical mythology.

Ascended his high Throne, which under state   445
Of richest texture spred, at th' upper end
Was plac't in regal lustre. Down a while
He sate, and round about him saw unseen:
At last as from a Cloud his fulgent head
And shape Starr-bright appeerd, or brighter, clad   450
With what permissive glory since his fall
Was left him, or false glitter: All amaz'd
At that so sudden blaze the *Stygian* throng
Bent thir aspect, and whom they wishd beheld,
Thir mighty Chief returnd: loud was th' acclaime: 455
Forth rushd in haste the great consulting Peers,
Rais'd from thir dark *Divan*, and with like joy
Congratulant approachd him, who with hand
Silence, and with these words attention won.

   Thrones, Dominations, Princedoms, Vertues,
     Powers,   460
For in possession such, not onely of right,
I call ye and declare ye now, returnd
Successful beyond hope, to lead ye forth
Triumphant out of this infernal Pit
Abominable, accurst, the house of woe,   465
And Dungeon of our Tyrant: Now possess,
As Lords, a spacious World, to our native Heaven
Little inferiour, by my adventure hard

445 *state*, a canopy.
448 *saw unseen*, looked at others being himself invisible.
451 *permissive*, permitted him (by God).
454 *Bent . . . aspect* (accent aspéct), directed their gaze (the choice of word being probably suggested by 'Starr-bright', 'blaze', etc.; cf. 658).
457 *dark Divan*, secret council (the Turkish word for a privy council).
458 *Congratulant*, congratulating him (Lat. present partic. *congratulans*).
460-2 i.e. I now call you by these titles in view of your possession (of the Earth), not only by your old right to them.
466 i.e. Hell is God's prison-house for his enemies.

With peril great atchiev'd. Long were to tell
What I have don, what sufferd, with what paine   470
Voyag'd th' unreal, vast, unbounded Deep
Of horrible confusion, over which
By Sin and Death a broad way now is pav'd
To expedite your glorious march; but I
Toild out my uncouth passage, forc't to ride   475
Th' untractable Abysse, plung'd in the womb
Of unoriginal *Night* and *Chaos* wilde,
That jealous of thir secrets fiercely oppos'd
My journey strange, with clamorous uproare
Protesting Fate supreame; thence how I found   480
The new created World, which fame in Heav'n
Long had foretold, a Fabrick wonderful
Of absolute perfection, therein Man
Plac't in a Paradise, by our exile
Made happie: Him by fraud I have seduc't   485
From his Creator, and the more to increase
Your wonder, with an Apple; hee thereat
Offended, worth your laughter, hath giv'n up
Both his beloved Man and all his World,
To Sin and Death a prey, and so to us,   490
Without our hazard, labour, or allarme,

469 *Long were,* it would be a long story.

471 *Deep,* i.e. Chaos.

475 *uncouth* (accent on first syllable), unknown, the original meaning of the word.   *ride,* traverse; cf. IX, 63.

477 *unoriginal,* without origin or beginning.

480 *Protesting Fate supreame,* calling to witness supreme Fate (against the violation).   *thence* (to tell, 469) *how.*

484 *exile* (accent on last, as in Spenser), banishment.

485 *Him.* The capital letter is for emphasis.

488 *Offended,* thwarted (stronger than nowadays).   (a thing) *worth your laughter.*

491 *allarme,* call to arms (and so almost 'fighting').

To range in, and to dwell, and over Man
To rule, as over all hee should have rul'd.
True is, mee also he hath judg'd, or rather
Mee not, but the brute Serpent in whose shape   495
Man I deceav'd: that which to mee belongs,
Is enmity, which he will put between
Mee and Mankinde; I am to bruise his heel;
His Seed, when is not set, shall bruise my head:
A World who would not purchase with a bruise,   500
Or much more grievous pain? Ye have th' account
Of my performance: What remaines, ye Gods,
But up and enter now into full bliss?

    So having said, a while he stood, expecting
Thir universal shout and high applause   505
To fill his eare, when contrary he hears
On all sides, from innumerable tongues
A dismal universal hiss, the sound
Of public scorn; he wonderd, but not long
Had leasure, wondring at himself now more;   510
His Visage drawn he felt to sharp and spare,
His Armes clung to his Ribs, his Leggs entwining
Each other, till supplanted down he fell
A monstrous Serpent on his Belly prone,
Reluctant, but in vaine: a greater power   515
Now rul'd him, punisht in the shape he sinnd,
According to his doom: he would have spoke,

493 *hee*, man.
499 *when*, the time.   *set*, determined.
506 *contrary*, on the contrary.
511 *drawn*, contracted.
512 *clung . . . entwining*, still after 'he felt'.
513 *supplanted*, tripped up (the original Latin sense from *planta* = the sole of the foot).
515 *reluctant*, struggling against (this) (Lat. *reluctari*).
517 *doom*, see 177.

But hiss for hiss returnd with forked tongue
To forked tongue, for now were all transformd
Alike, to Serpents all as accessories   520
To his bold Riot: dreadful was the din
Of hissing through the Hall, thick swarming now
With complicated monsters, head and taile,
Scorpion and Asp, and *Amphisbæna* dire,
Cerastes hornd, *Hydrus*, and *Ellops* drear,   525
And *Dipsas* (Not so thick swarmd once the Soil
Bedropt with blood of *Gorgon*, or the Ile
Ophiusa) but still greatest hee the midst,
Now Dragon grown, larger then whom the Sun
Ingenderd in the *Pythian* Vale on slime,   530
Huge *Python*, and his Power no less he seemd
Above the rest still to retain; they all
Him followd issuing forth to th' op'n Field,
Where all yet left of that revolted Rout
Heav'n-fall'n, in station stood or just array,   535
Sublime with expectation when to see

520 *accessories*, probably to be read as 'accessóries'.
521 *Riot*, revolt, outbreak.
523 *complicated*, intertwined.
524 *Amphisboena*, a mythical kind of serpent with a head at both ends
(Gk. *amphi* + *baino*, go).
525 *Cerastes*, a snake with horns (Gk. *keras* = horn).   *Hydrus*, a
fabulous water-snake (Gk. *hydor* = water).   *Ellops*, a kind of serpent,
usually a fish (Gk. *ellops* = mute).
526 *Dipsas*, a serpent whose bite caused thirst, which is in Gk. *dipsos*.
(The name occurs in Du Bartas.)   *soil*, i.e. of Libya.
528 *Ophiusa* (in reading slur the 'iu' into one syllable) isle of snakes
(Gk. *ophioussa*); now Formentera, one of the Balearic isles.
529 *than whom*, than the one whom.
530 *Pythian*. Pytho was the older name for the region of Delphi.
534 *Rout*, defeated army.
535 *in station*, at their post, on guard.   *just array*, drawn up in proper
order.
536 *Sublime*, towering up, lofty.

In Triumph issuing forth thir glorious Chief;
They saw, but other sight instead, a crowd
Of ugly Serpents; horror on them fell,
And horrid sympathie; for what they saw,   540
They felt themselves now changing; down thir arms,
Down fell both Spear and Shield, down they as fast,
And the dire hiss renewd, and the dire form
Catchd by Contagion, like in punishment,
As in thir crime. Thus was th' applause they meant,   545
Turnd to exploding hiss, triumph to shame
Cast on themselves from thir own mouths. There stood
A Grove hard by, sprung up with this thir change,
His will who reigns above, to aggravate
Thir penance, lad'n with fair Fruit, like that   550
Which grew in Paradise, the bait of *Eve*
Us'd by the Tempter: on that prospect strange
Thir earnest eyes they fixd, imagining
For one forbidd'n Tree a multitude
Now ris'n, to work them furder woe or shame;   555
Yet parcht with scalding thurst and hunger fierce,
Though to delude them sent, could not abstain,
But on they rould in heaps, and up the Trees
Climbing, sat thicker then the snakie locks
That curld *Megæra:* greedily they pluckd   560
The Frutage fair to sight, like that which grew

540 *sympathie,* fellow-feeling in the literal sense.
541 *changing* (into), becoming; cf. IX, 505.
545 *meant,* intended to give (Satan).
546 *exploding,* in its literal Lat. sense of driving off the stage with hisses.
549 (by) *His will . . . above,* an absolute construction, like *Deo volente.*
551 *the bait of Eve,* to catch Eve.
554 *For,* in place of.
555 *furder,* further.
556–7 *Yet parcht . . . could not,* yet, parched as they were . . . they could
not.   *Though .·. sent,* though they knew the trees were sent.

Neer that bituminous Lake where *Sodom* flam'd;
This more delusive, not the touch, but taste
Deceav'd; they fondly thinking to allay
Thir appetite with gust, instead of Fruit   565
Chewd bitter Ashes, which th' offended taste
With spattering noise rejected: oft they assayd,
Hunger and thirst constraining, drugd as oft,
With hatefullest disrelish writh'd thir jaws
With soot and cinders filld; so oft they fell   570
Into the same illusion, not as Man
Whom they triumphd once lapst. Thus were they
    plagu'd
And worn with Famin, long and ceasless hiss,
Till thir lost shape, permitted, they resum'd,
Yearly enjoind, some say, to undergo   575
This annual humbling certain numberd days,
To dash thir pride, and joy for Man seduc't.
However some tradition they dispers'd
Among the Heathen of thir purchase got,
And Fabl'd how the Serpent, whom they calld   580
Ophion with *Eurynome*, the wide-
Encroaching *Eve* perhaps, had first the rule
Of high *Olympus*, thence by *Saturn* driv'n
And *Ops*, ere yet *Dictæan Jove* was born.

562 *that bituminous Lake*, the Dead Sea or Lake Asphaltitis (cf. 298), near which was Sodom.

565 *gust*, taste (a common sense in the seventeenth century).

567 *assayd*, tried to eat.

568 *drugd*, drugged, nauseated (most medicines used to taste horrible!).

572 *whom they triumphed* (over), as in 186 above. *once lapst*, man had only fallen once.

574 *permitted*, i.e. by God.

577 *for Man seduc't*, over having seduced man, cf. 332.

579 *thir purchase got*, the prey they had won.

584 *Dictæan*, as having been brought up on Mt. Dicte, in Crete.

Mean while in Paradise the hellish pair   585
Too soon arriv'd, *Sin* there in power before,
Once actual, now in body, and to dwell
Habitual habitant; behind her *Death*
Close following pace for pace, not mounted yet
On his pale Horse: to whom *Sin* thus began.   590
    Second of *Satan* sprung, all conquering *Death*,
What thinkst thou of our Empire now, though earnd
With travail difficult, not better farr
Then still at Hells dark threshold to have sate watch,
Unnam'd, undreaded, and thy self half starv'd?   595
    Whom thus the Sin-born Monster answerd soon.
To mee, who with eternal Famin pine,
Alike is Hell, or Paradise, or Heaven,
There best, where most with ravin I may meet;
Which here, though plenteous, all too little seems   600
To stuff this Maw, this vast unhide-bound Corps.
    To whom th' incestuous Mother thus repli'd.
Thou therefore on these Herbs, and Fruits, and Flours
Feed first, on each Beast next, and Fish, and Fowle,
No homely morsels, and whatever thing   605
The Sithe of Time mowes down, devour unspar'd,
Till I in Man residing through the Race,

586 *Too soon*, only too soon.   *in power*, potentially.
591 *Second*, i.e. after me, his daughter.
593 (is it) *not better farr*.
594 *then*, than.   *to have*, cf. 12 of this book and Commentary there.
599 *There best, where*.   *either* being best in proportion as, *or* I am
happiest where.
601 *unhide-bound Corps*, body with slack skin (not stuffed with food).
602 *incestuous*, on account of her union with her father, Satan.
605 *no homely morsels*, food not obtainable at home in Hell, and so
choice.
606 *Sithe*, scythe.
607 *through the Race*, throughout mankind.

His thoughts, his looks, words, actions all infect,
And season him thy last and sweetest prey.
    This said, they both betook them several wayes,   610
Both to destroy, or unimmortal make
All kinds, and for destruction to mature
Sooner or later; which th' Almightie seeing,
From his transcendent Seat the Saints among,
To those bright Orders utterd thus his voice.   615
    See with what heat these Dogs of Hell advance
To waste and havoc yonder World, which I
So fair and good created, and had still
Kept in that state, had not the folly of Man
Let in these wastful Furies, who impute   620
Folly to mee, so doth the Prince of Hell
And his Adherents, that with so much ease
I suffer them to enter and possess
A place so heav'nly, and conniving seem
To gratifie my scornful Enemies,   625
That laugh, as if transported with some fit
Of Passion, I to them had quitted all,
At random yeilded up to their misrule;
And know not that I calld and drew them thither

---

609 *season him thy last*, prepare him to be thy last.

610–11 *several wayes*; *Both*, i.e. in different directions but both with the same purpose.

612 *mature*, make (all beings) ripe.

615 *Orders*, the orders of angels.

617 *havoc*, make havoc of, destroy (the noun occurs at IX, 30).

620 *Furies*, i.e. Sin and Death.

621 *so*, as (also).

622 *that*, in that, because.

624 *conniving*, by remaining inactive (as in *Samson Agonistes*, 465); originally to shut one's eyes to.

627 *quitted*, abandoned.

629 *and know not*, with 'that laugh'.

My Hell-hounds, to lick up the draff and filth   630
Which Mans polluting Sin with taint hath shed
On what was pure, till crammd and gorg'd, nigh burst
With suckt and glutted offal, at one sling
Of thy victorious Arm, well-pleasing Son,
Both *Sin*, and *Death*, and yawning *Grave* at last   635
Through *Chaos* hurld, obstruct the mouth of Hell
For ever, and seal up his ravenous Jawes.
Then Heav'n and Earth renewd shall be made pure
To sanctitie that shall receive no staine:
Till then the Curse pronounc't on both precedes.   640
    He ended, and the heav'nly Audience loud
Sung *Halleluiah*, as the sound of Seas,
Through multitude that sung: Just are thy ways,
Righteous are thy Decrees on all thy Works;
Who can extenuat thee? Next, to the Son,   645
Destind restorer of Mankind, by whom
New Heav'n and Earth shall to the Ages rise,
Or down from Heav'n descend. Such was thir song,
While the Creator calling forth by name
His mightie Angels gave them several charge,   650
As sorted best with present things. The Sun
Had first his precept so to move, so shine,

630 *draff*, dregs.

632–6 The construction is: 'till Sin and Death . . . , crammd and gorgd . . . obstruct the mouth of Hell'.

639 *To sanctitie*, changed into a sanctity.

640 *both*, Heaven and Earth.   *precedes*, must come first.

645 *extenuat*, lessen, diminish (Lat. *tenuis*=thin); hence our use, e.g. extenuate a fault.   *to the Son*, sc. they sang.

647 *to the Ages*, to last for ever and ever.   *rise*, as if from the ashes of the old.

650 *His mightie Angels*, i.e. the seven chief angels.   *several*, separate, individual.

651 *as sorted . . . things*, as best suited the situation (after man's sin).

As might affect the Earth with cold and heat
Scarce tollerable, and from the North to call
Decrepit Winter, from the South to bring   655
Solstitial summers heat. To the blanc Moone
Her office they prescrib'd, to th' other five
Thir planetarie motions and aspects
In *Sextile*, *Square*, and *Trine*, and *Opposite*,
Of noxious efficacie, and when to joine   660
In Synod unbenigne, and taught the fixt
Thir influence malignant when to showre,
Which of them rising with the Sun, or falling,
Should prove tempestuous: To the Winds they set
Thir corners, when with bluster to confound   665
Sea, Aire, and Shoar, the Thunder when to rowle
With terror through the dark Aereal Hall.
Some say he bid his Angels turne ascanse
The Poles of Earth twice ten degrees and more
From the Suns Axle; they with labour pushd   670
Oblique the Centric Globe: Som say the Sun

655 *Decrepit*, because Winter was depicted as an old man (e.g. by Spenser).
656 *Solstitial*, extreme (as at midsummer).   *blanc*, pale, white.
657 *they*, the angels (650).   *five*, sc. planets.
658 *aspects* (accent on last), i.e. the appearances that follow, each of which was thought by astrologers to have its special influence over events on earth.
659 *Sextile*, etc., technical terms describing various positions of the planets with reference to one another, which were thought harmful ('noxious') in their effect ('efficacie').
661 *Synod*, conjunction.   *the fixt*, fixed stars.
662 *showre*, pour out.
665 *corners*, quarters (from which to blow).   *when*, sc. and taught them.
667 *Aereal Hall*, the vault of heaven, the sky.
668 *ascanse*, sideways.
669 *The Poles*, i.e. the axis ('Axle').
671 *the Centric Globe*, our earth, centre of the Universe.

Was bid turn Reines from th' Equinoctial Rode
Like distant bredth to *Taurus* with the Seav'n
Atlantick Sisters, and the *Spartan* Twins
Up to the *Tropic* Crab; thence down amaine   675
By *Leo* and the *Virgin* and the *Scales*,
As deep as *Capricorne*, to bring in change
Of Seasons to each Clime; else had the Spring
Perpetual smil'd on Earth with vernant Flours,
Equal in Days and Nights, except to those   680
Beyond the Polar Circles; to them Day
Had unbenighted shon, while the low Sun
To recompence his distance, in thir sight
Had rounded still th' Horizon, and not known
Or East or West, which had forbid the Snow   685
From cold *Estotiland*, and South as farr
Beneath *Magellan*. At that tasted Fruit
The Sun, as from *Thyestean* Banquet, turnd

672 *Reines*, the reins of the Sun's chariot.   *th' Equinoctial Rode*, his course round the Equator.

673 *Like distant bredth*, an equal distance (viz. 20 degrees).   *Taurus*, a constellation.

674 *Atlantik Sisters*, the Pleiades, daughters of Atlas.   *the Spartan Twins*, the Gemini, Castor and Pollux, twin sons of a Spartan king.

675 *the Tropic Crab*, the Tropic of Cancer as opposed to that of Capricorn (677).   *amaine*, with force and/or speed.

676 *Leo*, etc., are constellations.

679 *vernant*, vernal, flourishing in spring.

682 *unbenighted*, not terminated by any night.

684–7 *not known . . . or West*, had not risen or set.   *forbid the Snow*, i.e. to come as far south as Estotiland from the north, or as far north as Magellan from the South Pole.

686 *Estotiland* was the old name for the part of N. America round Hudson Bay.

687 *Magellan*, the straits at the tip of S. America, called after an explorer. *At . . . Fruit*, when the apple was eaten (by Adam and Eve).

688 *Thyestean* (scan 'Thyéstĕan), served up to Thyestes.

His course intended; else how had the World
Inhabited, though sinless, more then now,   690
Avoided pinching cold and scorching heate?
These changes in the Heav'ns, though slow, produc'd
Like change on Sea and Land, sideral blast,
Vapour, and Mist, and Exhalation hot,
Corrupt and Pestilent: Now from the North   695
Of *Norumbega*, and the *Samoed* shoar
Bursting thir brazen Dungeon, armd with ice
And snow and haile and stormie gust and flaw,
Boreas and *Cæcias* and *Argestes* loud
And *Thrascias* rend the Woods and Seas upturn;   700
With adverse blast upturns them from the South
Notus and *Afer* black with thundrous Clouds
From *Serraliona*; thwart of these as fierce
Forth rush the *Levant* and the *Ponent* Windes
Eurus and *Zephir* with thir lateral noise,   705

689–91 *how had . . . avoided*, how would the world of innocent man
have avoided . . . any more than it does now?

693 *sideral blast* (sidereal), damaging influence from the stars (Lat.
sidera).

696 *Norumbega*, the east coast of N. America.   *Samoed shore*, the shore
of NE. Siberia.

697 *Dungeon*, prison-house (in which Aeolus kept them in classical
mythology).

698 *flaw*, hurt.

699 *Boreas*, north wind.   *Caecias*, north-east wind.   *Argestes*,
north-west wind.

700 *Thrascias*, a north-west wind from Thrace (to Greece).

701 *adverse*, from the opposite direction, meeting them.

702 *Notus*, south wind.   *Afer*, south-west wind from Africa.

703 *Serraliona* (accent Sérralíona), Sierra Leone on the NW. coast of
Africa, a name of Spanish derivation.   *thwart of*, athwart, at right
angles to.

704 *Levant and the Ponent windes*, winds from the directions of the rising
(Lat. *levo*) and setting (Lat. *pono*) sun.

705 *Eurus*, the east wind.   *Zephir*, a west wind.   *lateral*, coming
from the sides, as against coming from top and bottom of a map.

Sirocco, and *Libecchio*. Thus began
Outrage from liveless things; but Discord first
Daughter of Sin, among th' irrational,
Death introduc'd through fierce antipathie:
Beast now with Beast gan warr, and Fowle with   710
  Fowle,
And Fish with Fish; to graze the Herb all leaving,
Devourd each other; nor stood much in awe
Of Man, but fled him, or with count'nance grim
Glar'd on him passing: these were from without
The growing miseries, which *Adam* saw   715
Alreadie in part, though hid in gloomiest shade,
To sorrow abandond, but worse felt within,
And in a troubl'd Sea of passion tost,
Thus to disburden sought with sad complaint.

   O miserable of happie! is this the end   720
Of this new glorious World, and mee so late
The Glory of that Glory, who now becom
Accurst of blessed, hide me from the face
Of God, whom to behold was then my highth
Of happiness: yet well, if here would end   725
The miserie, I deserv'd it, and would beare

706 *Sirocco*, south-east wind, *Libecchio*, south-west wind; Italian names.
708 *th' irrational*, things living but not rational, i.e. the animals.
711 *leaving*, ceasing.
716 *though hid*, though he was hidden.
717 *but worse felt*, but he felt worse miseries.
719 *disburden*, unburden himself (intransitive, as in V, 319), the metaphor
from a ship unloading being suggested by 'Sea' in 718.
720 *of happie*, instead of, after being happy (and so again in 723).
722 *The Glory of that Glory*, the summit of that glory; cf. expressions
like 'King of Kings'.
722-3 *becom ... hide me*, having become ... am hiding myself.
724 *then*, i.e. when I was innocent.
725 *well*, all would be well.

My own deservings; but this will not serve;
All that I eate or drink, or shall beget,
Is propagated curse. O voice once heard
Delightfully, *Encrease and multiplie*,   730
Now death to heare! for what can I encrease
Or multiplie, but curses on my head?
Who of all Ages to succeed, but feeling
The evil on him brought by mee, will curse
My Head, Ill fare our Ancestor impure,   735
For this we may thank *Adam*, but his thanks
Shall be the execration; so besides
Mine own that bide upon me, all from mee
Shall with a fierce reflux on mee redound,
On mee as on thir natural center light   740
Heavie, though in thir place. O fleeting joyes
Of Paradise, deare bought with lasting woes!
Did I request thee, Maker, from my Clay
To mould me Man, did I sollicit thee
From darkness to promote me, or here place   745
In this delicious Garden? as my Will
Concurrd not to my being, it were but right
And equal to reduce me to my dust,

727 *serve*, suffice (to atone for my sin).

729 *Is propagated curse*, shall inherit the curse.

730 *Delightfully*, with delight.

733 *of all Ages to succeed*, in all succeeding generations.

735 *Ill fare*, sc. 'saying'; we should now put inverted commas from 'Ill' to 'Adam'.

737 *Shall ... execration*, will be a curse upon me.

738 *Mine own* evils, suggested by 734, rather than 'curses'.

739 *redound*, flow back.

740 'alight on me as the appropriate centre for evils, or curses, to come to rest on.' (*centre* = 'a point towards which things move or are attracted', *O.E.D.* s.v. 6b).

747 *my being*, my existence.

748 *equal*, fair, just (Lat. *aequus*).   *reduce*, bring back.

Desirous to resigne, and render back
All I receav'd, unable to performe   750
Thy terms too hard, by which I was to hold
The good I sought not. To the loss of that,
Sufficient penaltie, why hast thou added
The sense of endless woes? inexplicable
Thy Justice seems; yet to say truth, too late   755
I thus contest; then should have been refus'd
Those terms whatever, when they were propos'd:
Thou didst accept them; wilt thou enjoy the good,
Then cavil the conditions? and though God
Made thee without thy leave, what if thy Son   760
Prove disobedient, and reprov'd, retort,
Wherefore didst thou beget me? I sought it not:
Wouldst thou admit for his contempt of thee
That proud excuse? yet him not thy election,
But Natural necessity begot.   765
God made thee of choice his own, and of his own
To serve him, thy reward was of his Grace,
Thy punishment then justly is at his Will.
Be it so, for I submit, his doom is fair,
That dust I am, and shall to dust returne: 770

749 *Desirous*, since I am desirous.
752 *The good*, i.e. my life.
754 *sense*, feeling, consciousness.
757 *whatever* they were; so 'whenever' it comes, 771.
758 *Thou*. Adam now addresses himself, not God.
759 *cavil* (at), object to.
760 *thy* is emphatic.
761 *reprov'd*, when reproved.
764 *election*, choice.
765 *Natural necessity*, i.e. the human instinct for procreation, sexual desire.
766 *of his own*, either (1) as being one of his servants *or* (2) from his gifts.
769 *doom*, judgement.
770 From Gen. 3:19.

O welcom hour whenever! why delayes
His hand to execute what his Decree
Fixd on this day? why do I overlive,
Why am I mockt with death, and length'nd out
To deathless pain? how gladly would I meet   775
Mortalitie my sentence, and be Earth
Insensible, how glad would lay me down
As in my Mothers lap! there I should rest
And sleep secure; his dreadful voice no more
Would Thunder in my ears, no fear of worse   780
To mee and to my ofspring would torment me
With cruel expectation. Yet one doubt
Persues me still, least all I cannot die,
Least that pure breath of Life, the Spirit of Man
Which God inspir'd cannot together perish   785
With this corporeal Clod; then in the Grave,
Or in some other dismal place, who knows
But I shall die a living Death? O thought
Horrid, if true! yet why? it was but breath
Of Life that sinnd; what dies but what had life   790
And sin? the Bodie properly hath neither.
All of me then shall die: let this appease
The doubt, since human reach no furder knows.
For though the Lord of all be infinite,
Is his wrauth also? be it, Man is not so,   795
But mortal doomd. How can he exercise
Wrauth without end on Man whom Death must end?

773 *overlive*, live too long, survive.
774 *death*, i.e. a sort of living death, or death in life.
778 *as*, as being (a use of the Lat. *ut*; cf. 978).
783 *all*, entirely (as in Horace's *omnis non moriar*).
785 *inspir'd*, breathed into man (Gen. 2:7).
789 *yet why* (should it be true?)
795 *be it*, even if it is.   *so*, immortal.

Can he make deathless Death? that were to make
Strange contradiction, which to God himself
Impossible is held, as Argument   800
Of weakness, not of Power. Will he draw out,
For angers sake, finite to infinite
In punisht Man, to satisfie his rigour
Satisfi'd never; that were to extend
His Sentence beyond dust and Natures Law,   805
By which all Causes else according still
To the reception of thir matter act,
Not to th' extent of thir own Spheare. But say
That Death he not one stroak, as I suppos'd,
Bereaving sense, but endless miserie   810
From this day onward, which I feel begun
Both in me, and without me, and so last
To perpetuitie; Ay mee, that fear
Comes thundring back with dreadful revolution
On my defensless head; both Death and I   815
Am found Eternal, and incorporat both,
Nor I on my part single, in mee all
Posteritie stands curst: Fair Patrimonie
That I must leave ye, Sons; O were I able

798 i.e. can even God make Death deathless, and so make my punishment go on for ever?

800-1 'that would be a proof of his weakness'.

802 *finite*, mortal.

805 *beyond dust and Nature's Law*, beyond what man's nature lays down, viz. 770.

806-8 'all other causes act according to the nature of the subject (matter) which receives their action, not according to their own nature'.

808 *say*, suppose.

810 *bereaving sense*, extinguishing feeling (cf. 'insensible', 777).

812 *without me*, in the world outside.

814 *revolution*, return.

816 *incorporat both*, bound together in one body.

817 *nor* (am) I.   818 *Patrimonie*, inheritance.

To waste it all my self, and leave ye none!   820
So disinherited how would ye bless
Mee now your Curse! Ah, why should all mankind
For one mans fault thus guiltless be condemnd,
If guiltless? But from mee what can proceed,
But all corrupt, both Mind and Will deprav'd,   825
Not to do onely, but to will the same
With mee? how can they then acquitted stand
In sight of God? Him after all Disputes
Forc't I absolve: all my evasions vain
And reasonings, though through Mazes, lead me still 830
But to my own conviction: first and last
On mee, mee onely, as the sourse and spring
Of all corruption, all the blame lights due;
So might the wrauth. Fond wish! couldst thou support
That burden heavier then the Earth to bear,   835
Then all the World much heavier, though divided
With that bad Woman? Thus what thou desir'st,
And what thou fearst, alike destroyes all hope
Of refuge, and concludes thee miserable
Beyond all past example and future,   840
To *Satan* onely like both crime and doom.
O Conscience, into what Abyss of fears
And horrors hast thou driv'n me; out of which
I find no way, from deep to deeper plung'd!

820 *waste*, use it up.
825 'but that which is totally corrupt, depraved both in mind and will.'
828 *Disputes*, arguing with myself.
829 *Forc't I absolve*, I am bound to absolve.
831 *my own conviction*, self-condemnation.
833 *due*, as it is due, duly.
839 *concludes thee*, ends by making thee.
840 *future*, accent on last.
841 *like both*, alike in both (cf. 825 for syntax).

Thus *Adam* to himself lamented loud   845
Through the still Night, not now, as ere Man fell,
Wholsom and cool, and mild, but with black Air
Accompanied, with damps and dreadful gloom,
Which to his evil Conscience represented
All things with double terror: On the ground   850
Outstretcht he lay, on the cold ground, and oft
Curs'd his Creation, Death as oft accus'd
Of tardie execution, since denounc't
The day of his offence. Why comes not Death,
Said hee, with one thrice acceptable stroke   855
To end me? Shall Truth fail to keep her word,
Justice Divine not hast'n to be just?
But Death comes not at call, Justice Divine
Mends not her slowest pace for prayers or cries.
O Woods, O Fountains, Hillocks, Dales and Bowrs, 860
With other echo late I taught your Shades
To answer, and resound farr other Song.
Whom thus afflicted when sad *Eve* beheld,
Desolate where she sate, approaching nigh,
Soft words to his fierce passion she assayd: 865
But her with stern regard he thus repelld.

Out of my sight, thou Serpent, that name best
Befits thee with him leagu'd, thy self as false
And hateful; nothing wants, but that thy shape,
Like his, and colour Serpentine may shew   870
Thy inward fraud, to warn all Creatures from thee

853–4 *tardie execution . . . offence,* slowness in carrying out his office
(the death of Adam), which had been proclaimed on the day of his sin;
see X, 48–9.

864 *Desolate . . . sate,* from where she sat desolate.

869 *wants,* is lacking.

870 *Serpentine,* like a serpent's.

Henceforth; least that too heav'nly form, pretended
To hellish falshood, snare them. But for thee
I had persisted happie, had not thy pride
And wandring vanitie, when lest was safe,   875
Rejected my forewarning, and disdaind
Not to be trusted, longing to be seen
Though by the Devil himself, him overweening
To over-reach, but with the Serpent meeting
Foold and beguil'd, by him thou, I by thee,   880
To trust thee from my side, imagind wise,
Constant, mature, proof against all assaults,
And understood not all was but a shew
Rather then solid vertu, all but a Rib
Crooked by nature, bent, as now appears,   885
More to the part sinister from me drawn,
Well if thrown out, as supernumerarie
To my just number found. O why did God,
Creator wise, that peopl'd highest Heav'n
With Spirits Masculine, create at last   890
This noveltie on Earth, this fair defect
Of Nature, and not fill the World at once
With Men as Angels without Feminine,

872-3 *pretended To . . . falshood*, stretched or laid over to cover false-
hood (the literal sense of Lat. *praetendo*).

873-80 see Commentary.

875 *wandring vanitie*, careless vanity, or (perhaps) the vanity that made
you wander off on your own (IX, 214).   *when lest was safe*, when it was
least safe (for you to do so).

878-9 *him . . . to over-reach*, fancying in your pride that you could get
the better of him.

880 *I by thee*, as I was fooled by thee.

883 *understood*, I understood.

884 i.e. you were only a rib.

886 *sinister*, literally left, but also ill-fated (modern 'sínister').

887-8 'And it would have been well if that extra rib beyond the
number I required had been discarded altogether.'

Or find some other way to generate
Mankind? this mischief had not then befall'n,   895
And more that shall befall, innumerable
Disturbances on Earth through Femal snares,
And straight conjunction with this Sex: for either
He never shall find out fit Mate, but such
As some misfortune brings him, or mistake,   900
Or whom he wishes most shall seldom gain
Through her perversness, but shall see her gaind
By a farr worse, or if she love, withheld
By Parents, or his happiest choice too late
Shall meet, alreadie linkt and Wedlock-bound   905
To a fell Adversarie, his hate or shame:
Which infinite calamitie shall cause
To Human life, and houshold peace confound.

He added not, and from her turnd, but *Eve*
Not so repulst, with Tears that ceas'd not flowing,   910
And tresses all disorderd, at his feet
Fell humble, and imbracing them, besaught
His peace, and thus proceeded in her plaint.

Forsake me not thus, *Adam*, witness Heav'n
What love sincere, and reverence in my heart   915
I beare thee, and unweeting have offended,
Unhappilie deceav'd; thy suppliant
I beg, and clasp thy knees; bereave me not,
Whereon I live, thy gentle looks, thy aid,
Thy counsel in this uttermost distress,   920
My onely strength and stay: forlorn of thee,

898 *straight conjunction*, close union.
901 *whom*, her whom.
905 *already linkt*, (probably), when *he* is already linked.
916 *unweeting*, ignorantly; cf. 335.
917 *deceav'd*, i.e. by Satan.
921 *forlorn of*, forsaken by.

Whither shall I betake me, where subsist?
While yet we live, scarse one short hour perhaps,
Between us two let there be peace, both joining,
As joind in injuries, one enmitie   925
Against a Foe by doom express assign'd us,
That cruel Serpent: On mee exercise not
Thy hatred for this miserie befall'n,
On mee already lost, mee then thy self
More miserable; both have sinnd, but thou   930
Against God onely, I against God and thee,
And to the place of judgement will return,
There with my cries importune Heaven, that all
The sentence from thy head remov'd may light
On mee, sole cause to thee of all this woe,   935
Mee mee onely just object of his ire.
     She ended weeping, and her lowlie plight,
Inmoveable till peace obtain from fault
Acknowledg'd and deplor'd, in *Adam* wraught
Commiseration; soon his heart relented   940
Towards her, his life so late and sole delight,
Now at his feet submissive in distress,
Creature so faire his reconcilement seeking,
His counsel whom she had displeas'd, his aide;
As one disarmd, his anger all he lost,   945
And thus with peaceful words uprais'd her soon.
     Unwarie, and too desirous, as before,

924–5 *both . . . enmitie*, both joining in one enmity as we have both
been wronged.
926 *express*, explicit.
932 *will*, I will.
938 i.e. Eve would not rise from her knees till she obtained pardon for
her fault.
941 *so late*, so recently.
944 *His counsel whom*, the counsellor of him whom.   *aide*, helpmate.

or loss of life and pleasure overlov'd.
Or if thou covet death, as utmost end   1020
Of miserie, so thinking to evade
The penaltie pronounc't, doubt not but God
Hath wiselier armd his vengeful ire then so
To be forestalld; much more I fear least Death
So snatcht will not exempt us from the paine   1025
We are by doom to pay; rather such acts
Of contumacie will provoke the Highest
To make death in us live: Then let us seek
Som safer resolution, which methinks
I have in view, calling to minde with heed   1030
Part of our Sentence, that thy Seed shall bruise
The Serpents head; piteous amends, unless
Be meant, whom I conjecture, our grand Foe
Satan, who in the Serpent hath contriv'd
Against us this deceit: to crush his head   1035
Would be revenge indeed; which will be lost
By death brought on our selves, or childless days
Resolv'd, as thou proposest; so our Foe
Shall scape his punishment ordaind, and wee
Instead shall double ours upon our heads.   1040
No more be mentiond then of violence
Against our selves, and wilful barrenness,
That cuts us off from hope, and savours onely
Rancor and pride, impatience and despite,
Reluctance against God and his just yoke   1045

1026 *by doom*, according to (God's) judgement.
1028 *death . . . live*, cf. 'a living death' (788).
1032 *piteous amends*, a poor consolation (but stronger than this phrase).
1037–8 *childless days Resolved*, the determination to remain childless.
1041 (let) *no more be mentioned*.
1043 *savours*, smacks of, shows.
1045 *Reluctance*, struggle against; cf. 515.

So now of what thou knowst not, who desir'st
The punishment all on thy self; alas,
Beare thine own first, ill able to sustaine   950
His full wrauth whose thou feelst as yet lest part,
And my displeasure bearst so ill. If Prayers
Could alter high Decrees, I to that place
Would speed before thee, and be louder heard,
That on my head all might be visited,   955
Thy frailtie and infirmer Sex forgiv'n,
To mee committed and by mee expos'd.
But rise, let us no more contend, nor blame
Each other, blam'd enough elsewhere, but strive
In offices of Love, how we may light'n   960
Each others burden in our share of woe;
Since this days Death denounc't, if aught I see,
Will prove no sudden, but a slow-pac't evil,
A long days dying to augment our paine,
And to our Seed (O hapless Seed!) deriv'd.   965
    To whom thus *Eve*, recovering heart, repli'd.
Adam, by sad experiment I know
How little weight my words with thee can finde,
Found so erroneous, thence by just event
Found so unfortunate; nevertheless,   970
Restor'd by thee, vile as I am, to place

951 *whose*, of whose wrath.   *lest*, the least.
953 *that place*, see 932.
954 *louder heard*, heard pleading more loudly (than you).
957 *To mee committed*, as having been entrusted to my care.
959 *elsewhere*, *either* at the place of judgement, *or* in Heaven.
961 *in our share of woe*, in sharing our woe.
962 *this . . . denounc't*, the death proclaimed for us this day (cf. 48, 853–4 and 1049).
965 *deriv'd*, passed on.
967 *experiment*, experience.
969 *event*, issue, result.
971–2 *place Of new acceptance*, the position of being accepted back.

Of new acceptance, hopeful to regaine
Thy Love, the sole contentment of my heart
Living or dying, from thee I will not hide
What thoughts in my unquiet brest are ris'n,   975
Tending to som relief of our extreames,
Or end, though sharp and sad, yet tolerable,
As in our evils, and of easier choice.
If care of our descent perplex us most,
Which must be born to certain woe, devourd   980
By Death at last, and miserable it is
To be to others cause of misery,
Our own begott'n, and of our Loines to bring
Into this cursed World a woful Race,
That after wretched Life must be at last   985
Food for so foule a Monster, in thy power
It lies, yet ere Conception to prevent
The Race unblest, to being yet unbegot.
Childless thou art, Childless remaine: So Death
Shall be deceav'd his glut, and with us two   990
Be forc't to satisfie his Rav'nous Maw.
But if thou judge it hard and difficult,
Conversing, looking, loving, to abstain
From Loves due Rites, Nuptial embraces sweet,
And with desire to languish without hope,   995

976 *extreames,* extremity.
978 *As in our evils,* considering the evil plight we are in.
979 *descent,* descendants.
981–6 *and miserable . . . Monster* is all one long parenthesis.   *Our own begott'n* qualifies 'others'.
983 *of,* out of.
987 *prevent,* forestall, cut off beforehand.
988 *being* (noun), existence.
990 *deceav'd his glut,* cheated of his prey.
995 *hope,* i.e. of fulfilment.

Before the present object languishing
With like desire, which would be miserie
And torment less then none of what we drea
Then both our selves and Seed at once to fr
From what we fear for both, let us make sh
Let us seek Death, or hee not found, supply
With our own hands his Office on our selve
Why stand we longer shivering under feare
That shew no end but Death, and have the
Of many wayes to die the shortest choosing
Destruction with destruction to destroy.
    She ended heer, or vehement despaire
Broke off the rest; so much of Death her t
Had entertaind, as di'd her Cheeks with pa
But *Adam* with such counsel nothing sway
To better hopes his more attentive minde
Labouring had rais'd, and thus to *Eve* repl
    Eve, thy contempt of life and pleasure s
To argue in thee somthing more sublime
And excellent then what thy mind conten
But self-destruction therefore sought, refu
That excellence thought in thee, and imp
Not thy contempt, but anguish and regre

996 *Before . . . object,* with the object of your desir
here in front of you.
1000 *make short* (work).
1004 *and have the power,* when we have the power.
1005 'choosing the shortest of many ways to die'.
1006 'to destroy the power of death by destroying o
1009 *di'd,* dyed.   *pale,* paleness, pallor (a poetic li
in Shakespeare.
1011 *more attentive,* i.e. to God's purposes; see 1079 e
1015 *what thy mind contemns,* i.e. (love of) pleasure.
1016 *self-destruction* seems here to mean the refusal t
1017 *thought,* supposed (for the moment).

Laid on our Necks. Remember with what mild
And gracious temper he both heard and judg'd
Without wrauth or reviling; wee expected
Immediat dissolution, which we thought
Was meant by Death that day, when lo, to thee   1050
Pains onely in Child-bearing were foretold,
And bringing forth, soon recompenc't with joy,
Fruit of thy Womb: On mee the Curse aslope
Glanc'd on the ground, with labour I must earne
My bread; what harm? Idleness had bin worse;   1055
My labour will sustain me; and least Cold
Or Heat should injure us, his timely care
Hath unbesaught provided, and his hands
Cloath'd us unworthie, pitying while he judg'd;
How much more, if we pray him, will his ear   1060
Be op'n, and his heart to pitie incline,
And teach us furder by what means to shun
Th' inclement Seasons, Rain, Ice, Hail and Snow,
Which now the Skie with various Face begins
To shew us in this Mountain, while the Winds   1065
Blow moist and keen, shattering the graceful locks
Of these fair spreading Trees; which bids us seek
Som better shroud, som better warmth to cherish
Our Limbs benummd, ere this diurnal Starr
Leave cold the Night, how we his gatherd beams   1070
Reflected, may with matter sere foment,

1052–3 *soon recompenc't . . . Womb*, which would soon be recompensed with the joy of offspring (cf. Luke 1:42).

1053–4 'The curse pronounced on me glanced off sideways on to the ground.' Cf. 201–8.

1066 *locks*, metaphorical for foliage (as Lat. *comae*=hair is used).

1068 *shroud*, shelter (as in *Comus*, 147).

1069 *this diurnal Starr*, the sun which makes day and night.

1070 *how*, seek how.

1071 *with matter sere foment*, warm with dry matter, i.e. kindle a fire.

Or by collision of two bodies grinde
The Air attrite to Fire, as late the Clouds
Justling or pusht with Winds rude in thir shock
Tine the slant Lightning, whose thwart flame driv'n
    down   1075
Kindles the gummie bark of Firr or Pine,
And sends a comfortable heat from farr,
Which might supplie the Sun: such Fire to use,
And what may else be remedie or cure
To evils which our own misdeeds have wrought,   1080
Hee will instruct us praying, and of Grace
Beseeching him, so as we need not fear
To pass commodiously this life, sustain
By him with many comforts, till we end
In dust, our final rest and native home.   1085
What better can we do, then to the place
Repairing where he judg'd us, prostrate fall
Before him reverent, and there confess
Humbly our faults, and pardon beg, with tears
Watering the ground, and with our sighs the Air   1090
Frequenting, sent from hearts contrite, in sign
Of sorrow unfeignd, and humiliation meek.
Undoubtedly he will relent and turn
From his displeasure; in whose look serene,
When angry most he seemd and most severe,   1095
What else but favor, grace, and mercie shon?

1073 *attrite*, rubbed together (Lat. *attritus*).
1075 *Tine*, kindle (cf. tinder).   *thwart*, coming sideways; as in 703.
1077 *comfortable*, comforting.
1078 *supplie* (the place of) *the Sun*.
1079 *what may else*, whatever else may.
1081 *praying*, if we pray.   *of Grace*, for Grace.
1082–3 *not fear To pass*, have no fear about passing.
1091 *Frequenting*, filling (Lat. *frequentare*).

So spake our Father penitent, nor *Eve*
Felt less remorse: they forthwith to the place
Repairing where he judg'd them prostrate fell
Before him reverent, and both confessd   1100
Humbly thir faults, and pardon begd, with tears
Watering the ground, and with thir sighs the Air
Frequenting, sent from hearts contrite, in sign
Of sorrow unfeignd, and humiliation meek.

COMMENTARY ON BOOK IX

O.E.D. = *The Oxford English Dictionary* (complete edition).

C.D. = Milton's *De Doctrina Christiana* (Sumner's translation).

Newton = *Paradise Lost* with Notes of various authors, edited by
T. Newton (9th ed., 1790).

Verity = editions of separate books of *Paradise Lost* (1891, etc., one
volume edition, 1910).

The titles of works by other critics quoted will usually be found
in the section of Select Criticism.

1–47. *A Prologue in which the poet re-invokes the Heavenly Muse as
he comes to the crisis of his poem, and contrasts the nature of his epic with
those that had preceded it.* Previous prologues occur at the beginning
of Books I, III and VII. All are memorable as poetry, and also
because they give some insight into the author and his attitude to his
work. They have been compared to 'Act-drops' in signalling a
different scene or tone.

1–5. Milton marks the change from conversation and description
of what had happened in the past, especially the fall of the rebel
angels and the creation of man, to dramatic action; and from the
affability of Raphael's talk with Adam, which filled the last three
and a half books, to occasions of sadness and anger on the part of
Heaven.

The words 'Angel Guest' had already been used of Raphael, the
Archangel, when, at his first arrival, he had been entertained at a
meal (V, 328). So Abraham had entertained three angels, who
seem to be the mouthpieces of Jehovah (Gen. 18), while Moses is
described as speaking to God 'face to face, as a man speaketh unto
his friend' (Exod. 33:11). In view of these passages it is hardly neces-
sary to recall the stories of classical mythology which relate a descent
of gods among men.

Adam had related to Raphael how the 'Presence Divine' had
appeared to him and forbade him to eat of the Tree of Knowledge
(VIII, 314, etc.).

5. *Venial discourse unblam'd.* This flanking of a noun by two adjec-
tives is one of the most conspicuous features of Milton's style. Near

the beginning of *Lycidas* we have 'sad occasion dear', and another example here as soon as 45–6. Often the second adjective occurs with 'and', like a sort of afterthought, e.g. 'pleasing was his shape and lovely' (503–4, cf. 618–19); and in this form, at any rate, seems to be due to Italian poets of the Renaissance.

6. *Tragic* may be understood in the general sense, *and* in that of recalling a tragic drama like the Greek.

8. *disobedience*, the key word of the poem, of which the subject had been announced as

> Of Mans First Disobedience, and the Fruit
> Of that Forbidden Tree . . .

The sound of the word is picked up by the jingling 'distance and distaste'. Milton did not avoid puns, or something near puns on serious subjects, any more than Shakspeare had avoided them (e.g. that on 'light' in *Othello*, v. ii. 7). Other instances in this book are 144, 532–3, and 648. Aubrey described Milton as 'very satirical'.

11. *a world of woe*. The phrase is intended to take us back to the beginning of the poem: 'whose mortal taste/Brought Death into the World, and all our woe' (I, 2–3). The student would do well to note what other echoes of the phrase this book contains. It is almost a 'leit motif' till the last books, when it is replaced by a note of hope.

12. *Sin and . . . Death*. These personifications, which Milton carried further than other poets, had been described in II, 648–73; while their mention here prepares the way for their passage to Earth in X, 229, etc.

The repeated 'Death' takes up the hard initial letter of 6–8, a sinister prologue to the book.

13–19 and 27–41. Milton affirms that the subject of his epic is really a worthier one than that of the classical or Renaissance epics, and even of Spenser (if he would have counted *The Faerie Queene* as an epic at all).

In Homer's *Iliad* the chief hero, the Greek Achilles, chased the Trojan Hector thrice round the walls of Troy before killing him. In Virgil's *Aeneid* Aeneas took to wife Lavinia who was to have married Turnus, whom Aeneas eventually killed. In Homer's *Odyssey* the anger of Poseidon (Latin Neptune), the sea-god, prevented Odysseus ('the Greek') from reaching his home for ten years after the fall of Troy. Aeneas was the son of Cytherea (Venus) and a mortal, Anchises; while Juno, queen of the gods, was his enemy.

In the later passage (27–41) 'Races and Games' belong to classical epic, but the subsequent details are those of writers like Ariosto, Tasso, and Boiardo in Italy, and Spenser in England.

It need not be accounted arrogance in Milton to put his subject above that of previous epics (cf. I, 42–16). For a Christian, the relation of God and man must be the supreme subject, whether or not we consider it suitable for epic treatment. Tasso had written a Christian epic, but not on theological issues. An Italian friend of Milton had similarly exalted Dante over pagan poets thus: 'Nor has our tongue lacked its Homer or its Virgil. It has had its Dante, who is much greater than they ... as the conception he expounds is greater, as Heaven is nobler than earth, as things eternal and invisible are more prized than the temporal and visible'. (This is translated from Buomattei's oration of 1623 'In Praise of the Tuscan Language', and Milton in a letter to the author speaks of 'going eagerly to a feast of that Dante of yours'.)

Milton renews his estimate of war and warlike conquerors in XI, 683–97, and in *Paradise Regained*, III, 71, etc.; but he had himself fallen in with epic conventions so far as to describe in some detail the war in Heaven. It might be argued, however, that this had been a different kind of war, war on the spiritual level to quell the manifestation of disorder and rebellion, of which the originator was heroic only in his own eyes.

14. *wrauth* with 'rage' (16) and 'ire' (18) take up the 'anger' of 10. 'The anger of the true God is a more noble subject than of the false gods' (Newton).

21–4. Milton believed as firmly as Plato that the poet was 'inspired'. He seems to have found the early morning the time when the verses had formed in his head, ready for an amaneuensis to take them down (cf. 47). Aubrey tells us that his man used to come to him at 4.30 a.m., and that if he came later the poet would complain that he wanted to be milked; while his third wife recorded that when he woke in the morning he would sometimes make her write down twenty or thirty verses.

Note how the inversion of accent in the first foot of 24 ('Easie') produces a smooth and gliding effect, an onomatopoeia of the less obvious sort.

21. *my Celestial Patroness.* Who is she? It is tempting to answer, 'the Holy Spirit'. For in the section of *De Doctrina Christiana* devoted to the third Person of the Trinity Milton says:

'Sometimes it means the light of truth, whether ordinary or extraordinary, wherewith God enlightens and leads his people. . . . It is also used to signify the spiritual gifts conferred by God on individuals, and the act of gift itself.'

And again in another prose work *The Reason of Church Government urged against Prelaty* (1641) Milton looked forward to writing a work 'not to be obtained by the invocation of Dame Misery and her Siren daughters, but by devout prayer to that eternal Spirit who can enrich with all utterance and Knowledge, and sends out his Seraphin with the hallowed fire of his Altar to touch and purify the lips of whom he pleases'.

But in the Prologue to the whole poem we find Milton apparently distinguishing the 'Heavenly Muse' whom he first invokes (6) from the 'chiefly Thou O Spirit' of 17–22. Of 'the Heavenly Muse' H. Gardner has recently written:

'She is inseparable from the poet, and is no part of the universe he presents to us. She has another kind of reality. In his invocation of her Milton has summed up all his feeling about the sacredness of his vocation, the reality of his calling, and the truth of his subject, all his awe at his own temerity and his sense that through him great things are to be said. In invoking her aid he expresses also his sense that although he goes forward alone "in darkness, and with dangers compast round", he is not alone; he has great allies, others before him and others who will come after him "smit with the love of sacred song". Through his invocation of her he declares that inspiration is a reality, not a subjective fancy. She is the poetic embodiment of Milton's belief in his vocation, no more a convention than those "Powers" that haunt the poetry of Wordsworth.' (*A Reading of Paradise Lost*)

Perhaps, however, the distinction is not an ultimate one, or would not have appeared so to Milton. For Puritans frequently thought of the Holy Spirit as 'a spiritual perception analogous to the physical perception of the senses and given in "experience" as a whole' (G. Nuttall, *The Spirit in Puritan Thought*).

25–6. Milton began to choose a subject for his great work about

1640, and began to write about 1648. Details as to the subjects he considered will be found in Verity's introduction and in most books on Milton. Had he followed one plan, that of writing an Arthuriad, he would have involved himself in many of the trappings of chivalry which he here repudiates.

29. *dissect*, although here it means 'expound in detail', may have been suggested by the thought of knights cutting up one another.

30. *havoc* is the tumult and slaughter of battle ('Cry "Havoc",' and let slip the dogs of war', *Julius Caesar*, III. i. 273), while 'long and tedious' refers rather to the effect of writing and reading such descriptions of battle as we find, for example, in Malory's *Morte Darthur*. The epithets could be called 'transferred' if there were any other word in the text to which they could be attached. Surprisingly the boldness of the language seems to have escaped all comment.

31-2. So Sir Thomas Browne had said in *Religio Medici* that martyrs were the true and almost only example of 'fortitude'. John Foxe's *Book of Martyrs* had appeared in 1563, and continued to be very familiar.

When Adam has learned the lesson of his Fall that 'to obey is best' he concludes 'that suffering for Truth's sake Is Fortitude to highest victorie' (see XII, 493-7 and 561-73). Earlier in the poem 'the better fortitude' is illustrated by Abdiel, especially in the words which greeted his return to Heaven (VI, 29-33). Later in his life Milton returns to the thought of 'plain Heroic magnitude of mind' when the Chorus anticipates that Samson will through his blindness have to be numbered with those 'Whom Patience finally must crown' (*S. A.*, 1268-97).

41. *Mee* is a spelling used by Milton for emphasis: whatever other poets may choose for their subjects, *his* will not be chivalry. The importance the poet attached to spelling is proved by a list of Errata in the second and third issue of the first edition of *Paradise Lost* which includes: 'II, 414. For *we* read *wee*.

42-3. The words recall Virgil's *maius opus moveo* (*Aeneid*, VII. 45) when he begins the second half of his work, the conquest of Italy; but Milton is tackling an even loftier subject.

44-5. If the later part of the seventeenth century was not 'too late' for an epic, it may still be judged that there has been no true epic since *Paradise Lost*.

Writing in 1642, in *The Reason of Church Government*, Milton had hoped to accomplish a great work if the climate were not too adverse. He preferred that of Italy, where he had been in 1638–9. He once said that 'the sun, which we want, ripens wits as well as fruits'. His 'years' had reached fifty-nine when the first edition of *Paradise Lost* appeared.

46–7. We may notice the skill with which the author works back to the subject of inspiration, thus toning down, as it were, any impression of egotism which the unusually personal nature of the last few lines, or even of the whole prologue, might have given.

48–98. *Satan slips into Eden*. After the Prologue the narrative follows on Book IV, where Satan first saw Adam and Eve, but was prevented from approaching them by the archangel Gabriel. A conflict was imminent, but prevented by the Almighty:

> The Fiend lookt up and knew
> His mounted scale aloft; nor more; but fled
> Murmuring, and with him fled the shades of night.

It is now a week later by human reckoning of time (58 and 63). The intervening books have been filled with the discourse of Raphael and Adam, both concerned with earlier events. That Adam had a week in Paradise before the Fall was an idea common in Milton's time.

Satan once more begins the action, as in Book I.

54–5. Satan now knew all about the Tree since he had heard Adam talking with Eve (IV, 408, etc.), and could lay his plans accordingly.

60–2. Uriel, usually described as an angel, but once as an archangel (in 2 Esdras, a book of the Apocrypha), was connected by tradition with the sun. He had reported to Gabriel the arrival of Satan in Eden (IV, 125, etc., and 550, etc.)

63–6. Gives an astronomical account of Satan's journey, 76–82 a geographical.

71. The Bible gives four names to rivers of Paradise (Gen. 2:10–14), one being the Euphrates. A later addition to the story was

that a river (here called the Tigris) passed underneath the mountain on which Paradise was situated (cf. IV. 223–30). The Tigris is thought of as going underground for part of its course, like the classical Arethusa, and several streams in our own Yorkshire limestone. Its re-emergence is well brought out by the strong stress on the first syllable of 73.

73. *the Tree of life:* see Gen. 2:9; perhaps originally thought of as conferring immortality.

76–82. The journey was northward to 'Pontus' (the Black Sea) and the Sea of Azov, which opens out of it (called 'Poole' from Latin *Palus Maeotis*, used of an inland sea) and on to the 'Ob', a great river flowing to the Arctic just east of the Urals. The Fiend is then thought of as crossing the North Pole and going down to the South Pole; and lastly as going from the 'Orontes' in Syria (Turkey) westward to Panama (Darien), and across the Pacific to India. In the astronomical description the east to west journey came first, but here the order is reversed.

Milton liked to give colour and sound to his narrative by the use of place names; but he was also a man of the Renaissance in his interest in the geography of an expanding world. In both he recalls Marlowe and other Elizabethans.

87–8. The placing of object before subject is a Latinism, as also is the powerful conciseness of the whole sentence down to 96 (e.g. 'irresolute of . . .' = irresolute in respect of the thoughts he had revolved).

92–6. See Gen. 3:1; but the writer of that account did not associate the serpent with Satan.

98. Notice the onomatopoeia by which the b's and p's cause an opening of the lips suitable to a 'bursting passion'.

99–178. *Satan's speech to the Earth.* This speech is, as Mackail pointed out long ago, in Milton's latest manner, corresponding to the freedom of Shakespeare's style in his last plays, though the epic poet is always a stricter metrist than the dramatist. But it is appropriate that even Milton should allow himself greater freedom in a speech than in narrative. Notice the colloquial touch of 'Let it' (173).

99. When God created the Earth, we were told, in Raphael's

description to Adam, that 'Earth now Seem'd like to Heav'n, a seat where Gods might dwell' (VII, 328–9). Milton's description of Eden might seem to justify Satan's preference. A divine had written in 1654: 'Paradise was a little model of Heaven, and a sign of the great Heaven, assuring Adam that, if he continued in obedience to God, he should be translated into Heaven, to enjoy God supernaturally, as he then did enjoy him naturally' (Leight, *A System or Body of Divinitie*).

103. The beautiful word 'danc't' recalls old ideas of the music of the spheres in Plato and elsewhere, which has its most familiar expression in Portia's speech to Jessica towards the end of the *Merchant of Venice* (v. i. 58, etc.), and is more fully developed in *Orchestra*, a poem by Sir J. Davies of Hereford (1596), in which natural phenomena are reduced to an ordered motion or 'dancing'. This meant for Milton 'the liberation of energies of every kind harmoniously disposed' (H. Gardner). Cf. V, 617–27, and VII, 323–4 where 'last Rose as in Dance the stately Trees' at the Creation.

105. Milton had been equally cautious in his language earlier as to whether man was in fact the only inhabitant of the Universe (see VIII, 15–38). Shortly before writing these words the writer of this commentary listened to a scientist speculating as to whether certain waves could have originated from the inhabitants of other planets.

110. The last foot of this line has three syllables, two lightly followed by one strongly accented (an anapaest in classical terminology). The first foot of 152 is similar, but there it is easier to slide over or elide the first syllable of 'effected'.

114–15. Milton does not let us forget that Satan is 'Archangel ruined', so that he himself recognizes the possibilities of good which he had rejected when he said 'Evil, be thou my good'. Cf. 463–470.

126–8. It has been remarked that Satan no longer retains here his earlier pity for Adam and Eve.

141. *welnigh half* has replaced the 'third' of II, 692. Satan lies to himself more notably in 146–7, having previously referred to himself as created by God (IV, 43). Milton could have found in Augustine the devils' denial that they were created beings.

156-7. Cf. 'He shall give his angels charge concerning thee' (Ps. 91:11).

166. It is not without significance that Satan speaks scornfully of having to 'incarnate' divine being in human (and bestial) form, since this is what Christianity holds to have happened in the Incarnation, i.e. the earthly life of the Son of God. All through the poem we find reminders of what Love and Hate did respectively for and against man.

175-8. Satan supposes that God created man simply to spite the fallen angels. The reiteration of the words 'spite' and 'despite' express bitterness, and had been anticipated in Beelzebub's 'devilish Counsel first devis'd by Satan' which had been pleaded at the Council in Hell:

> Done all to spite
> The great Creatour. But their spite still serves
> His glory to augment. (II, 383-5)

Envy is nearly allied to spite, and commonly expresses itself through spiteful actions; while envy had been united to pride in Satan's character from the first book of this poem, as it had been long before Milton's time.

179-204. *Satan enters into the Serpent and awaits morning.*

180. In the *Iliad* Thetis rising from the sea to visit her son Achilles had been compared to a mist; and the picture is more fully developed by Milton a little later on when the Cherubim descended:

> on the ground
> Gliding meteorous, as Ev'ning Mist
> Ris'n from a river o're the marish glides
> And gathers ground fast at the Labourers heel
> Homeward returning. (XII, 28-32)

187-91. The idea that Satan was in the serpent, although not in Genesis, comes elsewhere in the Bible: 'That old serpent called the Devil and Satan' (Rev. 12:9), and 'The serpent beguiled Eve' (2 Cor. 11:3) when compared with 'By the envy of the devil death entered into the world' (Wisdom 2:24).

It was part of the Rabbinic tradition that after his fall Satan could only assume animal, not human, form. He had 'sat like a Cormorant' on the Tree of Life in IV, 194–6, and assumed other animal forms in IV, 401–8.

197. *Forth came the human pair*. Metre did not require the inversion of the prose order, but there is a gain in force and liveliness.

196–7. The source of this piece of anthropomorphism is in the Bible: 'And the Lord smelled a sweet savour' (Gen. 8:21, of Noah's sacrifice; cf. Lev. 1:9). We need not conclude that Milton really thought of God as having the form and passions of a man.

Eden is always fragrant; cf. 425 below, and IV, 264–5.

198. A specimen of this 'vocal worship' had been given in the morning hymn of Adam and Eve at V, 153–208.

200. Milton tells us in his prose treatise *Apology for Smectymnuus* that he liked to rise early; and there is a charming description of the early morning in *L'Allegro*, 41–68.

208–25. *Eve proposes to Adam that they should do their garden work apart.*

The proposal, and the reason given for it seem to have originated with Milton, who had already explained in IV, 623–32 that keeping enough of the garden clear provided ample occupation for our first parents. The Genesis story passes straight from the creation of Eve to her temptation by the serpent. Others before Milton had seen the need to explain the separation of Adam and Eve. In some of the miracle plays Adam left Eve alone while he explored the garden, and in one Eve went off alone to see the flowers (quotations in Evans, *Paradise Lost and the Genesis Tradition*, p. 198). But in order to safeguard God's providence and human responsibility Eve 'must be alone by decision and not accident, and also with Adam's acquiescence' (Burden). Milton therefore makes Eve take the initiative; although asking Adam for his ideas, she has already decided upon her task (212–13 and 217–19).

'The gardening is not primarily a matter of horticulture, but is at every point enmeshed with the imminent tragedy', says C. Ricks, pointing to the grave implications of the words 'luxurious', 'restraint', 'wanton', 'wild' and 'redress', considered from the point of view of the whole story and their use at other points. (In V, 295 Nature 'wantond' innocently in 'enormous bliss'.)

213. *hear.* The second edition of 1674 had 'bear', which, though intelligible, seems more likely to be a mistake.

222-3. *object new Casual discourse draw on.* Readers alert for irony and ambiguity, particularly critics who think irony indispensable to poetry worthy of much attention, may find it here in the fact that Eve was soon to meet a new object in the Satan-filled serpent, and her discourse with him was to lead to the Fall ('casual' is derived from Lat. *casum,* supine of *cadere,* which means 'to fall' before it means 'befall').

225. This line is metrically noticeable. The inverted first foot 'Early' with its comma causes a slight pause, after which the line seems to hurry downwards to the hour of supper. If Milton had not troubled to cut off the vowel of 'the' and insert the comma, we might have been tempted to read the first foot as 'early and', and so miss the full effect.

226-69. *Adam replies that there is no need to work so hard that they cannot pause to enjoy each other's society, and that the wife is safer by her husband's side.*

232-4. It is true enough that these words reflect Milton's view of woman; but they also reflect that of his age, and of many men in all ages. Nor did it prevent Milton holding that some women are superior to some men 'in prudence and dexterity'. It may be more valuable here to note that 'Adam speaks unwittingly to an Eve who is not exactly going to study household *good,* and who is about to promote in her husband not good works but the first act of evil' (Ricks).

249. The sentiment is found in Cicero *à propos* of Scipio Africanus (*nunquam minus solus quam cum solus*), but Milton has given it a different though equally memorable expression.

This line could be called an Alexandrine, i.e. a line of six feet instead of five, such as is common enough in Shakespeare but rare in Milton. Both here and in VIII, 216 where the last word is 'satietie', we have a sixth foot of two lightly stressed syllables.

263-4. The idea that Satan envied the 'conjugal love' of Adam and Eve began with Jewish expositors of the Old Testament. In the poem it occurs when Adam first sees 'these two Imparadis'd in one another's arms' (IV, 505-6). So also a good part of Iago's motive in ruining Othello's happiness may be seen as sexual jealousy.

266. The creation of Eve from Adam's rib is described in Gen. 2:21-2 and in *P.L.* VII, 465-71.

270-89. *Eve reproaches Adam for doubting her power to resist temptation if left by herself.* The syntax all through this paragraph is compressed and slightly difficult, especially to those who have not the familiarity with the classics that most of Milton's earlier readers possessed. The poet has been blamed for this syntactical difficulty, but it gives a weight and dignity to his epic that is not given by the looser style of (e.g.) Spenser. In the sentences beginning at 274, 279, and 282, the subject and main verb are placed after the object or object clause, an order which causes no difficulty in fully-inflected languages. But the last two lines of the paragraph are the climax of difficulty. Line 288 may be explained by supposing that Eve was going to say something like 'Thoughts which dishonour you', and then changes to the more dramatic question. In 289 'misthought' is best seen as a past participle of 'misthink' = think wrongly, applied to 'thoughts', while 'of her' = 'in respect of' or 'about her'. But these difficulties, as they seem to some, of style, should not blind us to the human feeling shown in 272 and 278.

273. Adam was the offspring of Heaven and Earth in a particular as well as a general way because God 'formed man of the dust of the ground' (Gen. 2:7) as well as 'in his own image' (Gen. 1:27).

274-7. A modern critic of repute has stigmatized Eve's eaves-dropping as 'comic'. It is equally permissible to see it as the courtesy and humility which would not intrude when she found her husband deep in conversation with his guest. After all she had no kitchen to retire to! It is more important to observe that Eve is not left unprepared for her Tempter; cf. 307-8 and 361.

282. Adam had not expressly said that he did not fear Satan's violence but implied as much in enlarging on his 'sly assault' (256).

288-9. Eve's argument is not exactly logical, since Adam's reluctance to leave her to face temptation alone was hardly a proof of lack of love; but Milton is not misrepresenting human nature in allowing her to appeal to the argument of love to get her own way.

290–317. *Adam tries to soothe the wounded pride of Eve.* A continued freedom of metre and syntax, at least when compared with the earlier books of the poem, corresponds to the colloquial tone.

296. This line has a trisyllabic third foot, 'though in vain', i.e. (in classical terminology) an anapaest instead of an iambic, and also an extra weak syllable at the end of the line, 'asper(ses)'.

309–12. Milton was doubtless thinking of the medieval knight fighting in the lists before his lady-love to show himself worthy of her favours.

> How sweet are looks that ladies bend
>   On whom their favours fall!
> For them I battle till the end,
>   To save from shame and thrall.
>   TENNYSON, *Sir Galahad*

As the advocate of married love rather than 'courtly' love (cf. 27–41 of this book), Milton makes Adam say that the presence of·Eve will strengthen him against temptation, and make him ashamed to succumb; leaving her to apply the opposite to herself.

314. *rais'd unite.* At first sight it seems easier to keep 'shame' as the subject of 'unite', which involves supplying 'vigour' with 'rais'd', in the Latin ablative absolute construction; but it gives better sense to make 'vigour' the subject.

318. *domestick Adam.* The epithet has been alleged to 'register Milton's opinion of his uxorious weakness' (D. Bush); but this is perhaps to anticipate. Adam is showing a proper care for his wife, and so for his home, ('attached to home' is one of the definitions in *O.E.D.*).

319–41. *Eve insists that if they cannot be trusted to stand up to temptation, whether single or together, their life in Eden is not worth much.* Contrast the earlier attitude of Eve in 'Unargu'd I obey' (IV, 636).

Eve is voicing one of the central thoughts of Milton, most fully developed in his *Areopagitica*, which is an argument against the censorship of printed matter before publication. To adapt one of the most famous sentences of that tract, Eve 'cannot praise a fugitive and cloistered virtue, unexercised and unbreathed, that never sallies out and sees her adversary, but slinks out of the race, where that immortal garland is to be run for, not without dust and hear.' But Eve has been said to 'confuse the sin of asking for trouble with the virtue of not avoiding the "dust and heat" of battle when they are necessary' (Tillyard). The theme of temptation is common to all Milton's longer poems.

It should, however, be noted that Milton only held that 'as the state of man now is' virtue can only be known by its opposite. Before the Fall knowledge was held to have been 'not gotten but infus'd' (Du Bartas). After it Adam bewails the price of Knowledge (1070–9).

322–6. Eve had not felt life in Eden to be restricted till she had listened to Satan.

342–75. *Adam reluctantly yields to Eve's persuasion that they should separate.*

343. *O Woman.* Contrast his last address to her, 291. Adam is about to give way to a woman's wiles, against his own better judgement and 'fondly overcome with Femal charm' (999).

352. We should not now put a comma between the subject 'what obeys Reason' and its predicate, but the slight pause indicated makes the word 'Reason' more emphatic—a kind of punctuation often found in the Folio text of Shakespeare.

351–6. Adam is anxious that Eve should understand the freedom of the human will to choose good or evil. This was set out by God in III, 96–128, and again by Raphael to Adam in V, 520–40; and there are close parallels in the prose treatise, e.g. 'the gift of reason has been implanted in all, by which they may of themselves resist bad desires'. After the Fall the position is somewhat changed:

> Since thy original lapse, true Libertie
> Is lost, which alwayes with right Reason dwells
> Twinn'd, and from her hath no dividual being,
>
> (XII, 83–4)

because passions now 'catch the government from reason, and to servitude reduce man, till then free'.

Reason he made right (352). The expression 'right reason' seems to be derived from Cicero's treatise *De Republica*: 'True law is right reason (*recta ratio*) in agreement with nature.' Milton equated the Law of Nature or Natural Law (which had been so powerfully expounded by Hooker at the end of the sixteenth century) with the law originally given to Adam by God. But when he speaks of Reason being deceived by some apparent good (354), he is adopting the Greek approach, which made wrong-doing proceed from intellectual error as to what was really good. (See also the extract from Bush in Select Criticism headed 'Right Reason'.)

354-6. Eve is here warned against the kind of specious reasoning with which she later deceives herself. For the prohibition see 651-4.

365. *mee.* The long spelling of the personal pronoun here may have been intended less for emphasis (see 41 and Commentary there), than because the run over of the sense into the next line might have made the ordinary spelling unduly weak.

370-2. The sense in which 'secure' and 'security' are often used in earlier English may be well illustrated by two quotations. Quarles writes in 1642: 'The way to be safe is never to be secure'; and Jeremy Taylor in 1655: 'By understanding our present state we may prevent the evils of carelessness and security'.

372-5. The more abrupt language here represents the unwilling consent of a man who has tried argument in vain. 'Adam', argues A. Stein ingeniously, 'is letting a short-sighted unselfishness conceal his real selfishness'.

376-472. *Eve carries out her desire to leave Adam, and meets the Serpent, who is enraptured by her person and by the place.*
The poet shows his sensibility both in the description of Eve's beauty and of her fragility. He clearly regards her as wrong in her defiance of her husband's wishes, let alone the greater sin of disobedience which will follow; but that no more prevents him from presenting her tenderly than it prevents Virgil raising our sympathy for Dido. There is a touch of domestic Eve in 400-3 to balance the 'domestick Adam' of 318.

377. We should be inclined to reverse the order, and say that the woman insisted on having the last word; but Milton does not quite say this.

385–6. The withdrawal of the hand may be regarded as symbolical of the disunion, which is finally repaired when they leave Eden 'hand in hand' (XII, 648), just as they had first been seen (IV, 21).

388. Homer had compared his Nausicaa to Artemis (*Odyssey*, vi. 102, etc.), and Virgil transferred the comparison to Dido and Diana (*Aeneid*, i, 498).

392. Although 'Guiltless' has first of all its archaic sense 'without experience of', it also suggests 'innocent', as opposed to the more sophisticated and dangerous use of fire for forging. The introduction of fire comes after the Fall (X, 1070–81), and it is usually associated with Hell.

393–6. Bentley thought that these lines were the interpolation of an editor on the ground that Eve could not be like both Artemis and the agricultural goddesses Pales and Pomona, and also that line 396 was 'a monster of an expression'. But Eve is first compared to Delia (Artemis) for her beauty, and then to the others for her gardening equipment; while the unusual expression in 396 is clear enough, and far more concise than prose could be. Pomona eventually yielded to her pursuer, as Eve yielded to Satan's temptation.

The mention of Proserpina takes readers back to one of the most beautiful and famous similes of the poem, describing the beauty of the Garden of Eden:

> Not that faire field
> Of Enna, where Proserpin gathering flours
> Her self a fairer Floure by gloomie Dis
> Was gathered . . . (IV, 269–71),

which itself foreshadowed the fatal event now to ensue.

404–7. Such apostrophes and anticipations occur in older epic poetry (e.g. *Aeneid*, x, 501, etc.), but never more effectively than here. Sin brings restlessness to men, as to the fallen angels (I, 65–7).

416. The two past participles in this line well illustrate the conciseness attained by such imitation of Latin: the whole human race being 'included' in the fate of their first parents, whom Satan has 'purposed' to make his prey.

420. This line may be considered to apply to the line before, as well as going with 'He sought them both'; and again in 422 the fact

that we are given only a comma after 'separate' allows us to make
'Eve separate' the object of 'he wish'd' as well as of 'find'.

431–3. *fairest unsupported Flour*: see Commentary at 393–6. Most
modern editions omit the comma after 'the while'. If Milton
intended it, it may have been to show that 'Her self' (herself) goes
with what follows as well as with what precedes. For Eve among
her flowers, cf. VIII, 44–7.

436. The word 'voluble', though it must refer primarily to a
snake's rolling, may also have a secondary allusion to the specious
volubility which Satan was soon to display. Milton uses the word in
its modern sense of ready speech in *S.A.* 1307.

439–40. The love of Venus for Adonis is described in Shakes-
peare's *Venus and Adonis*. The gardens of Adonis had been described
by Spenser in the *Faerie Queene* (III. vi. 29–49), and by the younger
Milton as 'the Gardens fair/Of Hesperus . . .

> Beds of hyacinth and roses
> Where young Adonis oft reposes,
> Waxing well of his deep wound
> In slumber soft, and on the ground
> Sadly sits the Assyrian Queen
> > *Comus*, 998–1002

A generation before Milton these gardens had been identified
with Eden: 'Lastly . . . what can *Adonis horti* among the Poets meane
other than Moses his Eden, or terrestrial Paradise?' (H. Reynolds,
Mythomystes).

439–43. Milton had already compared Eden with other more or
less imaginary gardens in IV, 268–85. [The whole topic has recently
been fully surveyed by A. B. Giamatti in *The Earthly Paradise and
the Renaissance Epic* (U.S.A., 1966).]

442. *not Mystic* is taken in the footnote as a contrast to the gardens
described in poetry, since this comes in the Bible; but Milton may be
asserting that the book Canticles describes a real earthly love, and
not allegorically the love of Christ for His bride, the Church, as it
had long been explained.

442–3. In view of the use of the word 'Sapience' of taste in 1048
and 'Sapient' here, it may be that the poet felt an affinity between

COMMENTARY ON BOOK IX

Adam and Solomon, both 'large-hearted and uxorious'. [The last words are those of Ricks, who, in an argument too long to summarize here, would apply 444 to Solomon as well as to Satan; see *Milton's Grand Style*, 135–7.]

445. The phrase 'populous city' occurs in *Othello* (I. i. 77). By itself this would not prove even unconscious reminiscence, but Satan's envy of the love of Adam and Eve reminds us more than once of Iago's malignity; so that it would be difficult to believe that Milton did not know the play, although he only alludes to Shakespear as a writer of such plays as *A Midsummer Night's Dream* (*L'Allegro*, 132–4).

There is no harshness in reading 'populous' as if it were two syllables, since the consonant between the two vowels is a liquid. So in 451 the second syllable of 'Dairie' is pronounced lightly before the following vowel, although there the comma makes the slurring less natural (but cf. 429 'Azure, or').

445–54. The simile may well reproduce the poet's own experience in a London still small enough to have fields within walking distance of the City. Milton, as his early poems show, was as susceptible to the beauty of nature as to that of woman. The stricture of Johnson that 'Milton saw nature through the spectacles of books' may be contrasted with the words of Landor: 'If ever there was a poet who knew nature well, and described her in all her loveliness, it was Milton.'

465–6. *Stupidly good*. Satan finds in Eve's 'Innocence' (459) a power like that of the Lady in *Comus*, and of Minerva, as described by the Elder Brother (418–52, especially 'blank aw').

467–70. Satan was 'One who brings/A mind not to be chang'd by Place or Time' (I, 252–3), a 'Hell within him' (see IV, 20–3 and 75), and his jealousy of pleasures denied him has already met us in this book, 263–4.

473–493. *Satan soliloquises*. This is the most difficult paragraph in Book IX so far, because, although there are no learned allusions, the style is so succint and the punctuation lighter than we are accustomed to. The first few lines, for example, would be easier if there had been a question mark at 'me'; but this would have obscured the construction of 'transported', and required another main verb. Again we might have expected a semi-colon or full stop at 'destroy' (477). The punctuation is probably Milton's choice, seeing how careful he was about such matters, but this cannot be regarded as certain in every case with a blind man.

489–93. A recent critic (Kermode) calls this elaborate word-play 'pseudo-rhyming', and notes the half-rhyme which concludes it.

490. So in *Paradise Regained* the fairest women are said by Belial to possess

> Virgin majesty with mild
> And sweet allay'd, yet terrible to approach (II, 159–60)

494–531. *The Serpent approaches Eve deviously, and attracts her attention to his beauty.*

495. *Inmate bad* seems an unusually flat expression for Milton; perhaps the point lies in the suggestion that 'serpent' would not have a bad connotation for us if Satan had not once assumed a serpent's form. That he did so on this occasion was an addition by the Fathers to the Bible story.

496–502. There are somewhat similar descriptions of snakes in Virgil (*Aeneid*, v. 84–9) and in Ovid (*Metamorphoses*, iii. 32, etc.), while Rabbinic writings made the Serpent upright. Dante gave Cerberus red eyes, a sign of passion, and the Player in *Hamlet* speaks of 'the hellish Pyrrhus', when he is devastating Troy, as having 'eyes like carbuncles'.

indented wave may be a reminiscence of Shakespeare's 'snake that with indented glide did slip away' in *A.Y.L.I.* (IV. iii. 113).

497. *as since* the Fall; for the punishment pronounced by God on the serpent was 'upon thy belly shalt thou go' (Gen. 3:14).

503. The inversion of accent in the first foot, followed by the marked caesura after 'redundant', gives an effective climax to a description.

504, etc. 'Ornamentation, such as the comparisons that follow, comes best in the pauses of the action. We now know for certain that Satan is to make his culminating attack on Eve, and in that certainty we are glad to pause and enjoy the digressive ornament that Milton gives us' (Tillyard). Milton is fond of these negative similes, as in the famous 'Not that fair field of Enna', etc. (IV, 269).

506. Hermione was in Greek story the daughter of Menelaus and Helen, and seems to have been put here by mistake for Harmonia, although the mistake has been found also in Sandys (the Elizabethan translator of Ovid) and others. The story of Cadmus and Harmonia retiring from Thebes to Illyria for rest, and being changed into snakes by Apollo, is told by Ovid (*Metamorphoses*, iv), and furnished Arnold with occasion for a beautiful bit of description in his *Empedocles on Etna* (427, etc.), which is better known than most of that work since it was printed as a separate poem (while the dramatic poem was suppressed) with the title 'Cadmus and Harmonia', beginning 'Far, far from here, The Adriatic breaks in a warm bay'.

506–7. *the God in Epidaurus:* Aesculapius, the Greek god of medicine, had his chief shrine at Epidaurus in the Peloponnese, where there are considerable remains, including the finest theatre in Greece. He was appealed to by ambassadors from Rome at the time of a plague, and accompanied them back to Rome in the form of a serpent (Ovid, *Metamorphoses*, xv).

508. *Jove* (Juppiter) was worshipped in North Africa under the title of Juppiter Ammon, the 'Libyan Jove' of IV, 277. Olympias was the wife of Philip of Macedon and the mother of Alexander the Great (born in 356 B.C.), who on account of his world-wide conquests was thought to be of divine descent. The mother of Scipio Africanus was likewise thought to have been visited by the supreme god of the Roman Capitol, since her son was the conqueror of Hannibal.

Milton as a staunch republican would be even more inclined than others to see the republic which survived the Punic wars as the greatest days of Rome.

521. Odysseus on his wanderings came to the land of the enchantress Circe, who turned his followers into swine. 'All around the palace mountain-bred wolves and lions were roaming, whom she herself had bewitched with evil drugs that she gave them. Yet the beasts did not set on my men, but lo they ramped about them and fawned on them, wagging their long tails' (*Odyssey*, x. 214, etc.).

Milton had made his Comus the son of Circe, inheriting her magic powers.

523. The semi-colon at the end of this line, where we might expect a comma, may be intended to make the following phrase stand out more prominently.

524-6. Dante had described on the mount of Purgatory 'a snake, perchance such as gave to Eve the bitter food' advancing through grass and flowers and turning back its head 'licking like a beast that sleeks itself.'

529-30. The alternatives are thus put by the first commentator on *Paradise Lost:* 'That the devil moved the serpent's tongue, and used it as an instrument to form that tempting speech he made to Eve, is the opinion of some: that he form'd a voice by impression of the sounding air, distinct from the serpent, is the opinion of others: of which our author has left the curious to their choice' (Hume). The second alternative, the 'impulse of vocal air', is clarified by Sylvester (Du Bartas) at this point thus:

> Locally absent, present by effect:
> As when the sweet strings of a lute we strike,
> Another lute laid near it, sounds the like.

532-48. *The Serpent's first speech to Eve:* a speech of pure flattery, appealing to a woman's vanity. Some extra-biblical Jewish sources represented Satan as desiring to kill Adam and get the woman for himself.

532-3. So Comus addressed the Lady in Milton's Mask as 'Hail, foreign wonder', and went on to suggest that she must be a goddess (*Comus*, 265-70); and in the dream of Eve, which prepares the way for this temptation, she hears a gentle voice say to her:

> Heav'n wakes with all his eyes,
> Whom to behold but thee, Natures desire,
> In whose sight all things joy, with ravishment
> Attracted by thy beauty still to gaze. (V, 44-7)

Satan's pun on 'Wonder', and the deification of a woman, both recall the love poetry of the Metaphysicals, with which Milton had little sympathy.

538–48. The language suggests not only metaphysical poetry, but also that courtly love which was repudiated in the prologue to this book, and perhaps also the loose morals of the Restoration Court. Milton, the Puritan poet of wedded love, puts into Satan's mouth the picture of feminine beauty as 'the cynosure of every eye'. 'To cry her up as a goddess was' says Newton, 'the readiest way to make her a mere mortal'.

549–66. *Eve expresses her surprise at an animal being endowed with the faculty of speech.* Milton may have remembered a passage at the beginning of Sir Thomas Browne's *Vulgar Errors* (1646) in which he says that some have been surprised that Eve should allow herself to be deluded by a serpent, or hear such a creature speak 'without suspicion of imposture'. But we must remember that Eve is still *innocent* in a way we can hardly conceive.

549. Satan had already shown his power of persuasion on his own followers in the early part of the poem.

The word 'gloz'd' takes us back once more to Milton's earlier picturing of temptation, when Comus prepares to attack his Lady:

> I under fair pretence of friendly ends,
> And well-plac'd words of glozing courtesie
> Baited with reasons not unplausible
> Wind me into the easie-hearted man,
> And hugg him into snares (160–6)

551. The biblical account does not attribute to Eve surprise at the Serpent's ability to speak, nor make the Serpent claim to have eaten the fruit first (575, etc.)

559. Milton's Eve anticipates many moderns in arguing for at least a limited intelligence in animals. God had said to Adam that the animals 'also know And reason not contemptibly' (VIII, 372–3), which need not be irreconcilible with IX, 239–40, if 'reason' here is taken rather differently from 'Reason' there.

567–612. *The Tempter's second speech to Eve describes the apples on the tree of knowledge. He tries to invest the Tree and its fruit with a special glamour.* The texture of this speech is, for Milton, loose, and gives an almost colloquial tone (e.g. 589–97). Mackail compared it to the manner of *Comus*.

568. We may notice the variety of forms used for Satan's address to Eve (cf. 532).

570. The spelling shows that 'commandst' is only two syllables and 'shouldst' only one; while the vowel of 'be' must be pronounced lightly, or even slurred over, before the following open vowel.

581. The idea that snakes were fond of fennel comes ultimately from Pliny's *Natural History*, and in one of his prose works Milton refers to the belief that a snake refreshed its sight in spring by rubbing against the fennel plant. Here, however, it is the flower that is in point; which, when crushed is (says *The Oxford Book of Wild Flowers*) 'very aromatic'.

585. *Apples* are not actually mentioned in the biblical story, though the tree was well known in Syria and is often mentioned in Canticles (the Song of Songs). The tree of Genesis is simply 'the tree of the knowledge of good and evil'. In English the fruit is called an apple as early as Caedmon; and anyhow the word 'apple' is 'used with the greatest latitude' of any fruit (*O.E.D.*).

586-8. Satan's 'perswaders' anticipate Eve's, 740-3.

606-8. This is very similar to what Adam confessed to Raphael about his feeling for Eve (VIII, 471-3). In the adjective 'Divine' (capitalized by poet or printer) Satan already insinuates that godhead to which he will tempt her to aspire.

612. *Dame* is one of those words that have gone down in the world; and its status has not been altogether restored by the institution of the order of Dames of the British Empire (D.B.E.). But at Eton the 'dames' once held almost the position of the modern housemaster, and 'the Dame of Sark' would hardly exchange her title for that of 'the Lady of Sark'.

613-24. *Eve's second reply to the Tempter* shows that her curiosity has been aroused. She does not yet know that the magical tree is the tree forbidden to them.

622. Presumably it was eternal spring or summer in Paradise, so that the fruit would no more decay than the leaves.

624. *Bearth* is the same word as 'birth', and is only here spelt in this way. The ordinary spelling can have the meaning of 'that which

is borne', and if the spelling here is due to the poet, as seems probable, it must be intended to stress the derivation from 'bear'. The present editor suggests a slight play on the idea that the tree has to 'bear' all its weight of fruit till it is picked. Milton has the same spelling in his translation of Ps. 8 (of 1653) where it has to rhyme with 'earth', but is exactly the ordinary word' 'birth' in sense.

625–46. *The Serpent leads Eve to the tree of Knowledge.*

625. The poet varies his names for the serpent, as he continues to do for Eve also in Satan's mouth. 'The line seems itself to exult' (Waldock). 'What a line, in its hard and snaky delight!' (Stoll).

626. The punctuation is, as usual, that of the first edition. We should require at least a colon at the end of this line.

631–2. Cf. IV, 247–50, where the inhabitants of Paradise are introduced:

> close the Serpent sly
> Insinuating, wove with Gordian twine
> His breaded train.

634–42. There are two points of comparison in the simile, as 643–5 indicates, the brightness of the light and its delusive character, in both resembling the Serpent.

The 'wandring fire' (634) or 'Friar's Lanthorn' (*L'Allegro*, 104) was presumably a commoner sight than it is now when so much of the land was not properly drained. It is caused by rotting vegetation under water, which sends up marsh gas (methane) which sometimes briefly ignites above the surface. Marsh gas is defined as 'the first member of the series of *paraffin* hydrocarbons', which may explain the epithet 'unctuous' (635). The light would naturally be more visible at nightfall (640), and Milton probably remembers Shakespeare's Puck, who 'misleads night-wanderers, laughing at their harm' (*M.N.D.*, II. i. 39); but Milton had already alluded to the folklore which saw in these lights an

> evil thing that walks by night
> In fog, or fire, by lake, or moorish fen
> (*Comus*, 432–3)

644–5. The Tree was not harmful in itself or God would not have planted it in Paradise, says Augustine, but it was forbidden.

root, cause, may well contain also a grim pun on 'tree', as 'bearth' above may have involved two kinds of bearing. The word 'root' suggests the rhyming word 'fruit', which, like the word 'woe', reverberates through *P.L.*

647–63. Eve recognizes the tree as the one forbidden to them by God. Soon after we first see the human pair in Eden Milton made Adam tell Eve of their 'easie charge'

> not to taste that onely Tree
> Of knowledge, planted by the Tree of Life . . .
> for well thou knowst
> God hath pronounc't it death to taste that Tree,
> The only sign of our obedience left
> Among so many signs of power and rule. (IV, 423–9)

In Genesis the Serpent first questions Eve about God's prohibition. In Milton Eve first states the prohibition.

648. For another tragic play on words cf. 11 of this book. Paronomasia, as this figure of speech is technically named, is common in Latin and Italian poets.

653. *Sole Daughter of his voice:* 'Another Hebraism. *Bath Kol.*, the daughter of a voice, is a noted phrase among the Jews, and they understand by it a voice from Heaven; and this command is called the 'sole daughter' as it is the only command that we read of that was given to our first Parents in Paradise' (Newton). Wordsworth remembered it when he addressed Duty as 'stern daughter of the voice of God' (*Ode to Duty*).

654. St. Paul had spoken of the Gentiles as 'a law unto themselves', since they had not the Jewish law and had to live by the natural law (Rom. 2:14).

655–63. Milton puts into metre with very slight change words from Gen. 3:1–3.

657. Satan grossly exaggerates the prohibition, unless we are to suppose that he means all trees of this species. But perhaps this is to look too precisely upon the event! We are not told in the Bible that the exact tree was pointed out to Adam.

659. Note the words 'yet sinless'. Milton held that evil could enter

the mind of God or man (V, 117), but that sin only began when the will consented to it. Milton did not hold, as Tillyard thought, that Eve's dream in Book V proved her already fallen.

664–732. *Satan wins over Eve by appealing to her pride and ambition.* He is inviting her to claim the total freedom, the independence of God, which he had claimed.

665–7. The Tempter now tries a new kind of guile, feigning sympathy with the beings he has designed to ruin.

Milton has a fair number of references to the stage and acting, of which he is said to have been a great frequenter as a young man.

670–8. Milton has in mind the orators of Athens in the fifth and fourth centuries B.C., such as Demothenes, who tried to arouse his city to the danger from Macedon, and Isocrates, one of whose speech supplied a title for Milton's *Areopagitica*; and those of republican Rome, especially Cicero, in the last century B.C., after which oratory was no longer free, under the Roman Empire. No slur is intended upon these orators by the comparison of Satan to them.

'Here as usual Milton uses a simile as a transposed description of what would be otherwise unimaginable; this image remains in the mind, and it is as an orator rather than a snake that we see Satan during the speeches that follow and throughout the scene of the temptation' (B. A. Wright).

675–7. The double use of 'highth', first in a metaphorical, then in a literal sense seems to me a slight flaw, such as might more justifiably have given Bentley ground for objection than most of what he censured or emended.

681–2. *Things in their causes* is probably a reminiscence of a line in Virgil (perhaps referring to Lucretius): *Felix qui potuit rerum cognoscere causas.*

683. *deemd however wise* may be regarded as a hit at God, like the new and scornful title of 'the Threatner' (687).

687–90. Satan's appeal to his own example is not explicitly made in the Bible. Milton brings out his egoism by his repeating of the lengthened spelling 'mee'. [In the first edition the 'me' of 690 is also printed 'mee', but it is clear that it should not there be emphasized;

hence Darbishire in the text adopted prints what she believes the poet would have intended if he could have overseen the printer.]

689–90. By using the pagan words 'Fate' and 'Lot' Satan avoids acknowledging God's supremacy. Cf. the complaint of the fallen angels, 'that Fate Free Virtue should enthral to Force or Chance' (II, 549–50).

697. Knowledge of evil, acquired as Satan suggested, was not to prove a guide to 'happier life'. 'Perhaps this is the doom which Adam fell into of knowing good and evil, that is to say of knowing good by evil' (*Areopagitica*). Plato had taught that 'to know what is good involves knowing that what is incompatible with good must be evil' (A. E. Taylor, summarizing Plato).

702. The first editor of Milton, Patrick Hume in 1695, nicely calls the argument of the following lines 'a Satanic syllogism'. The argument assumes that God is good, implicitly denying the title to a being, however powerful, whose actions offended the moral sense of man. It has been pointed out that Satan is inconsistent in saying first that God would have praised their courage in eating the fruit (693–4), and then that He did not want them to rival him in knowledge. But we must expect inconsistency from devilish rhetoric, which at any rate a woman would not detect.

708–18. *Gods* moves about between the sense 'God' or 'like a god' (involving a plurality of deities) and its fairly common Miltonic use for angels as being sons of God, put into the mouth of God himself at II, 352. The ambiguity of Gen. 3:5 recurs in John 10:34–5). Milton intends Satan to confuse Eve. 'He seems to use both numbers promiscuously, sometimes speaking of "God", sometimes of "Gods"; and I think we may observe that he generally speaks of "Gods" when the sentiment would be too horrid if it was spoken of "God"' (Newton). A medieval divine, Peter Damiani, commenting on Satan's words in Genesis remarked that the Devil was the first grammarian when he taught men to give a plural to the word 'God'. 'It should have neither a plural nor the indefinite article. It is a proper name' (Baillie). But in Hebrew *Elohim* could be plural.

723–5. The only knowledge gained by eating the fruit of the Tree was ironically of 'Good lost and Evil got' (1072); which hardly increased their 'wisdom'. Satan is no more specific about the nature of forbidden knowledge than Mephistopheles when he tempts Doctor Faustus. The attraction to pride lies in the very thought of its being forbidden to mere mortals.

728. *if all be his*, i.e. if He is omnipotent and can control the result of your act. This, of course, ignores the whole purpose of God in giving man freewill.

729-30. The suggestion of God's jealousy of man is ascribed to the Serpent in more than one Jewish source (see on 826-33). But 'We cannot suppose the Deity envious of truth, or unwilling that it should be freely communicated to man' (Milton's *Second Defence*). The *expression*, on the other hand, comes from near the beginning of the *Aeneid*: *tantaene animis caelestibus irae?* It is found in Shakespeare when he makes Gloucester rebuke a cardinal for his intemperate language (*2 Henry VI*, II. i. 24).

732. 'Human' and 'Humane' were originally the same word. The accent in the old French form was on the last syllable, but in English gradually got shifted backward, although the spelling with 'e' remained general till the beginning of the eighteenth century; after which it was only retained in the special sense of the Latin *humanus* = 'kindly'. There are three more instances in the epic where the spelling with an 'e' must bear the meaning of 'human' or 'mortal', viz. X, 793 and 908, and XI, 147. Patrick Hume, knowing current usages at the end of the seventeenth century, glosses 'Goddess humane' as 'Thou Earthly Deity'. The oxymoron would have been congenial to Milton (cf. 'darkness visible', I, 63); but it is difficult to believe that he would have pronounced the word here as 'húmăne' after the inversion of accent in the first foot. I conclude that the poet intended the word to be read with the accent on the second syllable, and perhaps to suggest both meanings. (Verity's note is, for once, inaccurate).

733-79. *Eve, deceived by the Serpent and further provoked by the appearance of the fruit and her own hunger, argues her right to follow the Serpent's example in attaining knowledge.*

739-40. 'This is a circumstance beautifully added by our author to the Scripture account, in order to make the folly and impiety of Eve appear less extravagant and monstrous' (Newton). But the dissection of the various sins involved in Eve's act was part of a long exegetical tradition. Modern critics have followed in their wake; e.g. 'Eve falls through self-confidence, wilfulness, conjugal insubordination' (Stoll). Others have asserted that her sin was gluttony, or 'triviality of mind'. But it is clear enough from the following speech that gluttony is quite subordinate to disobedience. The Bible says that 'the woman saw that the tree was good for food', and this allowed Milton to suggest midday hunger (cf. 'noontide repast', 403) as a subsidiary cause of her disobedience. He also adds the smell. The time of midday may have been assumed because the Crucifixion also took place at that hour.

751–2. On *the Tree of Knowledge*, see Introduction, p. 18.

756–7. Eve has caught something of Satan's kind of logic; just as Othello, when he has yielded to Iago's insinuations, begins to think and talk like him.

760. Milton himself had argued that supposedly divine (scriptural) prohibitions could not be binding when clearly inimical to human good, in the matter of divorce.

770–2. The reader, or hearer, if we may suppose ourselves for the moment present at the temptation, knows that envy is precisely the main force moving Satan, and that it is to her ruin that Eve does not suspect the Serpent's proffered gifts. The dramatic irony is appropriate to the dramatic form originally conceived of for the work. It is Satan's triumph to have brought Eve to ascribe implicitly to God his own attitude of envy for man.

780–833. *Eve picks the fruit, and congratulates herself on having done so. She decides to invoke Adam in the consequences.* Notice the brevity with which the fatal deed is related in contrast to the long preparation for it. The greater artist knows better than the lesser when to exercise restraint.

780. *rash hand.* Milton had used the phrase in *Comus*, when the second Brother thought that his sister's beauty needed defence against 'the rash hand of bold Incontinence' (397).

782–4. Cf. 'All nature is likewise subject to mortality and a curse on account of sin' (*C.D.*), and the details of the change in nature in X, 412–14 and 651, etc. Milton would have in mind the darkness that overspread the land in the gospel accounts of the Crucifixion accented monosyllable, 'Ran through his veins', while the spondee ('slack hand') in the next line slows down the movement—an effect completed by the spondee beginning the next line 'Down dropd'.

As so often in *Paradise Lost* the passage gains additional force from a back reference. 'Silence and the shower of rose leaves had marked the height of Adam and Eve's happiness in Milton's description of their bower (IV, 773). But Adam's present silence is the speechlessness of horror, not the quiet of untroubled sleep, and the rose leaves, which, in Eden's perpetual spring, had been renewed before morning, now fade irreparably' (Mahood).

Note also the contrast between the 'slack hand' of Adam here and the 'rash hand' of Eve in 780 (to which Mr. Midgley kindly drew my attention). Cf. Commentary on 385–6.

890. 'horror chill' was a favourite collocation in Virgil (e.g. *Aeneid*, ii. 120–1); fear drains away warmth from the body.

893. The roses of the garland (see 840) are made to fade in sympathy with Adam's horror—an instance of the 'pathetic fallacy' perhaps, but something without which poetry at least would be much the poorer.

900–1. Here Death first enters the Garden. The alliteration, is all the more effective because it is not so frequent in Milton as in Spenser.

'There rushes into "defac't" everything that the poem has shown us of sin and its effects: "A deminution of the majesty of the human countenance, and a conscious degradation of mind" (*De Doctrina Christiana*). "Deflour'd" too draws on those echoes and anticipations which are felt in the blood and felt along the heart of the poem. Eve, the gatherer and guardian of flowers, "herself though fairest unsupported flour" has been deflowered' (Ricks).

'Deflowered' is commonly used of a woman deprived of her virginity (as, for example, by Shakespeare and Cowley in that century). In the choice of the word here there may be a trace of sexual implication, since Milton would have known the tradition started by the rabbis that the Serpent's display (494–503) was a seduction scene. Cf. the following from T. Milles, *Treasurie of Auncient and Modern Times* (1613): 'Many authors affirme that Serpents have been noted to desire the companie of women. Who seeth not therin (but more in the action of Eve, than in all other) a

and perhaps also the Renaissance commentaries which elaborated 'the belief that nature fully reflected divine intentions' (Patrides). But it was also a feature of classical poetry to make nature sympathize with the doings of man, as in horror at the union of Dido and Aeneas (*Aeneid*, iv. 166–9). The present passage stands in marked contrast with the sympathy of nature at the first union of Adam and Eve (VIII, 511–20).

784. As Milton had glorified the Serpent in his approach to Eve (494–504), so his ignominious departure from his victim is given in the ugly monosyllable 'slunk'. In the whole passage (780–5) monosyllables are as weighty as in the line 'So clomb this first grand thief into God's fold' (IV, 192).

790. The line reminds us that pride or vanity, and not hunger, was the main prompter to disobedience. For the 'affecting (of) Godhead' see III, 207–10 and V, 75–7.

793. *as with Wine*. Note the 'as'; cf. 1008. If Milton had intended literal intoxication he would have been accepting a rabbinic idea. He may well have picked up the adjective 'jocond' here, although he does use it occasionally elsewhere, from Sylvester, whom I find applying it to the Serpent.

800. If the phrase 'due praise' is, as seems probable, still governed by 'not without', the omission of the comma after it may be due to a feeling that the end of the line gives enough pause in itself. But those who suppose that Milton was able to check everything, as we know he checked much, through his amanuenses, might find it difficult to explain why 'praise' has not the capital given to 'Song'!

800–25. Eve shows a kind of idolatry in that she who had joined in the morning hymn to her Maker (in V, 153–208) is now prepared to worship a tree (835). She goes on to speak of Him as one among many 'gods' (804–5), to adopt Satan's earlier suggestion that God grudged them knowledge, to speak of her own will as her best guide, to question His omniscience, and finally to crown her blasphemy by an opprobrious substitute for 'our great creator' and his throng of attendant spirits. In 825 she once more adopts the attitude of Satan in his rebellion; contrast V, 538–40.

811. The Eve of Grotius's play (see Appendix II, p. 244) hopes that perhaps God will not have noticed her.

813-15. Perhaps the poet remembers the taunt of Elijah to the priests of Baal on Mount Carmel (1 Kings 18:27).

826-33. The source of these lines was proclaimed by Saurat to be the Zohar, a Jewish commentary on the Pentateuch; but it is more probably the so-called Pseudo-Josephus, a work on Jewish history which had been printed in the fifteenth century and partially translated into Latin, French and English before Milton's day, who refers to it in his *Pro Populo Anglicano Defensio*. Parallels to the earlier lines in which the Serpent ascribes to envy on God's part the prohibition to eat from the tree, and to Eve's present fear of Adam being joined to another woman in her place are quoted in J. S. Fletcher's *Milton's Semitic Studies*. But Milton could have found the idea mentioned in biblical commentaries current in his day.

832-3. Milton may have remembered an ode of Horace which ends with a lover's wish to live and die with his lady (*Odes*, III. ix. 24, *Tecum vivere amem, tecum obeam libens*); but if he did, he improves on the original. Eve's assertion of her love for Adam is genuine enough, although her thoughts in this speech are self-regarding. When C. S. Lewis brands her as a murderess, he displays that love of paradox through the application of strict logic which also led him to call Satan a fool.

834-85. *Eve invites Adam to follow her example.*

838-42. There is a grim, even a ghastly, irony in Adam's occupation, which more resembles the irony of *Othello* where the handkerchief is concerned than the pathos of Andromache weaving a robe and preparing a bath against her husband, Hector's, return from battle (*Iliad*, xxii). The way is here prepared for 891-2.

843-52. The simple style of these lines of narrative are in marked contrast with that of the speeches of Eve which precede and follow.

845-6. The premonitions of trouble here attributed to Adam were anticipated in the poem called *Psyche* of Joseph Beaumont in 1648, from which the relevant stanza (VI, 294) is quoted by J. M. Evans.

851-2. In calling the fruit 'downie' Milton probably recalled a speaker in Virgil's second Eclogue who said he would pick apples with tender down on them; while he could have taken the 'ambro-

sial smell' from the Georgics (IV, 415). 'Nectar' (838) and ambr[...] were the drink and food of the gods in classical epic.

853-4. These lines are among the few in *Paradise Lost* wh[...] good scholars explain differently. Masson took the first part a[...] reference to Eve's beauty, and 'Apologie' as the object of the ve[...] 'prompt', thus: 'In her face, so beautiful it was, excuse for what sh[...] had done came already, as prologue to the very speech of excu[...] she was to make, and to prompt that apology which she no[...] addressed to him.' But it seems more likely that 'Apologie' is [...] nominative case, parallel to 'Prologue' and that the more forma[...] defence is thought of as backing up her excuse for absence.

A more drastic treatment of the passage was Bentley's reading of[...] 'too prompt' (printed by Newton): 'qui s'excuse s'accuse'; but few nowadays are prepared to suspect in Milton the corruptions common in ancient manuscripts, to which Bentley was accustomed.

It seems to the present editor that the rhythm of the line is much against what appears to be the usual view, of taking 'Apologie as the object of 'to prompt'.

856-85. The poet has with remarkable psychological insight and dramatic power given to Eve an ingratiating tone, bred of a bad conscience and expressing itself in a false gaiety summed up by the word 'blithe' (886). The familiar address 'Adam' is a contrast to the earlier respect of 273; (cf. 921 and 291.) The very compressed syntax of the paragraph may be intended to show her nervous eagerness to anticipate blame. In the later lines of the speech Eve invents a reason, original with Milton, for partaking of the fruit almost the direct opposite of that considered in 819-25; so quickly has deceitfulness come into her nature.

886-959. *Adam is dumbfounded at Eve's report, but first in soliloquy and then addressing his wife, determines to share her fate; which he hopes may not, after all, be death.*

888-93. The powerful effect of these lines is partly due to what i[...] described in 892-3 (called by a recent American critic 'the lovelies[...] symbolic act of all the poem') and partly to the poet's manipulatio[...] of the rhythm. We may notice the strong pauses in the middle [...] lines 888 and 890, and at the same time the reversal of the foot-stre[...] in the word 'Adam' which make the following words seem hasti[...] In 891 the first two feet become in effect a dactyl followed by [...]

strange efficacie and deceit in Satan? All the Rabbins are of this mind, that the devils (through Gods sufferance) have great power over ones concupiscence and privie members, saying that by an Allegorie Satan is meant the Serpent. Philo and the Hebrewes say, that the Serpent signifieth allegorically, Lecherie . . .' Milles goes on to give the instances of the fatherhood of Alexander the Great and Scipio Africanus used by Milton in 507-10.

906-7. Adam could be said to have some foundation for his resolution in the words put into his mouth in Genesis proclaiming man and woman as 'one flesh'; cf. VIII, 495.

908-10. These lines surely express true love and not the uxorious-ness of which C. S. Lewis accused Adam. They take us back to the lovely passage in Book IV, 650-6, in which Adam described the natural delights of Paradise which would not be sweet without Eve. So the 'wild words' would be all the wilder for lack of Eve's help in tending then.

When Adam confessed to Raphael in the previous book that he found himself 'here only weake/Against the charm of Beauties powerful glance' (VIII, 532-3), and was warned by the archangel to 'take heed least Passion sway/Thy Judgement to do aught, which else free Will/Would not admit' (635-7), Passion meant not so much sensuality as self-abnegation before a woman.

911-13. Milton makes Adam's thought of life without Eve contrast too much to his advantage with *her* thoughts of such a life (828-9).

913. The original punctuation, as here printed, gives a more dramatic feeling than the conventionalized texts of the nineteenth century with a comma inserted between the two negatives.

916. *parted* perhaps also suggests that the pair are 'parts' of one being, just as the sound of 'sole' twice repeated at 227 might be held to suggest one 'soul'.

920. The series of monosyllables slows down the rhythm to suit Adam's 'calmer mood'; ''Tis a deep, considerate melancholy' (Richardson).

922. *hast* is changed to 'hath' in the second edition of 1674, and may be Milton's own correction.

922–5. The syntax of these lines is difficult, and loose at the best. Many editors from early times have printed a comma after 'dar'd' (which Verity wrongly says is in 'the original editions') which makes the reader inclined to start a new sentence with 'Had it been' —only to find himself stranded. The two verbs 'to eye' and 'to taste' must be in parallel dependence on 'dar'd' if we are to get the general sense required out of the lines.

928. An early critic draws attention to Adam's reasoning as a good example of the tendency of the human mind to believe what it wants to believe. But it is possible that Milton has in mind also the reading of the Vulgate (Latin Bible) at this point 'ne forte moriamini' preserved in the Douai (R.C.) version 'lest perhaps we die' of Gen. 3:3.

932–4. Now Adam is accepting the Serpent's claim (705–15), as Eve had previously accepted it. He will end on 'a note of Satanic mockery of God' (B. A. Wright), very different from his later penitence.

947. the Adversary. This is the first occasion in this book on which this name has been used for Satan; but the title, which is in fact the meaning of the Hebrew word, occurs early in the poem:

> Meanwhile the Adversary of God and Man (II, 629).

See the first chapter of the book of Job for Satan in this role.

955–9. In addition to the words of Gen. (2:23), paraphrased at 914–15 above, Milton has behind him here Eph. 5:28–9, especially 'He that loveth his wife loveth himself.' Adam's final words have a terrible irony, since to keep Eve was also to lose himself.

960–89. *Eve welcomes the proof of Adam's love for her in his determination to share her fate, and recommends him to eat.*

The occasionally loose syntax of this paragraph may be intended to render the breathless excitement of Eve.

961–2. The words are a ghastly echo of what is said of the Messiah after His offer to die for man:

> 'O unexampl'd love,
> Love nowhere to be found less then Divine' (III, 410–11)

The irony of 'example high' as applied to Adam's disobedience of God, and of 'happie trial' in 975, mark the infatuation produced in Eve by her eating of the fruit.

966–7. The words 'One Heart, one Soul' are in apposition to 'our Union'. We may supply 'as being' after 'speak'. The prime reference is to 958–9; but speaking to Raphael Adam had also said that Eve's 'Love and sweet compliance' declared 'union of Mind, or in us both one Soule' (VIII, 604).

971. *mee.* We should not have expected the emphatic spelling here; but it has been accounted for on the ground that without it we should be tempted to overrun the medial pause (B. A. Wright, comparing 'shee' in 390).

977–80. A comparison of 826–33 shows that Eve had less noble ideas and is untruthful here.

986–9. These lines are doubly ironical in view both of the bliss of their unfallen state and of the misery to come.

990–1016. *Adam accepts the fruit at Eve's hands, and eats. Loss of innocence at once begins to show itself.* The short and simple style is in marked contrast to the excited words of Eve that had preceded.

997–9. Cf. 'Adam was not deceived, but the woman being deceived was in the transgression' (1 Tim. 2:14); and Calvin's 'The opinion has commonly been received that he was rather captivated by her allurements than persuaded by Satan's impostures.' Milton is also anxious to point the difference between the woman, deceived by the Serpent and hardly conscious of the importance of her action, and her husband, who is aware of what is involved, not deceived by Eve's arguments, but acts with his eyes open from love of his wife. ' "Femal charm" need not mean that Eve leered at Adam and waggled her hips' (Empson). The word signifies rather the irrational appeal of Beauty, 'the charm of Beauties powerful glance' (VIII, 533).

1002. Grammatical punctuation would require a comma after 'and', although some modernized editions do not supply one. This would still be needed even if 'muttering thunder' were taken to mean 'while thunder muttered'—which seems to the present editor impossible, although Newton called it 'ablative absolute'.

1003–4. This appears to be the only occurrence of the famous expression 'Original Sin' in Milton's poetry; 'original' meaning not only 'first' but also the *root* of all subsequent sin. The idea that the whole future human race was implicated in Adam's sin comes in the Apocryhpha (2 Esd. 7-48), and in St. Paul ('As in Adam all die, etc. 1 Cor. 15-22), though the expression does not come till Tertullian (*originis vitium*). Milton discusses 'original sin' at length in his prose treatise on Christian Doctrine (Book I, chapter xi), saying that 'undoubtedly all sinned in Adam'. Although the poet was no Church of England man, his view was pretty near that expressed in the ninth of the Articles of Religion, drawn up in 1562, to be found in the Book of Common Prayer. Modern theologians would make a distinction between the proneness to sin, which we all inherit, and the actual guilt of deliberate sin. (See for a brief note with references M. Ramsey, *From Gore to Temple*, Appendix II.)

1010–11. Eve had had 'expectation high' (789), and the metaphor here is a natural one, although Horace had spoken of 'spurning the earth with fleeing wing' (*Odes*, III. ii. 24).

1011–13. The biblical foundation here is the loss of innocence and the coming of self-consciousness and shame after the Fall (Gen. 3:7). Augustine held that the sexual desire before the Fall was devoid of 'concupiscence', i.e. lust. Cf. 'They felt a new motion in their flesh, which had become rebellious as a consequence of their own rebellion. . . . The motion of concupiscence is the consequence of sin' (Augustine, *De Civ. Dei*).

Milton manages, without involving his readers in the technical terms of theology, to convey effectively a difference between the sexual love of Adam and Eve before the Fall in Book IV (especially 492–502 and 736–75) and after it. Here the pair are in a state akin to intoxication, and physical union is sought more for its own sake than as an expression of love. Eve has become for Adam a woman to 'enjoy' (1032). Contrast 'Love unlibidinous' (V, 449) and 'Imparadis'd in one anothers arms' (IV, 506).

1017–33. *Adam provokes Eve to sexual pleasure.*

The phrase 'enjoy thee' (1032) suggests a selfish and merely bodily union, as it does on Dalilah's lips in *Samson Agonistes*, 807.

1017–20. Milton makes Adam display the unnatural exaltation engendered in him, as it had previously been in Eve (960–89), first by his facetiousness, and then (1024–6) by what the Greeks called *hybris* (infatuated pride), in wishing that they could have defied God by further disobedience. In the first lines he puns on the fact that both the Latin words for 'taste' or 'savour' (*sapor*) and that for 'wisdom' or 'sapience' are derived from the verb *sapere*. So in English when we speak of 'a man of taste' we mean more than taste in food and drink.

1029–32. The thought expressed here and the flowery setting that follows is parallel to a scene between Zeus and Hera in *Iliad*, xiv. 292–353. As usual, Milton interweaves his two chief sources—the Bible and the Classics (especially classical epic).

1034–66. *Sexual indulgence is followed by shame.*

1034–9. The blatant sexuality of this scene—a sexuality without love and without satisfaction—is intended to contrast with the unfallen sexuality of Adam's description of his first union with Eve in VIII, 509, etc.; but the introduction of flowers here as well as there seems unsuitable, unless it is designed to set the change in the human pair against unchanging nature. We may note also the difference between Eve's forwardness here and her 'sweet reluctant amorous delay' in the more ideal picture of IV (311 and 744–9).

1038. We should expect a comma at the end of this line since there is one at the end of the previous line; but perhaps the slight pause of the line ending was felt to be enough.

1042–4. Cf. 'Come, let us take our fill of love' in Proverbs (8:18); which, being the word of a loose woman seducing a young man, would have degraded the encounter in the mind of those who remembered the original. So 'Solace' is ironical; contrast 844.

1049. *grosser sleep*, in contrast with Adam's usual sleep which

> Was Aerie light, from pure digestion bred,
> And temperate vapors bland (V, 4–5).

1050. *conscious*, which essentially means self-conscious (of something), has come here, as occasionally the Latin *conscius*, to mean guilty. (This sense, ignored by Verity, is admitted by *O.E.D.*)

1053. The syntax here is a literal transference of the Greek idiom seen in the New Testament 'I know thee who thou art'.

1054. Contrast V, 383–5, where the innocence of Eve needed no veil, and IV, 312–14.

1058. *Hee covered*. This personification of Shame seems to us harsh, but may be a reminiscence of a sentence in the Psalms: 'Let mine adversaries be clothed with shame' (109:29). In the original text of Milton here there is no stop after 'Shame', which makes the line quite unintelligible. Darbishire has carried out what we may be sure was the author's intention in adding the full stop. On the difference between Shame and Modesty what H. Gardner says about the Eve of Book IV in *A Reading of Paradise Lost*, pp. 84–5, deserves attention.

1059–63. As Samson lost his physical strength when his hair was cut off (Judg. 16:4–20), so Adam lost his original virtue, his moral strength, through sin and the ensuing sensuality.

1061. In spite of the traditional pronunciation of 'Delíla', Milton undoubtedly chooses to place the stress on the first syllable here, and always in *Samson Agonistes*. Verity's attempt to preserve the common pronunciation in Milton's verse is hopeless. I am informed by a Semitic scholar that the first syllable bears the least accent in the Hebrew; so that the reason for Milton's choice is obscure.

1062. 'The simile becomes the vehicle of moral judgement' (Harding) in the first half of this line.

1067–98. *Adam suggests to Eve that they should cover their nakedness.* 'As this whole transaction between Adam and Eve is manifestly copied from the episode of Juppiter [Zeus] and Juno [Hera] on mount Ida . . . so it concludes exactly after the same manner in a quarrel . . . they are both overcome by their fondness for their wives, and are sensible of their error too late, and then their love turns to resentment, and they grow angry with their wives, when they should rather have been angry with themselves for their weakness in hearkening to them' (Newton).

1067. Milton's word-play suggesting that the word 'evil' might well have been derived from 'Eve, though it has, in fact, no connection with her name, is 'more of a knell than a jingle' (Ricks). See Commentary on 11.

1078. *evil store.* At first sight we should take 'store' as the noun, and, since no commentator touches the line, that has probably been usual. But it is more likely that 'store' is used adverbially = 'in plenty' (*O.E.D.* 4d) as in the poet's early translation of Ps. 88 'cloy'd with woes and trouble store' (verse 3) and in Pope's *Iliad* 'Ships thou hast store'.

1079. It is noteworthy that in the *C.D.* (I, 12) Milton does mention 'shame' *last* in the evils of 'the first degree of death'; but it should bear more meaning than this in the text.

1082. the open vowels of 'so oft' must have been felt as gliding into one another metrically, though not to be pronounced as 'soft'!

1086–8. The description is akin to Spenser's wood of Error (*F.Q.* I. i. 7) except for the 'brown' (probably from Italian use), whicn was to become a favourite adjective in the eighteenth century, e.g. Gray's: 'a broader, browner shade'. With 1084–8, cf. 910.

1088–90. So Marlowe's Faustus in his agony had exclaimed:

> Mountains and hills, come, come, and fall on me,
> And hide me from the heavy wrath of God!

1099–1133. *Adam and Eve 'made them selves aprons'* (Gen. 3:7); *but evil passions begin to assert themselves.*
Milton's source is, of course the Bible; but once more he had a literary parallel in Homer, when Odysseus, wrecked in Phaeacia, took part of a tree to cover himself before Nausicaa (*Odyssey*, vi).

1101. The Indian fig-tree is said to have been so called by the Portuguese from the resemblance of its fruit in appearance, not taste, to the fig. It is otherwise called the banyan tree. Since this has small leaves, it has been confused with the banana tree which does have large leaves (1110–11)—a confusion going back to Pliny. But Milton takes his information from the standard Elizabethan book on botany, Gerard's *Herbal* of 1597, as we can be sure from such details as: 'they cut certain loopholes or windows in some places . . . that they may see their cattell that feed therby'; cf. 1109–10.

1114–15. See the description in IV, 288, etc., and 319–20.
of late, nearly two hundred years before the time of *Paradise Lost*;

but the Creation of man was thought to be over five thousand years earlier.

1115–18. 'The simile shows the degree of the Fall. From their old dignity Adam and Eve have become like the lowest of mankind, conscious only of their human shame' (Bowra).

1121–3. Cf. Satan at IV, 18–20.

1125. *State of Mind* is perfectly intelligible to us now, but we may remind ourselves that the 'little kingdom' of man was interpreted more literally in Elizabethan psychology. It suffers 'an insurrection' when the lower parts of the body ('sensual Appetite)' overrule those situated higher in the body. Cf. *Julius Caesar*, II. i. 67–9.

1128–31. Every phrase drives home the complete subjection of mind to body. 'The notion that the conformity of the sensitive appetite to reason was destroyed as a result of the Fall is fairly frequent in seventeeth-century divinity' (Rajan).

1132. Although Milton would have been quite capable of inventing for himself the change in Adam's appearance after the Fall, it seems probable that in this and some other things he was indebted to a book written in his century from which his nephew, Edward Phillips, says that he collected his 'Tractate of Divinity' (i.e. the *C.D.*). This was *The Marrow of Sacred Divinity* by W. Ames published in English in 1634. So, when Adam feared that he would no longer be able to look upon God (1080), the poet may have remembered from Ames: *hinc sequitur horror et fuga presentiae divinae.* (See Sewell in *Essays and Studies of the English Association*, XIX, 40–66.)

1134–61. *Adam reproaches Eve for the desire for independence which led to her fall; and Eve reproaches Adam for giving way to her.* In the fourth draft for the contemplated tragedy Adam and Eve 'accuse one another, but especially Adam lays the blame to his wife'.

1139. *naked* should be understood in a moral sense, as naked of virtue or innocence, as much as in a literal sense; in so far as it is literal it must mean 'conscious of nakedness'.

1140. *henceforth* takes us back to Eve's words in 335–6, which had put little value on 'Virtue unassaid'. With that in view it is possible to take 'approve' here in the rarer and obsolete sense of 'test', 'make trial of', which occurs also in Shakespeare. Milton, however, does not appear to use the word thus elsewhere in his poetry, but always in the sense of 'prove', 'make good', as in 367 and in X, 31.

1144. *What words have past thy Lips* is an expression ultimately derived from one in Homer (*Iliad*, xiv. 83), which is literally translated: 'What word has escaped the hedge of thy teeth'.

1155. *the Head.* Cf. 'The head of the woman is the man' (1 Cor. 11.3), as Eve had already admitted in IV, 443.

1161. *mee* has been explained thus: 'The normal speech stress is on *with*; the emphatic spelling is needed to secure the stress on *me* in what would otherwise be a bad line' (B. A. Wright). But we can never be quite sure that variant spellings were intended by the blind poet.

1162–end. *Adam again blames Eve, this time more bitterly.* Cf. 1067, etc., and 1134, etc.

1178. *overmuch admiring.* Raphael had rebuked Adam for the same thing in VIII, 565–8, though there the actual words used here were separated by others.

1183. *Woman.* All the early editions of the text read 'Women'; but this is one of the very few emendations made by Bentley in the following century which has much to commend it. The singular suits better with the subsequent 'her' and 'she', while it could easily happen that, when the text was read over to the author, the plural might escape notice as an unaccented syllable.

The sentiment is here so appropriate to Adam that it is irrelevant to connect it with the author himself, however true.

1189. *appeerd,* but in fact it was not so. Milton prepares the way for the noble reconciliation of the next book.

COMMENTARY ON BOOK X

1–33. The angels from Eden report man's sin in Heaven.

1. *hainous*: it has been suggested that this should be taken as 'inspired by hatred', parallel with despiteful; but this is unnecessary and there is no parallel.

6. *God All-seeing* answers, as it were, IX, 811–16.

9–16. Milton once more insists on man's free will; cf. 43–7 below and III, 98–9 and IX, 351.

12. The fifth foot of this line is 'to have still' of which the first two syllables can be slurred together; and there is an extra syllable after the sixth foot.

16. *manifold in sin*, is best illustrated from Milton's prose: 'For what sin can be named which was not included in this one act? It comprehended at once distrust in the divine veracity, and a proportionate credulity in the assurances of Satan; unbelief; ingratitude; disobedience; gluttony; in the man excessive uxoriousness, in the woman a want of proper regard for her husband, in both an insensibility to the welfare of their offspring, and that offspring the whole human race; parricide, theft, invasion of the rights of others, sacrilege, deceit, presumption in aspiring to divine attributes, fraud in the means employed to attain the object, pride and arrogance' (*C.D.*, I, xi).

20–1. See IX, 69–76.

24–5. 'It is plain that Milton conceiv'd sadness "mix'd with pity" to be more consistent with heavenly bliss than sadness without that compassionate temper' (Newton).

28–31. This seems to me a good instance of the ambivalent use of words which is often admired in modern poetry, as it was in the seventeenth century. I have ventured to suggest in the gloss that 'towards' does not merely double, but triple duty, which it could not have done but for the position in which 'towards the Throne Supream' is placed. At the same time 'made haste' has double force, since the angels hasted towards the throne and hasted to exculpate themselves.

32-3. This is primarily based on passages in the Bible such as Exod. 33:9-10 and Rev. 4:5; but it also fits in with the classical depiction of Juppiter or Zeus thundering.

34-42. *God speaks to the assembled angels, and appoints His Son to judge fallen man.*

34. *Powers* were strictly the second of the three groups into which the angels had been divided before Milton's time; but he uses the term loosely here.

42. Satan had employed flattery particularly against Eve, and had lied, for example as to God's motives, IX, 705-9.

43-7. Man's freedom was particularly insisted on in II, 93-9. Milton is no Calvinist, but preserves the same balance as St. Paul and St. Augustine between Divine Grace and human effort.

Milton had used the picture of scales to describe the contest between Satan and Gabriel at the very end of IV, when the former 'knew His mounted scale aloft', i.e. the lighter. Here the scales are equal, and it is for man to throw his weight in that of right or wrong and make it prevail.

50-2. See IX, 927-37. In his *C.D.* (I, XIII) Milton explains that Death was not only bodily, which did not immediately follow the sin of Adam, but also included spiritual death of various kinds.

53. There was a proverb 'Omittance is no quittance', found in *As You Like It* (III. v. 132), where 'quittance' means letting a thing go for good, which probably led to the form 'acquittance' here; but the word was commonly used for release or payment of a debt.

54. *scornd* can be taken either with 'Justice' or with 'bountie', or perhaps better still with both.

56. Cf. 'The Father judgeth no man, but hath committed all judgement unto the Son.' (John 5:22); and, for 62, words which come a little further on in the same chapter: 'and hath given him authority to execute judgement also because he is the Son of man'.

59. *collegue*, though more familiar to us as a noun, was once a recognized verb, commonest in the past participle. In Ps. 85 we have

'Mercy and Truth are met together' (v. 10), and the three are brought together in the *Nativity Ode* st. xv. In medieval allegory Peace, Mercy, Justice, and Truth were four daughters of God; and this ancestry has left its trace in the third draft of Milton's drama which proposes as subject of Act I Justice and Mercy 'debating what should become of man if he fall'.

60. 'For there is . . . one mediator between God and men, the man Jesus Christ' (1 Tim. 2:3). In his *Christian Doctrine* Milton devotes a whole chapter (I, xv) to 'The Office of the Mediator and (of) His Threefold Function'.

61. *Ransom* enshrines the idea of Christ paying the *price* of man's sin to restore him to God's favour.

63–84. *The Son accepts the mission to judge mankind.*

63–7. Milton follows the Bible in making God the source of Light, and having his dwelling in 'light unapproachable'. Only the Son and the Spirit were thought of as being able to bear its brilliance. For what is here said of the Son cf. III, 138–42. The basis is Heb. 1:3, which must have suggested the word 'express'd' in 67: 'Who, being the brightness of his glory, and the express image of his person . . . sat down on the right hand of the Majesty on high'.

64. Metrically 'toward' counts as one syllable, and the foot is one with reversed accent.

66–7. 'manifest' and 'milde' (like 'bright' in 63) might be described shortly as adjectives used as adverbs; but it would probably be truer to say, bearing in mind classical analogies, that 'manifest' is an adjective in predicative position, (as in such a sentence as 'he made this clear'), and that 'milde' similarly agrees with the word 'answer' implied in the verb.

68–71. These lines furnish good examples of how pervaded with the Bible Milton's language is, quite apart from the small portion which furnishes his overt plot. For 69 see John 4:34 and for 70–1 Matt. 3:17 and parallels in other gospels.

72. *Those* is a correction by Darbishire of 'these' of the printed editions. The correction suits 'those' in 82, and the error can be easily explained through misreading of handwriting of the time.

74. *I undertook*: see III, 227–65; and for 'the strife Of Mercy and Justice' (ib. 406–7) all the first half of Book III.

77. Modern usage would put at least a semi-colon before 'yet'. We may remember, as Milton may have done, even when he changed the verb, Portia's plea to Shylock to 'season' Justice with Mercy.

80. This use of 'need' for 'be needed' was archaic even in Milton's time. Cf. 'For regal scepter then no more shall need' in III, 340, and 'pass' in 48 above.

79. It would be tempting to take 'them' as referring to the 'transgression' (72) *if* we could suppose that Milton could have used 'satisfied' to mean 'having made satisfaction'. Buxton's paraphrase 'give them full opportunity to realize heroic stature' respects the grammar but has to import a good deal of the meaning.

82–4. The first contrast here seems to be not between a serpent and a rebel angel, as the condemnation of the Serpent in 164–5 shows, but between Satan who had confessed his guilt by flight, like any human fugitive from justice, and man. But in 84 we may give 'conviction' its fullest meaning as a demonstration of error which brings conviction of the truth (cf. 831). The point will then be that the Serpent, being an animal, cannot be brought to understand his guilt, but can only be punished (as were animals which had caused a man's death by the Jewish Law).

85–102. *The Son descends to Eden in the cool of the evening.*

86–7. *Thrones . . . Dominations* are different orders of Angels, to which 'Virtues' were added in the thundering line
    Thrones, Dominations, Princedoms, Vertues, Powers (V, 601)
Milton knew 'thrones or dominions or principalities or powers' from the A.V. of Col. 1:16, and would not have worried himself too much about later elaborations of the orders of angels. There is a fuller picture, of the Son setting out to create the world, in VII, 192–201, where the escort does not stop at 'Heaven Gate'.

90–1. This is one of the harder phrases in Milton when we come to examine it closely. Time is thought of as flying on the swiftest of wings, but being still unable to keep up with, and so reckon the speed of, God or the angels. The difficulty lies in the idea of being winged with minutes. Minutes means only the shortest measure of time possible, and 'wingd' is transferred in thought from the instruments of angelic flight.

Hereabouts are two examples of Milton being influenced by such English predecessors as are dealt with in Appendix II. Cowley says of an angel's flight

> Slow Time admires, and knows not what to call
> The motion, having no account so small

while 'cooler ayres gently . . . fanne the fields' occurs in Phineas Fletcher (cf. 93–4).

92–3. 'With the help of "airs" Milton momentarily lends the beauty of a dying fall [in music] to evening in Eden' (Ricks). The cool of the day is, of course, from Genesis (3:21).

95. Milton wants to convey that God judges man more in sorrow than in anger; but however true it may be that our metaphor of 'cooling off' is based on a real affinity between nature and man, some may still find the play on words unattractive. But what Johnson said of Shakespeare is only somewhat less true of Milton and his contemporaries: 'A pun was the fatal Cleopatra for which he thought the world well lost'.

101. *God* is in the Bible here 'the Lord God', i.e. the Father; but Milton says in *C.D.* (I, v) that the Son was entitled to the name of God in his capacity as Judge.

103–56. *Adam, summoned to appear before Messiah, confesses his yielding to Eve, and is blamed for so doing.*

103–6. These lines well show the free use of participles which Milton imitates from Latin (where case inflections make it more natural), and which give so much compression to his style.

106. Although the modern meaning of 'obvious duty' may not be entirely absent here, it is clear that the former word must bear primarily its original sense, and we should note that the first meaning of 'duty' is 'an action of respect towards a superior'.

111–14. These lines are noteworthy as marking further the effects of the Fall; and it is true in everyday experience that a sense of guilt often brings on these other faults, or some of them.

116-23. In these lines Milton keeps as near to the words of Scripture as his metrical form allows; and presently (137-42) enlarges on his original in praise of woman (with the implication, as some think, of involving God in his Sin); whereas 143, in which Adam transfers the blame to Eve, is straight from Genesis, and not Milton's. In Adam's praise of Eve one is reminded of what Milton too may have known, Florizel's words about Perdita in *The Winter's Tale*, beginning 'What you do/Still betters what is done' (IV. iv. 135-46).

127-31. 'Unlike any previous Adam, he has at least some qualms about putting the blame on his wife' (Evans).

128. *My other self:* so God had called Eve 'thy other self' to Adam before her creation (VIII, 450). The expression is classical rather than biblical, but is there used of friends, not wives. Sir Thomas Browne still calls his friend his *alter ego*.

145. *Was shee thy God:* The wording may derive from 'Am I in God's stead' of Gen. 30:3, and 'Am I God to kill and to make alive' of 2 Kings 5:7; but the thought is nearer St. Augustine's 'As if there were anything to be believed or obeyed before God, or rather than the Most High' (*De Civ. Dei*, XIV, 14).

145-56. The Divine judgement is important in any discussion as to the nature of Adam's sin, especially when we observe how closely it confirms the warning Raphael had given to Adam against subordinating his wisdom to love. Adam's words in 141-2 echo what he had confessed to Raphael in VIII, 546-53, and form the basis for the charge of uxoriousness.

148. *Place* denotes spiritual and moral condition as well as spatial position, as when Satan speaks of 'this place', i.e. Hell in I, 625.

149-50. Eve had spoken of herself to Adam as 'Thou for whom and from whom I was formed' (IV, 440-1).

157-208. *Eve confesses her guilt, and Christ pronounces judgement on the Serpent and upon the human pair.* 'The Lord God' comes from Genesis, although Milton thinks of the Son as acting for the Father in this (X, 101). The Persons are only distinguished in the scenes in Heaven.

161-2. Eve had been 'bold' in sin, and 'loquacious' when she met Adam afterwards. Her simple sentence of confession, taken from the

Bible with one change of order, contrasts with Adam's, which the poet had much lengthened.

69–71. Milton is here in the difficulty that he accepts the Jewish tradition, not in Genesis, that Satan was speaking through the serpent. The 'yet' of 171 modifies the statement of 165 which suggested that Satan had escaped punishment. 'The phrase "though brute" (165) points to Milton's uneasiness' (Burden).

173. The judgement, 'mysterious' to Adam at the moment, becomes clearer to him in 1030–5 below, and in XII, 541–51.

181–91. Milton follows the universal Christian interpretation of the conclusion of God's judgement on the Serpent in Gen. 1:15, as fulfilled in Christ's redemption of man. The passage was known as *Protevangelium*, the first gospel or good news. Adam does not fully understand its meaning till after Michael's exposition (XII, 375–82). The following paragraph is made up of a number of biblical phrases, and inferences from some of them, not very familiar to modern Christians. Everyone can see the conquest of Death (so intimately connected with Satan) in the Resurrection of Christ (185), but the three following lines treat literally the symbolic pictures of Christ overcoming the powers of darkness. Evil spirits were thought to rule the air near the earth; so Christ is described as leading the powers of darkness as a Roman conqueror led his prisoners in his triumph. An apocryphal gospel described the 'spoiling' or 'harrowing' of Hell by Christ after His ascension (cf. *Piers Plowman*, Passus xviii in the B text).

The biblical passages underlying Milton's language here will be found in Eph. 2:2; Col. 2:15; Ps. 68:18 and Rom. 16:20.

183. *second Eve* the phrase is repeated from V, 287. So St. Paul had spoken of Christ as the 'last Adam'. Milton here speaks of Christ simply as a man 'Son of Mary', as he was to do in *Paradise Regained*; but no inference should be based on this line in isolation.

184. When the Seventy returned from their mission and reported their success in healing and casting out devils Jesus said that he beheld Satan as lightning fall from heaven, and added that he gave them power to tread on serpents and over all the power of the enemy (Luke, 10:18).

197–208. More departure from the normal metrical pattern than usual in some lines of this passage is accounted for by Milton's desire to keep close to the very words of Gen. 3:17-19.

209–28. *The Son clothes Adam and Eve, and returns to the Father.*

211–23. Milton here elaborates the simple statement of Genesis that 'the Lord God made coats of skins and clothed them', by taking this as an example of the humility which Christ showed in his Incarnation, when he 'took upon him the form of a servant' (Phil. 2:17), and particularly when he washed His disciples' feet before the Last Supper (John 13:5). Similarly the poet has widened the idea of covering man's physical nakedness by calling man's sin an 'inward nakedness' which, as Isaiah had expressed it (61:10), God had 'covered' with 'the robe of righteousness'. Thus Milton manages to avoid, as in the paragraph beginning at 182, direct reference to Christ's Passion, which Paul saw as the supreme instance of his humiliation in the next verse to that quoted above (Phil. 2:8), and also as the chief means of reconciliation between man and God. Milton, however, is in full accord with Christian tradition in applying to Christ things said of God the Father in the Old Testament.

217–18. The suggestion that other animals might have sloughed off their old skins besides snakes, although Pliny affirms it, is probably due to an unwillingness to introduce the idea of animals being killed in Paradise as unavoidable. Death has yet to enter the world. But cf. X, 586 and Commentary there.

The Bible merely says that God made coats of skin and clothed them. Milton almost seems to be thinking aloud in speculating where the skin came from, as also around 580 below.

229–71. *Sin, sitting with her son Death at the gates of Hell, proposes to him that they should prepare a way from Hell to the Earth.* We now enter on an episode (continuing till 610) which follows on II, 629–89, where Satan had forced his way out of Hell past these guards. The figures, which are not personified in the Bible, are here treated somewhat after the manner of characters in the Morality plays, and of Spenser's allegorical figures, such as Error in the *Faerie Queene*, 1. Addison did not consider 'such beautiful extended allegories . . . agreeable to the nature of an heroic poem', and Dr. Johnson gave reasons for a similar condemnation (see the extracts in Select

Criticism). Tillyard on the other hand, called it 'one of the grandest of all episodes in the poem'.

229. The transition would have been easier if it had been marked by a new paragraph.

235. Death was the son of Sin through her incestuous union with her own father.

241. *Avengers.* The plural is a correction in the second edition of 1674, required by 'their'.

246. *sympathie* has not quite reached its loose modern meaning, but is expanded and explained by the two and a half lines that follow. Even inanimate things were supposed to share this 'secret amity', as can often be seen in the poetry of Vaughan, a contemporary of Milton. When it is, as here, between persons, it resembles what we now call 'telepathy'.

267. *sent.* Milton uses this spelling for 'scent' in conformity with the derivation from Lat. *sentire* and Fr. *sentir*, but it died out with the seventeenth century.

Milton is as sensuous with regard to smells as with the other senses. Contrast the fragrance of Eden (IX, 425), and also the references at IX, 193-7 and 852. Aeschylus had spoken of the scent of blood (*Eumenides*, 251), and, as does not appear to have been observed before, in connection with the Furies pursuing Orestes—an appropriate analogy for this passage.

269. *The savour of Death.* The second foot is trisyllabic, but an elision or slurring is made easier by the liquid ending the word 'savour'.

272-353. *Sin and Death complete the bridge from Hell to Earth, and win their father's admiration for their work.* The rich style and clustering images hereabouts take us back to the earlier books of *Paradise Lost.* There are four similes between 282 and 311.

Tillyard (in his *Studies in Milton*) drew attention to a sort of parody here of the work of the Trinity in the Creation of the Universe (VII, 210-42). As God acted through His Word, the Son, and the Spirit, so Satan's children make the bridge, and are spoken of as 'hovering upon the waters' (285), just as the Spirit of God outspread his brooding wings on the watery calm (VII, 234-5).

273–6. Pliny had said that vultures would fly three days before-hand to places where there were destined to be carcases, and Lucan tells of the vultures following the Roman camps before the battle of Pharsalia between Caesar and Pompey (48 B.C.) Newton, who pointed out these parallels, added: 'I shall not undertake absolutely to defend Milton's introducing a fabulous story by way of simile; yet I think in this place it may be pardoned, since no other illustration could have been found so pat to the present case.'

279–81. This magnificent picture depends for part of its effect on the vagueness of the term 'grim Feature'—too horrible for detailed specification—as against the precision of the upturned nostrils. If the last phrase was suggested by Virgil's *patulis naribus* of a heifer sniffing a coming storm (*Georgic*, i. 276), Milton improved in the borrowing.

282–4. 'The rhythmic impulse of the *w-w* is upward and out-ward, of the *d-d* downward' (A. Stein). I should prefer to call the first collocation of sound expansive, but the second grim and forbidding.

283. The *Anarchie of Chaos* is described in II, 894, etc., 'where eldest Night/And Chaos, Ancestors of Nature, hold/Eternal Anarchie.'

291–3. Early voyagers were always seeking North-West and North-East passages, round the top of America and Asia to the riches of the far East. Cathay is loosely used for China in poetry as, e.g. in Tennyson's famous 'Better fifty years of Europe than a cycle of Cathay' (*Locksley Hall*); but down to Milton's time it seems to have denoted a kingdom in north China and what is now Siberia, which in XI, 388 is distinguished from 'Paquin of Sinaean Kings', i.e. Pekin in China.

294. *Mace* is the word used for Death's sceptre in older poetry; and in the play of *Dido* by Marlowe and Nash there occurs 'death's stony mace'.

296. *Delos*, the Aegean island sacred to Apollo, was supposed to have been a floating island till Zeus fastened it to the sea-bottom. There is supposed to be a floating island in our Derwentwater.

296–8. These lines attracted much comment from earlier editors, since it was felt to be strange that 'the rest' should be held together by the combination of a moral and a physical agency, a 'look' and 'slime'. The difficulty can be got over by interchanging the comma after 'move' with the semi-colon after 'slime'; but this gives a weak 'And', as well as somewhat imparing the rhythm. The collocation, even if slightly grotesque, does not seem in this context un-Miltonic.

298. *Asphaltic slime.* The builders of the tower of Babel are said to have had slime for mortar (Gen. 11:3).

305-6. The former line seems to contain a reminiscence of *facilis* ('easie') *descensus Averni* (*Aeneid*, vi. 126, where Aeneas is visiting the underworld), and the latter is certainly close to Virgil's *Si parva licet componere magnis* (*Georgic*, iv. 176).

307-10. Xerxes, king of Persia, whose winter palace was at Susa (founded by Tithonus, whose son, Memnon, built its acropolis, hence 'Memnonian') led the second Persian invasion of Greece in 480 B.C., but was defeated at Salamis and Plataea. Herodotus describes the expedition (vii. 33-6), and relates how the tyrant vented his wrath on the sea which had destroyed part of the bridge of boats he had built at the Dardanelles. In 308 Milton may be recalling a phrase in the play of Aeschylus about the expedition, the *Persae*, which means 'to cast a yoke of slavery upon Greece' (l. 50). So man is now enslaved by the tyranny of Sin and Death.

313. *Art Pontifical.* In choosing this expression and inventing the word 'Pontifice' in 348 Milton was probably making a grim hit at the Papacy, since the title of the chief priest at Rome, *pontifex maximus*, was preserved by the popes.

314-24. The bridge built by Sin and Death followed the track taken by Satan when he first went to the world, and terminated at the spot on the top of the outer shell where the universe was suspended from Heaven by a golden chain (II, 1051). At this point three ways met, to Heaven, Earth, and Hell. In the later part of Book III (418 onward) Satan was described walking about on the outer shell of the Universe, the Primum Mobile, and later as directed down by Uriel to the Earth through the opening.

319. The repetition (technically 'epanalepsis') is a figure of speech occasionally used in epic poetry. 'Too fast' is equivalent to the prosy 'only too fast', in view of the undesirable connection

between Earth and Hell thus facilitated; and is one of the poet's few interventions in the narrative of this book.

322. In the parable of the last Judgement the goats are placed to God's left (Matt. 25:41), and Hell lies to the left of Aeneas (*Aeneid*. vi. 542)—always the ill-omened side.

327. Cf. 'Satan himself is transformed into an angel of light' (2 Cor. 11:13).

328-9. 'Satan, to avoid being discovered (as he had been before IV, 569, etc.) by Uriel, regent of the sun, takes care to keep at as great a distance as possible, and therefore "while the sun rose in Aries" he steers his course upwards "betwixt the Centaure and the Scorpion", two constellations which lay in quite a different part of the Heavens from Aries' (Newton).

348-9. Contrast the language used of this unexpected meeting with that used of expected meetings in 104-6.

354-82. *Sin greets Satan on his return to Hell.*

358-9. Cf. 245-50, where the secret sympathy between Sin and Death was described. Once more we have a sort of parody of the divine Trinity.

362. *Worlds between* appears to be a sort of fusion of two constructions; we might say either 'This is worlds away (from that)' or 'There is a world (of difference) between this and that.'

372. There seem to be three syllables in the last foot, but the voice passes lightly over the open vowel which ends 'vertue' before the 'h' following.

373-80. Sin means that as Satan has made man sin, which alienates him from God, Satan has now got command of all things except the true Heaven where God lives and rules completely. Satan himself had claimed that he had held 'Divided Empire with Heav'ns King' (IV, 111).

381. The Empyrean heaven is thought of as square because the 'heavenly city' is said to lie 'four-square' in Revelation (21:16), although Milton had called it 'undetermined square or round', in II, 1048. The Universe or Cosmos, including the Earth, is always thought of as an orb suspended in Chaos.

383–409. Satan congratulates Sin and Death on their handiwork, and sends them to develop the sway he has won for them on Earth.

383. *The Prince of Darkness* occurs as a title for Satan in Spenser, Shakespeare, and Sylvester, and is ultimately based on Ephesians (6:12) 'the rulers of the darkness of this world'.

384. *Fair Daughter.* Satan's appreciation of Sin here, as at 352, is in contrast to his earlier reaction to Death as an 'execrable shape' (II, 681).

391–3. These lines are in ironic contrast with those where (in Raphael's narrative to Adam, VII, 160, etc.) God hopes that man may at length open to himself the way to Heaven: 'And Earth be chang'd to Heav'n, and Heav'n to Earth,/One Kingdom, Joy and Union without end.'

399–402. Milton has behind him such passages as: 'Death reigned from Adam to Moses' (Rom. 5:14) and 'the wages of sin is death' (Rom. 6:23). Earlier on Satan had promised his son and daughter to bring them to a place where they would dwell at ease, and be fed immeasurably: see II, 839–49.

504. *mee:* the spelling marks Satan's egotism.

409. The stop at the caesura makes the last words terrible in emphasis. They reproduce the words of Moses to the people of Israel to 'go in and possess' the Promised Land, and, just before his death, to Joshua (and others) to 'be strong and of a good courage' (Deut. 31:8).

410–59. Satan returns to Hell, and finds his followers in Council and eagerly awaiting his return.

413. 'We say of a thing when it is blasted and withered that it is "planet-struck"; and that is now applied to the planets themselves. And what a sublime idea doth it give us of the devastations of Sin and Death' (Newton). Milton may well have remembered *Hamlet* (I. i. 162): 'The nights are wholesome; then no planets strike.'

416–18. *exclaimd.* There is no instance of this word not involving speech, and Chaos has been fully personified in II, 895, etc.; but Milton may be using the word metaphorically of Chaos beating upon the framework of the bridge like the waves of a sea. Virgil had anticipated the 'indignation' when he spoke of the sea falling back before the barriers of an artificial harbour as 'indignatum magnis stridoribus aequor' (*Georgics*, ii. 161).

424. Milton invented the name *Pandemonium* for the 'high Capital Of Satan and his Peers' (I, 765-7), and in this case his word has been adopted in common speech to express noise and confusion.

425-6. Lucifer was the Latin translation of the Greek name for a morning star, meaning 'light-bringer'. The name was applied to Satan from the verse in Isaiah which reads in the A.V. 'How art thou fallen from Heaven, O Lucifer, son of the morning' (Isa. 14:12: translated in R.V. 'day-star') in combination with that in Luke ascribed to Christ 'I beheld Satan as lightning fall from heaven' (10:18). It is the planet Venus which appears as above the eastern sky before sunrise and in the western sky after sundown. In fact the verse from Isaiah is simply an ancient astral myth, based on the disappearance of Venus at day break, used to illustrate the inevitability of Babylon's downfall.

431-6. Ostensibly the point of the simile is simply withdrawal; in fact it gives the poet a chance to introduce exotic proper names and to utilize his interest in geography and maps. He had written a short *History of Moscovia*, i.e. Russia. The Tartars were on the lower Volga, and Astrakhan is situated where the Volga flows out into the Caspian. Bactria is the old name of part of Persia, and the Persians were often at war with the Turks in the sixteenth century. Aladule was part of Armenia in Asia Minor, Tauris is modern Tabriz, in north Persia, and Casbeen is Kazvin, north of Teheran.

441-8. This account of Satan's return seems to be based on that of Aeneas at Carthage in *Aeneid*, i. 439, etc.

445. Satan's throne forms the magnificent opening of Book II:

> High on a Throne of Royal State, which far
> Outshone the wealth of Ormus and of Ind, etc.

460-503. *Satan relates his adventures to the Council in Hell.*

458-9. Cf. IX, 670-6.

460. This grand line, which Milton uses more than once, in Homeric fashion, gives the names of five of the nine orders of

angels, as they were reckoned in medieval times. 'Vertues' corresponds to one of the Greek words for 'powers' (*dunameis*), 'Powers' to another (*exousiai*). Milton's spelling is due to the old French, through which the word came from Latin.

461–2. Satan's logic is no sounder than on some other occasions. The fact that man had been perverted did not restore the fallen angels to the rank they had lost by revolt, before which God had indeed addressed all the angels thus (V, 601). Satan is equally deceitful in pretending (475–80) that Chaos had opposed his journey (contrast II, 988–1109).

473. *a broad way* recalls 'broad is the way that leadeth to destruction' (Matt. 7:13).

477. The arrangement of nouns and adjectives in this line is not uncommon in the classics, where it is called chiasmus, from the shape of the Greek letter chi (like our X), a cross arrangement.

480. This line may also be taken to mean 'Protesting that Fate is supreme', and therefore Satan should not try to interfere with it.

481–2. See II, 345–51, where Beelzebub proposes to attack God through man.

486–8. The poet seems here to be recognizing part of the difficulty of his subject. As Rymer a little later called *Othello* 'the tragedy of the handkerchief' (*A short View of Tragedy*, 1693), so a scoffer might have dubbed *P.L.* 'the tragedy of the apple'. The fruit of the tree had not been specified in the Bible, but by patristic and rabbinic writers.

496–7. 'Our author understands the sentence (as the most learned and orthodox divines do) as referring partly to Satan the author of malice, and partly to the Serpent the instrument of it' (Newton).

503. 'On the very word "bliss" Satan's own voice turns to a serpent's hiss' (J. C. Maxwell).

504–84. *The rebel angels are transformed into serpents.* The idea of serpents in Hell is found elsewhere, but the process of the transformation of the rebel angels appears to be Milton's invention. Two previous accounts of men changing into serpents which he would have known well are those describing the transformation of Cadmus and his wife in the *Metamorphoses* of Ovid (to which we have already had an allusion in IX, 505–6), and Dante's account of five criminals changed to serpents in the Inferno (Cantos XXIV–V). Phineas Fletcher in his *Purple Island* of 1633 had said of the rebel angels in Hell

> There turn'd to serpents, swol'n with pride and hate
> Their Prince a Dragon fell.

and 'These while the snake they hear, they turn to snakes'.

Satan now disappears from the epic, where all interest can now centre on Adam. Satan is back where he started, in Hell, and the pattern is so far complete.

514. This effective line owes something to Ovid's *In pectusque cadit pronus*. A Jewish Apocalypse has 'On thy breast and thy belly shalt thou walk' as part of God's judgement on the Serpent.

517–25. 'We need never expect words and metre to do more than they do here' (Lascelles Abercrombie, in *The Idea of Great Poetry*).

521. Editors have usually taken 'Riot' as referring simply to the original rebellion; but it seems better to refer it to the violation of God's intended order brought about through Satan's temptation of man, to which the other angels were accessories, in welcoming his offer to make the attempt and in welcoming his return.

521–6. The alliteration first of hard 'd' and then of 's' extends right down to the proper names. Most of these occur in a passage of Lucan's *Pharsalia* (ix. 696, etc.), an epic of the Civil War between Pompey and Caesar; but the 'Cerastes' is from Dante or Du Bartes and the Ellops from Pliny.

526–7. The legend was that Perseus after killing the Gorgon (see 297), carried its dripping head across Libya, as Lucan relates in the same passage as that just referred to.

529. The 'great Dragon' is identified with Satan in Rev. 12:9; while Lucan mentioned the dragon as the largest of the snakes in Libya.

531. The *Huge Python* was a monstrous serpent bred out of the slime left behind from the pagan Deucalion's flood, and slain by Apollo.

541-2. Notice the rhythm and the alliteration of 'd' as in 521, etc., and compare the 'Down drop'd' of IX, 893.

545-6. The pun is more obvious when we know that 'applause' and 'exploding' both contain the Latin *plaudo*.

561-2. Josephus had recorded that apple trees growing in the ashes near Sodom bore fruit which, when plucked, dissolved in the hand. Although this supposed fact was repeated by other writers down to the later Middle Ages (e.g. Mandeville), it was probably only an inference from the wickedness ascribed to the 'Cities of the Plain' in Genesis.

569. *writh'd their jaws* may be a reminiscence of an expression in Virgil *Ora/Tristia tentantum sensu torquebit amaror* (*Georgics*, ii. 246); where, however, the context is of no significance. Jewish rabbis had imagined that the Serpent's diet was dust.

572. *once lapst:* According to what seems an almost invariable rule of Miltonic spelling 'lapst' must be the past participle, the past tense being 'lapsed'.

573. It is tempting to remove the comma after 'Famin' and insert it after 'long', since this would give a better rhythm, and remove the awkward assyndeton which appears to make the 'hiss' an explanation of 'Famin' instead of another cause of their exhaustion.

The following lines illustrate the extreme compression of style which can be produced by a Latinate use of participles.

575-7. The poet's authority for this statement has not been discovered. The nearest parallel is in the Italian romance of Ariosto, the *Orlando Furioso*, where a Fairy says (in Harrington's Elizabethan translation):

> Each seventh day we are compelled to take
> Upon ourselves the person of a snake.

578-84. Remembering that Milton accepted the identification of the fallen angels with heathen deities, we see how he comes to conjecture that two early deities of Greek legend, with names resembling the word for serpent in Greek (*ophis*) and Eve respectively may be a version of the biblical story. Ophion was one of the Titans, the first rulers of Olympus, and his wife was Eurynome, which means 'wide-ruling'. Milton thinks this appropriate to Eve because she extended her rule further than she should have done over her

husband, and even affected godhead. He may have read the sug-
gested identification of Ophion with the Serpent in the Elizabethan
edition of Ovid's *Metamorphoses* by Sandys, who says: 'Pherecrates
the Syrian writes how the Divels were thrown out of heaven by
Juppiter (the fall of the Gyaunts perhaps an allusion to that of the
Angells) the chiefe called Ophioneus which signifies Serpentine:
having after made use of this creature to poyson Eve with a false
ambition'. The dynasty of Ophion gave way to that of Saturn and
his wife Ops, only to be superseded in turn by that of Juppiter
(as is told in Keats's *Hyperion*).

The legend has been thought to have been taken by Milton from
the *Argonautica* of Apollonius Rhodius (i. 503, etc.); and this is
confirmed by the mention there of Dicte, the mountain in Crete
where Jove was brought up (cf. 'Dictaean Jove', 584).

In these lines Milton almost seems to be thinking aloud; and the
hyphened word across the line ending is unique.

585–609. *Sin and Death discuss the destruction of man.*

586–7. Three stages seem to be distinguished: Sin was there
potentially since Adam and Eve were free to sin, *actually* when they
did sin, and *in body* after Sin (personified) reached the Earth. 'Actual
Sin' was distinguished by theologians of Milton's time not from sins
of thought but from 'original sin'.

598–90. The image comes from Revelation (6:8): 'behold a pale
horse; and his name that sat on him was Death'.

593. We should have expected a question mark at 'difficult', and
a new sentence beginning with 'Is not this' or something similar;
but the poet prefers the utmost compression of syntax and forward
movement of the verse.

600–1. Cf. 'Hell and destruction are never full' (Prov. 27:20).
Down to about 1700 'Corps' was used of a living as well as of a dead
body; after which the spelling 'corpse' was used in the latter sense.
'Hidebound' is now used metaphorically, but originally referred to
the skin of an animal tight through emaciation; and in that sense is
here negatived.

609. *season* is a finely chosen word, because it may suggest not
only the art of the cook, but also the maturing of the meat, in this
case the heaping up of human wickedness through lapse of

time, so making more prey for Death. C. S. Lewis makes his Devil say: 'We want [men to be] cattle who can finally become food; he [God] wants servants who can finally become sons' (*The Screwtape Letters*, p. 45).

610–40. *The Almighty observes Sin and Death, and foresees the end of their power.*

616. *These Dogs of Hell.* In putting such an expression in the mouth of the Almighty (offensive as it may well be to Christians) Milton is drawing on biblical passages like Ps. 22:16 and Rev. 22:15, in both of which the wicked are called dogs. In II, 654 Sin was described as having 'a cry [i.e. pack] of Hell Hounds' about her middle; cf. 630 here. It has also been noted that Apollonius Rhodius speaks of 'the dogs of Hades'; so that once more classical and biblical sources fuse in Milton.

617. *havoc.* Cf. IX, 30, where the noun occurred. The word here may have come to the poet's mind from the association of 'dogs' and 'havoc' in Shakespeare's 'Cry "Havock", and let slip the dogs of war' (*Julius Caesar*, III. i. 273); and we, at least, may be reminded by 630 of how Shakespeare hated the messiness, as well as the fawning, of dogs.

620. Sin and Death are naturally compared to the vengeful and dreaded Furies of Greek legend (cf. 560 'Megaera'). But it is notable that Du Bartas (see Appendix II) has a whole book called *The Furies* devoted to the results of the Fall (pp. 327–54 of Sylvester's translation of 1605), including

> O, am I not near roaring Phlegeton?
> Allecto, sad Megera and Phlegeton?

626. Modern grammatical punctuation requires a comma after 'as if'; but Milton is, as often, content with the comma only at the end of the qualifying phrase.

633–5. *one sling of thy victorious arm* recalls David's victory over Goliath (I Sam. 17:49); while the next line recalls Paul's triumphant words read at the P.B. Burial Service 'Death is swallowed up in victory', etc. (I Cor. 15:54).

638. This *Heav'n* is not the dwelling place of God, but the atmosphere above our earth, as when it is said that 'the heavens are cloudy';

cf. 647 below. The renewal is based on the 'new heaven and a new earth . . . new Jerusalem, coming down from God out of heaven' (Rev. 21:1–2), where we get this double use of 'heaven'. 'Heaven and Earth' is the Jewish phrase for our world. Milton believed in the final conflagration of our universe (XI, 896 and XII, 547–51).

641–719. *The Almighty through his angels changed the climate of the earth.*

641. The adjective 'loud' replaces an adverb with the verb 'sung', but can also be felt as a second epithet of 'Audience'—loud when it replied. Cf. 'And I heard as it were the voice of a great multitude and as the voice of many waters . . . saying Alleluia' (Rev. 19:6); but Milton preferred a spelling closer to the Hebrew form. The substance of their song in 643–4 is also drawn from Revelation, while the poet had also announced *his* purpose as that of justifying the ways of God to man (I, 26).

647. *to the Ages:* to last for the ages. It does not appear to have been observed that Milton is translating literally the Greek words (*eis tous aionas*) translated as 'for ever', e.g. in the Lord's Prayer.

650. *His mightie angels* would naturally be the seven, including Uriel,

> Who in God's presence, neerest to his Throne
> Stand ready at command (III, 648–9)

651. Milton had to some extent prepared the way for this change in the outward circumstances of man's lot on earth by making Nature sympathize with Eve's, and again with Adam's, sin, and by making Satan boast that he would cause destruction to range widely (IX, 134). The biblical basis is 'cursed is the ground for thy sake' (Gen. 3:17), and 'the whole creation groaneth and travaileth together until now' (Rom. 8:22). In his prose treatise Milton elaborates this to 'All nature is subject to mortality and a curse on account of man', while in the third draft of his projected tragedy he set down a number of 'mutes' such as Envy, Pestilence, and Death.

The changes here described have been taken as proof of the harshness of Milton's God. Certainly He is the God of the Old Testament rather than of the New; but that is true of most Puritan writers. May it not also be that these changes stand symbolically for the inevitable results of sin? Contrast 'influence malignant' (662) with the 'sweet influence' of the Pleiades at the Creation (VII, 375). In any case these changes were only for the present, since it was God's ultimate plan to cleanse and renew the Earth (629–40). Evil is held to be finally self-destructive (639–8)—a faith which had already been affirmed as early as *Comus* (591–7).

657. *th' other five* planets were Mercury, Venus, Mars, Juppiter, and Saturn.

668–78. 'It is poetically assumed here that before the Fall the ecliptic or Sun's path was in the same plane as the Earth's equator, and that the present obliquity of the two planes, or their intersection at an angle of 23½ degrees, was a modification of the physical Universe for the worse, consequent on the Fall. There were two ways in which the alteration might have been produced; and Milton states both. Either the axis of the Earth might have been pushed askance (i.e. aside) the required distance; or the sun himself might have been compelled to deviate the required distance from his former path. To indicate what the second would amount to, Milton follows the Sun in the imagined deviation. First he traces him in his ascent north from the equatorial road, through the constellations Taurus and Gemini (in the neck of the former of which are the Pleiades), and so up to his extreme northern distance from the equator at the Crab in the Tropic of Cancer; then he descends with him again, by Leo and Virgo, till he retouches the equator at Libra, or the Scales, merely suggesting the equal vagary southwards beyond the equator as far as the Tropic of Capricorn' (Masson).

678–9. The idea of a perpetual spring once prevailing on Earth was common to some of the Church Fathers and to classical mythology, which spoke of a Golden Age in the past.

687–91. Milton is arguing that the sun must have changed his course on account of man's sin; for, if it had *not* then changed its course, the *original* course would have subjected even sinless man to great hardships. Greek legend said that the sun had turned aside from its course at the horror of beholding Thyestes devour the flesh of his own children served up to him by his brother Atreus, king of Mycaenae. This was the beginning of the curse of the House of Atreus, which forms the subject of the Aeschylean trilogy of plays.

696. *Samoed:* Samoedia occurs as part of a chapter heading in Milton's *History of Moscovia*, but it would appear from other names like 'Estotiland' (686) and 'Norumbega' (696) that the poet liked looking at contemporary maps and collected thence as well as from the classics some of the proper names with which he sprinkled parts of his narrative.

707. *Discord* personified was one of the powers Satan had met in Chaos during his voyage to Earth: 'Discord with a thousand various mouths' (II, 967). *Discordia demens* occurs in one of the most famous passages of Virgil (*Aeneid*, vi. 280), and in Book IV, Canto I, of the *Faerie Queene* (as Atē).

710–14. This passage is a deliberate contrast with that in which 'All Beasts of th' Earth' playd frisking' about Adam and Eve (IV, 340, etc.)

Sylvester (Du Bartas) makes discord among the animals, and their revolt from man, the most prominent feature of the change on earth after the Fall:

> 'Tis but a Dungeon and a dreadful Cave,
> Of that First World the miserable grave.

and goes on to the introduction of Famine (Dearth), War, and Sickness, rather than to the change of climate and seasons.

711. Milton has to assume that before the Fall no animals fed on one another; but he had authority for this in Gen. 1:30; to which he specifically added the fishes which 'Graze the Sea weed thir pasture' (VII, 404).

712–13. Contrast the peaceable approach of the beasts to Adam for their naming, described in VIII, 349–52. Bentley objected to animals fleeing from someone whom they did not hold in awe; which gave another eighteenth-century commentator the opportunity to make the nice distinction: 'Awe is a respect or reverence paid to one whom we love, and love excludes fear' (Pearce).

714, etc. 'The transition to Adam here is very easy and natural, and cannot fail of pleasing the reader. We have seen great alterations produced in nature, and it is now time to see how Adam is affected with them, and whether the disorders *within* are not even worse than those without' (Newton).

718. For the mood cf. IX, 1121–6; and for the metaphor Hamlet's 'take arms against a sea of troubles' (III. i. 59) and Isaiah's 'the wicked are like the troubled sea when it cannot rest' (57:20).

720–844. *Adam bewails his lot and desires death.*
This is the longest speech in *Paradise Lost*, if we do not count the long narratives put into the mouths of Raphael and Michael; and it has been called 'one of the loneliest scenes in literature'. Some students may be interested in a study of it by K. Svendsen reprinted in *Milton: Modern Essays in Criticism*, ed. A. E. Barker (O.U.P., New York, 1965).

720. *O miserable of happie.* Adam addresses himself in an idiom like the Latin exclamation *Me miserum.* His mood of despair finds its counterpart in the Samson of the earlier part of *Samson Agonistes.*

726. Adam acknowledges his deserts, unlike Satan. It would be normal to put a heavier stop after 'miserie'; but sometimes Milton prefers a lighter punctuation, like Shakespeare (if the printed texts represent his intention)

728–9. 'Meat and drink propagate it (the curse) by prolonging life, and children by carrying it on to posterity' (Newton).

730. *Encrease and multiplie* is almost God's words to Adam 'Be fruitful and multiply' (Gen. 1:28), which were reproduced exactly at VII, 531.

736. What might seem to us to be a colloquialism strikes somewhat strangely in the style of *Paradise Lost*; but the ironical use in fact goes back to the sixteenth century (*O.E.D.* s.v. 5), however this passage may have familiarized it.

740–1. Milton seems to be employing the contemporary idea that objects only had weight under the force of gravity till they reached their proper place, where they had no weight. Cf. this quotation of 1625: 'Gravity or heaviness is nothing else but an inclination of the parts of the Earth returning to their natural place' (*O.E.D.*). But misery, although settled in its right place, on him was still heavy. No doubt the verb 'light' suggested the play on the adjective which is its homophone. We may find this kind of punning as little to our taste as the half rhyme of 'joyes' and 'woes' in the two lines that follow.

742-3. The word 'clay' is probably a reminiscence of Isaiah's 'Shall the clay say to him that fashioneth it, What makest thou?' (45:9); but the general thought finds more parallels in the book of Job.

762. Isaiah continues 'Woe unto him that saith unto his father What begettest thou?'

764-7. The argument is that natural desire of offspring, partly a physical passion, causes Adam to beget children, whereas God created Adam from deliberate choice, not necessity, to serve Him.

773. *this day* (cf. 962) is an oversight since the poet has made a night intervene since God judged man. It was 'that day' in 49 and 210, and will be also in 1050.

778. *my Mother's lap;* the phrase (anticipated by Spenser) is beautiful enough to excuse a certain anachronism on the lips of one who had not known a human mother. But in fact the Earth was Adam's mother since he was moulded from it, cf. XI, 526 and 533.

779-80. 'God thundereth marvellously with his voice' in Job (37:5), and the Roman spoke of *Juppiter tonans;* but it is as noteworthy that Adam again reverts to the language about God that Satan taught him (see IX, 687).

781. *torment me:* the extra metrical syllable at the end is as rare in Milton as common in the Elizabethan dramatists; cf. 831 and 872. We may notice at the same time the scansion of 795 as 'man's not so'.

783-92. Earlier critics were content to point out a merely verbal parallel with Horace, and earlier readers to regard the argument of the passage as merely Adam's; but more recently it has been pointed out by a comparison with Milton's *Christian Doctrine* that he himself appears to have held a view, found elsewhere in his time, called Mortalism, that body and soul die together and would be raised

together at the Resurrection. [The group who held this belief was
first fully brought to light in Saurat's *Milton, Man and Thinker*,
Appendix II 'The Mortalists 1643–55', (added in his second edition
of 1944). Saurat found modern successors, perhaps lineal descendants,
of the Mortalists in the Christadelphians. Patrides argues that since
Adam does not yet know what Death is (cf. XI, 462) we are not
dealing with full Mortalism here (*Milton and the Christian Tradition*,
266).]

The words in the prose treatise most closely resembling the
argument ascribed here to Adam are: 'What could be more absurd
than that the mind, which is the part principally offending, should
escape the threatened death; and that the body alone to which
immortality was equally allotted . . . should pay the penalty of sin
by undergoing death, though not implicated in the transgression?'
(from chapter XIII of Book I, where Milton argues at length against
the common definition which supposes death to consist in the
separation of body and soul).

The conclusion of Adam's reasoning 'All of me then shall die'
forms a contrast with what Christ was made to say of *his* foreseen
death for man 'All that of me can die' (III, 246).

798–800. It was a point commonly made by medieval theologians
that God could not be guilty of contradictions; for which Milton
refers to 'He cannot deny himself' (2 Tim. 2:13) and to Heb. 6:18.

806–8. Adam is arguing that he is incapable of receiving any
punishment heavier than death, since it was an accepted axiom,
that the nature of the object, not simply that of the subject, deter-
mined the result of the latter's action on the former.

The subject matter of the last two notes serve to show that
Milton could be as scholastic as Donne when he chose!

813–15. 'The thought is as fine as it is natural. The sinner may
invent never so many arguments in favour of annihilation and utter
extinction of the soul; but after all his subterfuges and evasions, the
fear of a future state and the dread of everlasting punishment still
pursue him: he may put it off for a time, but it will return "with
dreadful revolution"' (Newton).

816. *Am found eternal*. The grammar is irregular, but dramatically
effective, being dictated by the desire to emphasize the oneness of

'Death and I', as Paul speaks of 'the sin that dwelleth in me' (Rom. 8:20), and 'Who shall deliver me from the body of this death?' (8:24).

822–8. See IX, 1003–4 and the Commentary there on Original Sin.

824. The emphasis on 'mee' here and in 827 and 831 may be said to show signs of a regenerate will.

830. *Mazes*, and other wandering ways, are always evil in *Paradise Lost*.

840. *past example* must refer to Satan and the fallen angels. The thought that every sinner shared Satan's 'inner hell' (cf. IV, 18–23) was apparently a commonplace.

842. *Conscience* was one of the *dramatis personae* in the early drafts. *Abyss*. Cf. 'If by *abyss* we understand a great depth, is not man's heart an abyss?'—quoted from St. Augustine by MacCaffrey in an interesting discussion of the word (*Paradise Lost as Myth*, 116–18).

843–4. Adam's words recall the language of Satan at IV, 76–7:

> And in the lowest deep a lower deep
> Still threatening to devour me opens wide.

But when we compare Adam's speech here with Satan's soliloquy on Mount Niphates (IV, 32–114), we see that there is hope for Adam just because he fully admits his fault.

845–908. *In his misery Adam repels Eve's attempt to comfort him, and abuses the institution of marriage.*

846–50. A critical, perhaps over-critical, scrutiny has detected inconsistencies in Milton's time scheme. The 'damps' which Adam now feels are clearly due to the changes in climate which God made after he saw Sin and Death reach Earth (650, etc.). But Satan stayed on Earth long enough to hear the laments of Adam and Eve (341, etc.), and met Sin and Death still on their way to Earth.

850–1. The repetition adds to the pathos. Such repetition is technically termed 'epanaphora', but here deserves to be called 'incremental repetition'.

858–9. *Death comes not at call* may be a reminiscence of a similar phrase in Sophocles (*Philoctetes*, 793) and in Spenser (*Daphnaida*, 355); while the slow pace of Divine Justice recalls Horace's *Pede Poena claudo* (*Odes*, III. ii. 32).

860–2. In their morning hymn Adam and Eve had taught their Creator's praise to Hill, Valley, and Fountain (V, 202–4); while 'resound' might suggest a grim contrast with the shepherd in Virgil's *Eclogue* causing the groves to 'resound' the name of his mistress: *Formosam resonare doces Amaryllida silvas.*

867. *Out of my sight:* So Samson upbraids Dalila: 'Out, out, Hyena' (*S.A.*, 748). Readers may well differ as to how far they think the denunciation of women and of marriage that make up this paragraph are prompted by Milton's own first unhappy marriage. It is dramatically appropriate that Adam should transfer his own blame to another; but 898–908 goes beyond his experience.

873–80. This is one of the most complex sentences in *P.L.* The skeleton is: 'I would have remained happy, if thy pride had not rejected my forewarning, and disdained not to be trusted . . . but, meeting with the Serpent, been fooled and beguiled by him, as I was by thee into trusting. . . and not understanding that there was no solid virtue in thee, who art nothing better than an unwanted rib from my side which had better have been thrown away.' (This paraphrase treats 'understood' as if it was 'understand', parallel with 'to trust' (881); but in fact the poet had substituted a main verb, as it is glossed in the foot-note to 883.)

887. The Bible merely says that God took one of Adam's ribs when he was asleep (Gen. 2:21–2); legend added that it was an extra rib and in Adam's left side, which allows the play on the literal and metaphorical meanings of 'Sinister'. The creation of Eve is described at VIII, 465, etc.

The 'crooked by nature' has been illuminated by this quotation from a late medieval book on witchcraft: 'there was a defect in the formation of the first woman, since she was formed from a bent rib, that is a rib of the breast, which is bent as it were in a contrary direction to man's. (*Malleus Maleficarun* of Krämer and Springer, quoted by Svendsen).

888–95. The thought that it would have been better for the human race to have been propagated without the need of women occurs in Milton's favourite Greek tragedian Euripides twice (*Hippolytus*, 616–24 and *Medea*, 573–5), in Shakespeare's *Cymbeline* (in the mouth of Posthumus), and in Sir Thomas Browne's *Religio Medici* of 1642. Hazlitt makes Lamb say 'Who would not be curious to see the lineamants of a man who, having been himself twice married, wished that mankind were propagated like trees?' (*Of persons one would wish to have seen*).

909–46. *Eve humbly implores Adam to let her take all the blame upon herself; and receives his forgiveness.* Here, if anywhere, said Tillyard, is the crisis of *Paradise Lost*. It is somewhat perverse to put the crisis anywhere else than in the Fall itself; but it is hardly possible to over-estimate either the importance or the beauty of the passage. This time the influence of 'female charm' on Adam is for good. 'Eve's love makes the reconciliation to God possible by removing the hardness and bitterness from Adam's heart, and by reviving the human love that can alone reopen the way to the love of God' (B. A. Wright). Observe the broken rhythm and the overflowing line (924, cf. 943), suiting the speaker's agitation. Further remarks on the style of the passage will be found in Select Criticism, p. 227.

910–12. We are naturally reminded of the woman who washed the feet of Jesus with her tears in the gospel (Luke 7:38).

911. Adam had previously been surprised to find Eve 'with tresses discomposed' after the bad dream which prefigured her temptation. Then also she had embraced Adam (V, 10 and 27).

914. The words 'Forsake me not thus' and 'forlorn of thee' are perfectly appropriate here; but older critics liked to note that the former correspond to those of Philoctetes imploring the young Neoptolemos not to abandon him alone on an island in the *Philoctetes* of Sophocles, and the latter to words of Tecmessa to Ajax in his play the *Ajax*.

926. The *doom express* was God's judgement on the Serpent: 'I will put enmity between thee and the woman' (Gen. 3:15).

929 (and 935–6) take us back to Messiah's taking upon himself the guilt of man in III, 236–41. In all these passages, as also in XI, 32–4, we have a triple 'Mee', like that in Virgil (*Aeneid*, ix. 427):

Me, me, adsum qui feci, in me convertite ferrum.

931. Cf. 'Against Thee only have I sinned' (Ps. 51:4).

935. *all this woe:* almost a *leitmotif* of the epic from the third line 'all our woe'; cf. 'all that pain' of Ceres, IV, 271.

940–3. 'Probably Milton's reconciliation with his wife was present to his thoughts' wrote Verity, following older critics, only to provoke a strong protest in 1962 that 'to substitute Mary Powell for Eve is an impious fraud' (Wright)! There is no need to know the story of Milton's reconciliation with his first wife to justify these lines; but it seems pointless to deny that the poet's own experience may have contributed something to the pathos of 899–900 and 943, and the humanity of the whole passage.

947–65. *Adam thinks that nothing but mutual love can lighten the punishment that both must share.*

960–1. *light'n Each other's burden:* cf. 'Bear ye one another's burdens' (Gal. 6:2).

963. *slow-pac't evil.* Did Milton (subconsciously perhaps) recall the 'lazy-pacing clouds' of Shakespeare (*Romeo and Juliet*, II. ii. 11)?

965. Later on Eve is encouraged by a dream to feel that not all her Seed will be 'hapless':

> though all by me is lost,
> Such favour I unworthie am vouchsaft,
> By me the Promis'd Seed shall all restore. (XII, 621–3)

966–1006. *Eve proposes that they should remain childless, or, if that would be too difficult, commit suicide.* There is, of course, no biblical foundation for Eve's proposals; but it has been noted that the second proposal occurred in the drama by Andreini mentioned in Appendix II.

968–9. The words of Eve that had proved most erroneous were those in which she argued that they should garden separately, and those by which she persuaded Adam to taste the Tree.

976–7. The *relief* is the proposal to avoid having children (979–91); the *end* is the proposal of self-destruction (992–1006).

989–90. It is curious that till the sixth edition of 1695 these lines were divided unmetrically at 'remaine', although there was no other case of such a serious error in the early editions.

1007–the end. *Adam replies by recommending fortitude instead of despair, and proposes that they should seek alleviation of their new condition, but, above all, that they should show contrition and beg mercy from God.*

1008–9. Similarly Dido's cheeks had become pale at the thought of death (*Aeneid*, iv. 499 and 644).

1016–19. The argument seems to be that Eve showed excellence in not rating too highly the pleasures of sense which their life had enjoyed, but that in seeking to prevent life for their offspring because it would not be so pleasant and easy as before their parents' sin, she was overrating these things. 'Self-destruction' here probably means prevention of offspring, since suicide comes later, in 1020.

But it is possible that Adam is only imputing to Eve two motives for coveting death, viz: (1) contempt for life, 1012–15 and (2) a desire to end their present and future misery, 1016–19.

1024–6. So Ames (see Commentary at IX, 1132) had said that Death was not mere extinction of life (*nuda privatio vitae*).

1033–5. Contrast 169–73. Adam now realizes that the words did not apply simply to the Serpent. He is saved from despair by the thought of the offspring promised him.

1046–7. Cf. 'mild Judge' (96).

1053, etc. 'Adam here shows that "better fortitude" of patience [IX, 41] which Milton set against the inferior fortitude of the conventional epic hero' (Tillyard).

1065. *Mountain:* The Garden of Eden had been placed on a hilltop by Dante and others, following Ezek. 28:13–14. The position is described in IV, 134 as 'champain head', i.e. a tableland.

1070–3. Milton fathers on Adam the idea of collecting the sun's rays in a mirror or some other reflecting surface to set light to dry matter, and goes on to an alternative method of making fire by friction, which he compares with fires started by lightning. The idea that fire started from lightning is in Lucretius (V, 1091, etc.).

Milton thinks of the air as being compressed between flint and flint, or flint and stone, and so producing fire. The technical process involves a Latinate diction (as in VI, 514).

1085. 'For dust thou art, and shalt to dust returne' (X, 208) = Gen. 3:19.)

1089–90. *With tears Watering the ground* is a Virgilian expression (*Aeneid*, xi, 191), while the (humble) confession of sins is of course biblical (Jas. 5:16, and 1 John 1:9); so that the two books which Milton almost knew by heart remain together at the end.

1092. This long line can be brought within the pattern by elision of the open vowel sound at the end of 'sorrow' before the following vowel, and by slurring the adjoining vowels in the third syllable of 'humiliation'; but perhaps the inevitable slowing down may be meant to be appropriate to the mood described.

1086–96. Jewish legend had assigned elaborate penances to Adam and Eve, which Milton's good taste, as well as his Protestantism, rejected.

1098–1104. repeats with very slight change 1086–1104, a device which occurs more elaborately at IV, 641–56. But it is more important to see it as emphasizing the essential step in man's restoration—penitence and confession—in contrast to the 'mutual accusation . . . neither self-condemning' which ended Book IX. At the same time the 'togetherness', which began to break up when Eve withdrew her hand from Adam in IX, 385–6, has been restored to the 'mutual help And mutual love, the Crown of all our bliss' (IV, 727–8). But the regeneration is not completed till Book XII.

SELECT CRITICISM

[THE edition of *Paradise Lost I and II* published in 1962 by the O.U.P. contained one appendix of ten pages in which Professor Prince surveyed 'Milton's Critics' from Addison to C. S. Lewis and Douglas Bush. The present volume offers something complementary in a selection from those critics themselves, so far as they provide matter relevant to the content of Books IX and X. The critics are grouped, as far as possible, by subject, with the addition of the date and the exact title for those who feel inclined to follow up that writer. The choice of passages has been dictated partly by what seemed to the editor intrinsic merit, but also by the wish to illustrate what topics in these books have interested critics, and what has been their reaction to the poetry of Milton. It is not intended that all the opinions quoted should be found consistent with one another. To the student who wishes to begin with a few more general books the following may be recommended:

D. Daiches: *Milton.*
K. Muir: *Milton.*
W. Raleigh: *Milton.*
B. A. Wright: *Milton's Paradise Lost.*
C. S. Lewis: *A Preface to Paradise Lost.*
D. Bush: *Paradise Lost in our Time.*
J. H. Summers: *The Muse's Method.*
C. Ricks: *Milton's Grand Style.*
H. Gardner: *A Reading of Paradise Lost.*

The two best books for the *background* of *Paradise Lost* are now:

J. M. Evans: *Paradise Lost and the Genisis Tradition* (1968).
C. A. Patrides: *Milton and the Christian Traditions* (1966).]

A Christian Poem

I should like for a moment to insist on the Christian character of the poem in all its explicitly stated doctrines. Milton's lesson is not contained in any new reading of Christian theology. *Paradise Lost* is not a theological poem in the measure in which Dante's is. This has been a little obscured of late by the interest awakened by M. Saurat's study of the *De Doctrina*. But if one is to understand how the poem was welcomed by Protestant Christianity from Ellwood, Addison, and others to Cowper, Foster, and the nineteenth-century Evangelicals, one must recognize that all the main and prominent doctrines of the poem are those of Evangelical Protestantism, unless we are to make the Calvinist doctrine of determinism a cardinal doctrine of all Protestantism, which I do not think it is. For this is the only doctrine which the poem expressly rejects, and it was rejected by the Quakers and by the Wesleyans at the outset. Everything else is in the poem—the Fall (through man's own free will); the corruption (though not the *complete* corruption) of man's will through the Fall; the Atonement through the Death of Christ; the renewal of Man's will through the Spirit, the Grace of God. . . .

In his treatment of the doctrine of God's prevenient grace there seems to me to be the same difference between his express recognition of the doctrine and the value which he attaches to it. To recover the full freedom forfeited by the Fall man needs the grace of God: [XI, 1–5 quoted]. But as a fact he seems to lay small stress on grace as communicated directly or through the mediation of sacraments. Man's will, is free, and on himself it depends whether, tempted, he falls like Adam, or overcomes every temptation like Christ, or, falling repents and sincerely repenting recovers his freedom like Samson. Man is free and thereby responsible for what happens to him in this world and the next—that is the whole burden of the message in these closing poems.

H. Grierson, *Milton and Wordsworth*, 1937.

More subtle and less easily refuted by concrete evidence is the second method by which certain scholars have sought to modernize Milton, for their method can best be described as a sort of critical mysticism. Determined primarily by the sceptical temper of our present time, and having its basis in modern psychological criticism, this approach to literature seeks to divorce Milton from his age less by warping or overlooking the *De Doctrina* than by openly acknowledging the treatise and then setting above it, as a court of higher and final appeal, the intuitions of the twentieth century critic. . . . To illustrate this impressionistic approach, let us consider the following remarks of E. M. W. Tillyard on the unconscious meaning of *Paradise Lost*:

The meaning of a poem is not the story told, the statements made, the philosophy stated, but the state of mind, valuable or otherwise, revealed by the sum of all the elements of the poem . . . and the only way to arrive at this meaning is to examine our minds as we read.

Mr. Tillyard, unsatisfied with the 'professed' meaning of *Paradise Lost* seeks for other, covert, but to him more valid, meanings by reading the epic and then comparing his reactions with Milton's explicit statements. When the two conflict, Mr. Tillyard pronounces his own impressions Milton's unconscious beliefs—the real convictions that Milton did not dare admit or did not realize that he held. . . .

By a study of the language of the seventeenth century and of contemporary documents that throw supplementary light on *Paradise Lost*, its author, and his age, the historical critic approaches an understanding of what the epic meant to Milton; and the critic approaches that understanding in direct proportion to the degree that he masters the supplementary material . . . I am unwilling to deny the value of historical criticism as a check on unbridled impressionism, especially when the impressions of Mr. Tillyard and his kind smack less of the seventeenth century than they do of our own, contemporary, Christian agnosticism. And finally, I am sufficiently ingenuous to hold that what men of the seventeenth century said in their writings is indicative of what they believed, even though modern psychologists dismiss the professions of these men as merely so many 'rationalizations' offered consciously or unconsciously to hide their more profound and unrealized convictions. For these reasons, therefore, I must reject Mr. Tillyard's conclusions and the intuitive approach to literature in which his conclusions originate. What Mr. Tillyard calls seventeenth-century unconscious meanings are actually twentieth-century impressions; and what he offers as an intimate psychological portrait of Milton is in reality little more than Mr. Tillyard himself.

If the 'New Movement' fails for one basic reason, that reason is the unwillingness of its exponents to recognize that one of our major English poets not only professed but also employed for serious artistic purposes a body of Christian belief that is today generally rejected or given at best perfunctory lip service. And failing to recognize this fact, they could offer no sound or considerable interpretation of Milton and his works. Behind *Paradise Lost* and its high argument is an aetiological explanation of the problem of evil, which is Christian, Protestant, and seventeenth-century to the core: Christian in its acceptance of the Hebraic explanation, Protestant in its reliance on the Bible and the Spirit alone, and seventeenth-century in its dogged assertion of Independency and the dignity of the common man. To understand *Paradise Lost*, we must not ignore this theological content or warp the poem from its chronological context.

M. Kelley, *This Great Argument*, 1941 (U.S.A.)

The new school emphasize what Milton says of temperance, the pagan virtue; but what Milton has most to say of is obedience and righteousness. The new school draw attention to his passionate and sensuous nature; but Milton scorned it and never gave it reign. The new school, some of them, make Milton out to have been a Puritan less and less as time went on and more of a freethinker and philosopher. But the course of his thought as it appears in his poetry and prose from first to last reveals him as more of a dissenter, to be sure, but unflinching in his belief in God and (if not in the Church) in the Bible, and less and less indulgent to the sense and earthly pleasure. He is more of a Puritan than ever, though just as he had left the Presbyterian chapel he now leaves the meeting house. Extreme dissent may look a little like free-thinking and paganism, but it is worlds away. The Bible is between.

E. S. Stoll, *Poets and Playwrights* 1930 (1965 ed.)

I cannot believe that Milton dedicated himself to the writing of his epic in the hope that he might in the writing of it convince himself and his readers of the 'reasonableness of Christianity'. Instead I believe that he chose this subject as allowing him the greatest possible scope for imagination and invention on the basis of known and accepted truths. Instead of concentrating on the difficulties of the subject, criticism is better employed in seeing what Milton made of its vast opportunities. . . . The doctrines to which Milton gives grand expression are of God's goodness and over-flowing bounty in creation, of his mercy to fallen man, and of his will and power to bring good out of evil. It is in man's response to the divine bounty and to the divine mercy that the religious feeling of the poem is purest and strongest, as its ethical and moral force lies in the strength with which it affirms the freedom of the will with the consequent dignity that this bestows on man as a responsible being, and the beauty with which it displays the joys and consolations of mutual love. Such dark questions as to why an ill will rose among the angels, natives of heaven, the poem is not concerned to answer. . . . Milton could rely here, as he could throughout his poem, on what Grierson elsewhere calls 'an unbounded reverence for the Bible', and invent and elaborate on a base that he could not imagine would ever be questioned. He knew that the whole story was in a sense a fiction, a divinely inspired fiction as he believed. The God of the Bible, and the God of his poem, was not the God who dwells in light inaccessible, who is 'higher than our highest thoughts and more inward than our inmost', but an image of him, capable of being grasped by minds living in space and time. Throughout his poem he reminds us of the existence, behind the drama he presents, of this God 'dark with excessive bright'. He can no more have thought the Father of his poem to be God as He is than Michelangelo can have thought his mighty Ancient creating Adam to be anything but a faint image of the Author of all being. To think of Milton as conceiving of God as the strategist and ironist of his poem is as naïve as to think of Michelangelo as believing that God possessed a pair of powerful legs. Both Milton and Michelangelo had to accept the limitations of their art, through which they expressed conceptions beyond the reach of narrative and pictorial images. I think we read *Paradise Lost* best if we read it in the spirit in which we look at great Renaissance paintings of Christian subjects. Much modern criticism of the poem seems to me as beside the point as asking, when we look at a superb painting of the Adoration of the Magi, how these magnificent figures have managed to traverse the snowy landscape in the background without getting snow on their boots, or complaining as we look at a paint-ing of the Assumption of the Virgin that the artist still has not managed to convince us of the possibility of solid bodies being suspended in mid air without visible means of support.

H. Gardner, *A Reading of Paradise Lost*, 1962

THE FALL

The first couple of mankind show how delightful and complete life can be in a state of innocence. This perfect harmony is broken, and in showing how this happens Milton follows a scheme that recalls Greek tragedy. The material from which the tragic crisis arises is the conflict of Adam's loyalties to God and to Eve. The power that starts the crisis comes from outside in Satan, but his power makes use of the potential weakness which it finds in Adam and drives him to choose wrongly, to break the harmony of existence by disobeying God, and so to precipitate a tragic situation in which life has lost all its charm and death seems desirable. Milton uses the ancient device of the Warner in Raphael, and treats Adam's fault in the Greek manner as the excess of what is in moderation a virtue. . . .

He finds himself torn between his love of God and his love
of Eve, and he decides to follow the second. He cannot
endure to live without Eve, and since he believes that she
is now doomed to die, he prefers to die with her [IX, 908–
10 quoted]. In this state of mind, knowing well how
wrongly he is acting, Adam gives in to his love for Eve,
and the irreparable evil is done. Like other tragic heroes,
he has been faced by choice between two conflicting
desires, and he follows the wrong one.

C. M. Bowra, *From Virgil to Milton*, 1945

THE FALL AND ORIGINAL SIN

God's plan for mankind is that it should be 'one body'.
But something has gone wrong. The organism has some-
how failed to function as one body. It has come to be
divided into countless little bits of life, each person trying
to be a quite independent cell, a self-sufficient atom,
dancing on a pattern of its own, instead of joining in the
great communal game of universal love. Each person
makes himself the centre of his universe, caring little for
the fellowship of the whole, but seeing things from his
selfish point of view; becoming his own God, and wor-
shipping himself. That is the universal aberration sym-
bolized in the 'myth' of the Fall of Man (it is the kind of
thing that can only be described in a 'myth', since we
cannot conceive of it as an event that occurred at a par-
ticular date in human history on earth, but as something
supra-historical, infecting all our history). In the story of
Eden the serpent says to the woman; 'Ye shall be as gods'.
That is the temptation to which mankind has succumbed:
we have put ourselves, each one individually, in the centre
of our universe, where God ought to be. And when persons

do that, it separates them both from God and from each other. That is what is wrong with mankind. That is original sin.

D. M. Baillie, *God Was In Christ*, 1948

ADAM'S CHIVALRY(?)

We have here, I would suggest . . . a perfect example of the sort of clash that we must sometimes expect in *Paradise Lost* between Milton's theory of a matter and the matter as he has actually presented it . . . 'Fondly overcome with Femal charm' (IX, 999) is simply Milton's comment on the recent course of events: events the true nature of which he has just been demonstrating to us. And between a comment and a demonstration . . . there can never be real question which has the higher validity. 'Femal charm' is merely Milton's way of inciting us to take a certain view of a matter that he has already presented with a quite different emphasis and to a quite different effect. . . . The matter may be summed up quite bluntly by saying that Adam falls through love—not through sensuality, not through uxoriousness, not (above all) through gregariousness—but through love as human beings know it at its best . . . and yet this noble (or at the very least half-noble) act constitutes the Fall of Man.

A. J. A. Waldock, *Paradise Lost and its Critics*, 1947

First let us make sure that we know what the offending words mean. 'Against his better knowledge, not deceav'd', that is as Eve was by Satan; Adam knows what he is doing, sins with his eyes open. 'Femal charm' is the seemingly preternatural, the irresistible power Eve exercises over him; and as he had told Raphael, this is a matter not only of her physical attractions but of all she means to him as the companion of his life—all that is expressed again in those two passages of passionate refusal to desert her. From the humanistic standpoint this may be 'love as human beings know it at its best'; but it is not for Milton the kind of love that leads up to heavenly love, any more than the love of Paolo and Francesca is for Dante. Adam prefers his love of Eve to love of God, and the immediate consequences is the corruption of the love he prizes so highly. As he eats the fruit he, like Eve before him, is all sensual appetite, and the immediate sequel is lust, 'in Lust they burne'. This is what Raphael had warned him of.

To say then that 'fondly overcome with Femal charm' is inconsistent with what went before is to say the reverse of the truth. As to Waldock's distinction between demonstration and comment, comment in narrative poetry is a proper means of demonstration if it comes at the right moment with the whole force of the argument and its action behind it. Here the comment falls like a hammer hitting its nail home; it is the consummation of the argument that started in Book VIII and has been worked out in the story. Milton has not once swerved from his course, even while living and pleading as Adam: he has kept control and brought us to his own foreseen conclusion. Of course Adam's words 'prove to us his feelings'; but Waldock assumes that they prove more, that they prove Adam to be in the right. Thus is a pathetic fallacy the great poet does not fall into; he feels strongly, thinks strongly and sees truly. Waldock on the contrary supposes that his irrepressible humanity unconsciously betrayed Milton into a sympathy with Adam that founders his conscious intentions. I find it more sensible to assume that so deliberate an artist as Milton knew just what he was about. Supposing he had not let Adam speak in a way that warms our hearts and commands our sympathy, making us feel he has no alternative but to act as he does, where then would have been the force of the situation, where the moral? We must feel to the full Adam's predicament, feel that he has no choice, before the poet comes down with his stern and measured judgement. We do not like it; it hurts our susceptibilities; it shocks us, as, in a contrary way (not acting 'against his better knowledge') Aeneas's desertion of Dido shocks us. Like Virgil, Milton puts religious duty above human desires.

B. A. Wright, *Paradise Lost*, 1962

Eve sins because her faculty of reason is deceived, while Adam sins by surrendering his reason to his passion . . . though we may applaud such sacrifice as a romantic gesture, we have to condemn it as a responsible act.

Rajan, *Paradise Lost and the Seventeenth-Century Reader*, 1947

Those who understand this alternation of the gentle and the stern understand Milton; here is the tenderness of the poetic mind, unseduced by the pathos it so exquisitely feels and portrays. Ruskin in his famous passage on the pathetic fallacy observes that the great poet feels strongly but also thinks strongly and sees truly: 'his mind is made up . . . it is not this or that which will at once unbalance him. He is tender to impression at the surface, like a rock with deep moss on it; but there is too much mass of him to be moved . . . Dante, in his most intense moods, has entire command of himself, and can look around calmly'. The words apply equally to Milton, who at the supreme moment of his story can make us feel the agony, the heartbreak of Adam's love for Eve, can make us sympathize wholeheartedly with his decision to sin with fallen Eve rather than desert her, and then can conclude

> he scrupl'd not to eat
> Against his better knowledge, not deceiv'd,
> But fondly overcome with Femal charm.

This shocks your modern humanist who has a touching faith in the sanctity of human weakness and folly. . . .

These words [IX, 952–9] are as irresistible as those of his silent resolution not to desert Eve, and leave us in no doubt of the compulsion of his love; and it is love untouched by sensuality. The poet is putting the issue in its most extreme form, piling up the odds as he moves to the climax of his story.

B. A. Wright, *Milton's Paradise Lost*, 1962

Adam fell by uxoriousness. We are not shown the formation of his decision as we are shown the formation of Eve's. Before he speaks to her, half-way through his inward monologue (896–916) we find the decision already made—'With thee Certain my resolution is to die'. His sin is, of course, intended to be a less ignoble sin than hers. Its half-nobility is, perhaps, emphasized by the fact that he does not argue about it. He is at the moment when a man's only answer to all that would restrain him is: 'I don't care'; that moment when we resolve to treat some lower or partial value as an absolute—loyalty to a party or a family, faith to a lover, the customs of good fellowship, the honour of our profession or the claims of science. If the reader finds it hard to look upon Adam's action as a sin at all, that is because he is not really granting Milton's premises. If conjugal love were the highest value in

Adam's world, then of course his resolve would have been the correct one. But if there are things that have an even higher claim on a man, if the universe is imagined to be such that, when the pinch comes, a man ought to reject wife and mother and his own life also, then the case is altered, and then Adam can do no good to Eve (as, in fact, he does no good) by becoming her accomplice. What would have happened if, instead of his 'compliance bad' Adam had scolded or even chastized Eve and then interceded with God on her behalf, we are not told. The reason we are not told is that Milton did not know. And I think he knows he does not know: he says cautiously that the situation 'seemed remediless' (919). This ignorance is not without significance. We see the results of our actions, but we do not know what would have happened if we had abstained. For all Adam knew God might have had other cards in His hand; but Adam never raised the question, and now nobody will ever know. Rejected goods are invisible.

C. S. Lewis, A Preface to Paradise Lost, 1942

Obedience is the proper order of the universe in relation to universal law.

C. Williams, preface to
Poems of Milton in 'World's Classics', 1941

'RIGHT REASON' [SEE IX, 351–6]

Right reason is not merely reason in our sense of the world; it is not a dry light, a non-moral instrument of inquiry. Neither is it simply the religious conscience. It is a kind of rational and philosophic conscience which distinguishes man from the beasts and which links man with

man and with God. This faculty was implanted by God
in all men, Christian and heathen alike, as a guide to truth
and conduct. Though its effectual workings may be
obscured by sin, it makes a man, in his degree, like God;
it enables him, within limits, to understand the purposes of
a God who is perfect reason as well as perfect justice,
goodness, and love. Hence the ancient pagans, to whom
the evangelical Christian is indifferent or hostile, are for
the Christian humanist men who achieved very positive
steps towards ultimate truth and virtue. Though even the
highest pagan wisdom, like Plato's, was the product of
only the natural reason, and must be fortified and illu-
minated by Christian revelation and love, that natural
reason was itself a divine gift and it sought the true light.
Since all truth is one, since man and the universe and God
are rational, the human reason is an ally, not an enemy, of
Christianity. Thus the Christian father Lactantius, quoting
Cicero's assertion that morality is founded on the eternal
law of right reason written in every human heart, could
claim that the utterance was well-nigh inspired. Thus
Erasmus could declare that there were perhaps more saints
than those named in the calendar and could add that
unforgettable phrase, 'Sancte Socrates, ora pro nobis'.
Thus Hooker, whose first book is such a magnificent
picture of the reign of law and reason in the universe and
in the mind of God and man, could affirm: 'The general
and perpetual voice of men is as the sentence of God
himself. For that which all men have at all times learned,
Nature herself must needs have taught; and God being the
author of Nature, her voice is but his instrument.' Thus
Jeremy Taylor, who so constantly quoted the ancients,
could say that 'the Christian religion in all its moral parts
is nothing else but the Law of Nature, and great Reason'.

Thus Benjamin Whichcote, the seminal mind of Cambridge Platonism, reinterpreted, and established as the sign-manual of the group the biblical phrase 'The spirit of man is the candle of the Lord', and insisted that right reason is found wherever true faith is found, that 'To go against Reason is to go against God. . . .' And thus Milton, to cite only one utterance maintains that the unwritten law of God 'is no other than that law of nature given originally to Adam, and of which a certain remnant, or imperfect illumination still dwells in the heart, of all mankind.

D. Bush, *Paradise Lost in our Time*, 1945

SATAN'S TEMPTATION OF EVE [IX, 679–732]

The speech itself is a feat not so much of logic as of legerdemain. It is crammed with specious argument, with sequences that look like syllogisms but stop before they have arrived, with stretches of reasoning that sound as if they are reaching a conclusion but do not quite reach it; and the ground is shifted every few seconds. What seems the same argument has turned in the twinkling of an eye into one that is really its opposite. It is a flashing string of incompatibilities, a glittering exhibition of plausible thought and spurious logic; and Eve, naturally, is bewildered. It is asking altogether too much of her to expect her to sort out and classify the fallacies in such a speech while she is listening to it. She has no more chance of *thinking out* what the tempter is saying than most of us have of detecting the flaws in what a bond salesman is telling us—while he is telling us. Our only defence (as hers would have been) is a closed mind. And that, of course, is the point: her mind has been opened: his words have 'too easie entrance won'.

The movement of thought is very interesting: There is the brilliant suggestion that the prohibition may be a trick of God's to test their courage, for if they risk death ('whatever thing death be') to achieve knowledge of Good and Evil they will have earned their Creator's praise indeed. If God punishes for this he will not be just; but if he is not just, how can he be God? So, momentarily, God is argued away. But the next moment he is back again, not this time as the God who may be testing them in an unexpected way, but in quite a different guise, as a God jealous of them, bent on keeping them down. God keeps slipping in and out of the argument like this and undergoes lightning changes in the process.

A. J. A. Waldock, *Paradise Lost and its Critics*, 1947

THE ALLEGORY OF SIN AND DEATH [BOOK X]

We are, in the last place, to consider the imaginary persons, as Death and Sin, who act a large part in this book. Such beautiful extended allegories are certainly some of the finest compositions of genius; but as I have before observed, are not agreeable to the nature of an heroic poem. This of Sin and Death is very exquisite in its kind, if not considered as a part of such a work. The truths contained in it are so clear and open, that I shall not lose time in explaining them; but shall only observe, that a reader who knows the strength of the English tongue, will be amazed to think how the poet could find such apt words and phrases to describe the actions of those imaginary persons, and particularly in that part where Death is exhibited as forming a bridge over the chaos; a work suitable to the genius of Milton. . . .

It is plain that these I have mentioned, in which persons

of an imaginary nature are introduced, are such short allegories as are not designed to be taken in the literal sense, but only to convey particular circumstances to the reader, after an unusual and entertaining manner. But when such persons are introduced as principal actors, and engaged in a series of adventures, they take too much upon them, and are by no means proper for an heroic poem, which ought to appear credible in its principal parts. I cannot forbear therefore thinking that Sin and Death are as improper agents in a work of this nature as Strength and Necessity in one of the tragedies of Aeschylus, who represented those two persons nailing down Prometheus to a rock, for which he has been justly censured by the greatest critics.

Addison, *The Spectator*, no. 357, 1712

Milton's allegory of Sin and Death is undoubtedly faulty. Sin is indeed the mother of Death, and may be allowed to be the portress of hell; but when they stop the journey of Satan, a journey described as real, and when Death offers him battle, the allegory is broken. That Sin and Death should have shown the way to hell, might have been allowed; but they cannot facilitate the passage by building a bridge, because the difficulty of Satan's passage is described as real and sensible, and the bridge ought only to be figurative. The hell assigned to the rebellious spirits is described as not less local than the residence of man. It is placed in some distant part of space, separated from the regions of harmony and order by a chaotic waste and an unoccupied vacuity; but Sin and Death worked up a 'mole' of 'aggregated soil', cemented with 'asphaltus'; a work too bulky for ideal architects.

Johnson, 'Milton' in *Lives of the Poets*, 1779

BASIC THEMES AND RHYTHMS

The poem is based on a series of massive antitheses, or if you like huge structural pseudo-rhymes, and the central pseudo-rhyme is *delight/woe*. The delight and woe are here and now, which is the real point of all the squeezing together of the time-sequence that Milton carries on in his similies, in upsetting allusions to clerical corruption, in using expressions like 'never since created man' or 'since mute' . . . The poem is absolutely contemporary, and its subject is human experience symbolized in this basic myth, and here made relevant in a manner not so different from that to which our own century has accustomed us. . . .

Paradise Lost deals most directly with this basic theme, the recognition of lost possibilities of joy, order, health, the contrast between what we can imagine as human and what is so here and now; the sensuous import of the myth of the lost Eden. To embody this theme is the main business of *Paradise Lost*; thus will life be displayed in some great symbolic attitude and not be the poet's explanations of the how and the why. His first task is to get clear the human experience of the potency of delight, and its necessary frustration, and if he cannot do that the poem will fail, no matter what is added of morality, theology or history. . . .

Milton saw the chance in Book IX, of presenting very concretely the impact of Death on Life; and it would be hard to think of a fiction more completely achieved. The moment is of Eve's return to Adam enormously ignorant and foolishly cunning, 'with Countnance blithe . . . but in her Cheek distemper flushing glowd'. This flush is a token of unimmortality; and then, since 'all kinds' are to be affected, the roses fade and droop in Adam's welcoming garland. He sees that Eve is lost, 'Defac't, deflowrd, and now to Death devote'. He retreats into Eve's self-deception; but all is lost.

F. Kermode in The Living Milton, 1960

The entire poem is built upon a few themes: love, creation, battle, fall, and praise. Each theme implies its opposite (hate, destruction, peace, rise, and disdain) and each is almost endlessly repeated and varied as it occurs in Hell or Heaven or Paradise, in and out of time and in the sequence of the poem. Partial units composed of all five themes repeatedly occur in the three major settings of the poem, and all of them together unite to form that one 'action' which is the subject; the patterned relationship between God and man throughout time and eternity. Eve's speech [X, 914–36] is crucial to the earthly and the total pattern. It is a speech of human love after man's fall, and it marks an end to the battle between man and woman —otherwise as endless as the war between the angels would have been without the direct intervention of the Son. It is the prelude to renewed praise, and it makes possible continued·life and a new creation. Eve offers herself as a redeemer, and however inadequate she is to fulfil that role, her attempts mirror the redemptive actions of the Son, both in His first moment of undertaking and throughout the poem. It also reflects the previous distortions of that action by Satan, Adam, and herself. And it points forward to Adam's attempts at the redeemer's role and to her own role as the mother of the Redeemer, when the second Eve will be addressed by the angel with 'Hail'.

J. H. Summers, The Muse's Method, 1962

Milton's Style

It is true of course that the more one knows of all thought and learning and literature, the richer one's understanding and enjoyment of Milton are. But the same thing may and must be said about any serious writer, the learned Donne and the unlearned Shakespeare among others. The more important fact is that Milton used to be and still is, an essentially popular poet. For many generations a great many ordinary people read *Paradise Lost*—very often, no doubt, with a more or less unaesthetic scale of values—as ordinary people never did or could read Donne's *Anniversaries*. If those fastidious intellectuals whose noses are in great indignation at anything popular are moved to ejaculate, 'so much the worse for Milton!' they must also outlaw most of the really great writings of the world, from Homer and the Bible onward. After we have listened to all that is said about Milton's remote learning and his un-English obscurity of style, we may still safely guess that about 90 per cent of his verse can be understood with sufficient ease and fullness by a modern reader of normal education and intelligence without special literary training. That reader might miss much in the way of aesthetic and philosophic refinements, though perhaps not more than sophisticated anti-Miltonists miss, and he might see a good deal more than they of what Milton strove to utter. Could that same reader comprehend 10 per cent of Mr. Eliot's major poems? The question is not a peevish *argumentum ad hominem*; it has to do with the whole character and standing of poetry in Milton's age and ours.

D. Bush, op. cit.

THE STYLE OF X, 914-36

I wish that this passage could be read again and again by those who believe that Milton could only write the grand style grandly, that his 'natural port' was always 'gigantic loftiness'. Nothing Eve says could be said more simply and directly, yet those words, so ordinary and so humanly contrite, ring always with that secure and steadfast gravity by which the finest of Milton's writing is sustained. The order, the grace of it is undeniable; yet the cadence is one of feeling rather than logic and once again it is the sound and syntax which make this cadence possible. The repeated couplings ('love . . . and reverence', 'beg and clasp', 'strength and stay') together with the varying but recurrent supplication ('Forsake me not', 'Bereave me not', 'On me exercise not') establishes very quietly the reiterative mood of the passage. Then, after the fifteenth line, these devices are discarded and over the persistent throbbing *mes* the emotion rises gently to its climax, the measured acceptance of responsibility, so different and yet so inevitable a consequence of the plea for protection with which the passage began.

B. Rajan, *Paradise Lost and the Seventeenth Century Reader*, 1947

MILTON AND THE MODERN WORLD

The superiority of the *Paradise Lost* (to the *Iliad*) is obvious in this respect, that the interest transcends the limits of a nation. But we do not generally dwell on this excellence of the *Paradise Lost*, because it seems attributable to Christianity itself . . . nay, still further, inasmuch as it represents the origin of evil, and the combat of evil and good, it contains matter of deep interest to all mankind, as forming the basis of all religion, and the true occasion of all philosophy whatsover.

S. T. Coleridge, from the *Lectures on Milton* of 1818

Basic to the whole ethic [of Milton] is the doctrine of free choice and the correlative doctrine of individual responsibility for individual actions of which we have made so much. We make so much of it because Milton does, primarily, but also because it is the fashion of our age (and its greatest danger) to deny the inner freedom in which Milton believed and the responsibility which goes with it. For our age has accepted a determinist philosophy which explains human weakness solely in terms of shaping environment and heredity, and completely excuses it. . . . Grierson is a generation behind the fashion in appealing only to the 'heredity' of Adam and Eve, and not to the enervating environment of Eden, as Tillyard does: for modern sociology prefers to blame environment. But the philosophical determination implicit in either explanation of human misconduct is widespread. It pervades not abstract philosophy alone, but also much of our political and social thought and the most successful of our contemporary literature. Certainly Milton would have none of it.

For in the terms of this philosophy or any other form of determinism, whether springing from a belief in a pre-destinating god or from the acceptance of a mechanistic metaphysic, men are not responsible for their deeds. Praise and blame become meaningless, right and wrong non-existent. The only question proper about an action are 'What is it?' and 'What' (not who) 'brought it about?' For in a sense one not responsible for his deeds does not do them. His grandfather does them, or the neighbourhood in which he was born, or the fates, or the stars, or something he saw in the woodshed at the age of three. This is the weakling's effort to shift responsibility; and it is not only untrue, it is unworkable. Therefore even modern determinists, when they have the courage to deal with problems of conduct, affirm the necessity of acting *as if we had a choice*, and their ethic is based upon a fiction. . . . Every age invents its own excuse, and the wise of every age reject it. Milton believed the human spirit capable of standing firm and uncorrupted in the presence of danger or desire and capable of rehabilitation if it failed.

J. S. Diekhoff, *Milton's Paradise Lost. A Commentary on the Argument*, 1946

The modern world has moved quite away from the old assumptions and doctrines of religious, ethical, social, and cosmic order and right reason. It is perhaps a fair guess that among the general reading public three out of four persons instinctively sympathize with any character who suffers and rebels, and pay little heed to the moral values and responsibilities involved, because in such cases the sinner is always right and authority and rectitude are always wrong. We have much more sympathy with *virtù*, which is always exciting, than with virtue, which is always smug. This instinctive response has of course grown the stronger as religion and morality have been increasingly sapped by romantic naturalism and sentimentalism. So thoroughly are we debauched by these flabby 'liberal' doctrines that when we encounter an artist who passionately affirms the laws of justice, reason, and righteousness, the laws that grow not old, we cannot understand his high convictions and purposes, and either turn from them in disgust or explain them away. . . . To celebrate Milton therefore as the great champion of a religious and ethical orthodoxy is to bring ignominy upon him. As Hooker said in opening his defence of divine and human reason against dogmatic and irrational Calvinism, a rebel always finds a ready and admiring audience, whereas one who maintains things established has to meet a number of heavy prejudices. And Milton, the great Puritan enemy of the Anglican church, was in the same tradition of Christian humanism as Hooker. . . .

Indifference or hostility to Milton is not a mere matter of liking or disliking a particular poet; it belongs to the much larger question whether the tastes and standards of our generation reflect spiritual health or disease. It is rather doubtful whether we do hold the faith and morals which Milton held. . . .

Our modern worship of science and technology has revealed its inadequacy, and in losing hold of the classical Christian tradition we have lost our way. Milton is one of the greatest of the men whose experience and whose writings can help us to understand the meaning of that tradition and the true nature and goal of mankind.

D. Bush, op. cit. (near the beginning and at the end)

THE POETRY

After I have been reading *Paradise Lost*, I can take up no other poet with satisfaction. I seem to have left the music of Handel for the music of the streets, or, at best, for drums and fifes. . . . Averse as I am to anything relating to theology, and especially to the view of it thrown open by this poem I recur to it incessantly as the noblest specimen in the world of eloquence, harmony and genius.

Landor, *Imaginary Conversations* (Southey and Landor),
1824–9

One reads great poetry, not to agree or disagree, but to grow.

W. M. Parker, *Milton: A Biography*, 1968

The following are the names of books by critics quoted in the Commentary where that title is not already given there or in Select Criticism:

Burden, D. H.: *The Logical Epic.*
Empson, W.: *Milton's God.*
Mackail, J. W.: *The Springs of Helicon.*
Mahood, M.: *Poetry and Humanism.*
McCaffrey, I. G.: *Paradise Lost as Myth* (U.S.A.).
McColley, G.: *Paradise Lost* (U.S.A.).
Stein, A.: *Answerable Style* (U.S.A.).
Taylor, A. E.: *Plato.*

APPENDIX I

Text, Spelling, Punctuation, Metre

THE Text printed in this edition of Books IX and X is, like that in Prince's edition of Books I and II published by the O.U.P. in 1962, the text edited by Helen Darbishire in *The Poetical Works of Milton* (two volumes, 1952), and reprinted in one volume in the Oxford Standard Authors series in 1958. It is based on the first edition (as had been the earlier Oxford edition of Beeching), but with a few corrections to bring it into line with what would appear to have been the poet's intentions as seen in the corrections of the second edition and the surviving manuscript of Book I.

The present editor recognizes that the original spelling and punctuation here preserved create some difficulties for a modern reader; but serious students of English poetry, who will constitute most of the users of an edition like this, have the right to read a poem in the form intended by its author, more particularly when that author is among the world's greatest artists, and one so particular about details as to insert the correction 'for *we* read *wee*' (at II, 414). Editions of *Paradise Lost* in modern spelling and punctuation are readily available; and those who are capable of studying Milton profitably are not likely to have their spelling disturbed by unfamiliar forms. Those who wish to have at hand the rest of the poem will find a good compromise in the re-edited *Everyman* Milton of B. A. Wright, where the spelling is modernized *except* where the original form seemed to the editor significant.

Most of the spellings in Milton's text can be found in other books printed in the seventeenth century; but on some points the poet was more concerned to show the pronunciation he desired than his printers would have been. He will, for example, vary the spelling of 'been' to 'bin' where he wants the voice to pass lightly over the unaccented syllable (e.g. IX, 806), or defy etymology in favour of sound by giving 'perfet' rather than 'perfect' (from Latin *perfectum*). Again in four successive lines (IX, 62–5) we find three cases of an apostrophe instead of an 'e' where the syllable does not count metrically, in the words 'driv'n', 'sev'n', and 'circl'd'.

The chief peculiarities of Milton's spelling may be summarized thus:

(1) Where a word can be pronounced as either one or two syllables, the distinction is made by the spelling: e.g. 'Heaven' or 'Heav'n'. The former is corrected to the latter in the manuscript at I, 136.

(2) Where a word can be accented in different ways, that desired may be indicated by the spelling: e.g. 'supreme' is to be accented on the first, but the usual spelling is 'supream', accented on the last; and 'femal' indicates that the last syllable is more lightly accented than in our usual speech. As in this example, final 'e' is generally dropped when it is not needed to lengthen the previous vowel.

(3) Personal pronouns may be given a more emphatic pronunciation by spelling, e.g. 'mee' for 'me', 'their' for 'thir'. This does not, however, seem to be quite consistently carried out in the text as we have it, perhaps on account of the poet's blindness. (Wright lays down that the longer spelling is not used where the pronoun is in a position of metrical stress already; but this is not borne out by X, 832 and 935–6).

(4) Where possible, the past tense of a verb is spelt with a 'd', and the past participle with a 't'. An apostrophe is only inserted where the omitted 'e' would have shown the preceding vowel to be long, e.g. 'rob'd' stands for 'rōbed', but 'robd' for 'robbed'.

(5) Words of identical sound but different meaning ('homophones') are distinguished, where possible, by spelling, e.g. 'counsel' and 'council'.

The editors of both the Oxford and the Everyman texts of Milton have applied these principles (which will be found more fully treated in their introductions) to places in the text where the printers appear to have ignored his intentions, which are chiefly derived from his own corrections in the surviving manuscript of Book I.

It may also be noted here that Milton used an initial capital letter not only at the beginning of verse lines, and for proper names, but also for many important words, not always nouns.

Punctuation will give less trouble than spelling. In general the stopping is lighter than in the following centuries, as it has been tending to become again recently; but it is not always as clear a guide to grammatical construction as that of prose normally is. For example, where we should place a comma at each end of a qualifying clause, we often find it at only one end in the text of *Paradise Lost* (e.g. X, 7). It may also be noted that a colon often replaces a full stop.

It has not been thought necessary to set out here the pattern of Milton's blank verse. Any students who are unfamiliar with it are advised to consult the Appendix on 'The Verse' in the excellent edition of the first two books by F. T. Prince. Irregularities of metre in Books IX and X are treated in the Commentary.

APPENDIX II

Milton's Sources

THERE are three main sources of *Paradise Lost:* The Bible, the Classics and Hexaemeral tradition. Speaking roughly, we may say that Milton took his subject matter from the first and last, but the structure and style of his epic from the second. His general debts to classical epic are not specially relevant to the study of these two books; while detailed debts are recorded in the Commentary. But there are no books, with the possible exception of Book VII (The Creation), more closely dependent on the Bible and connected literature. Milton's mind was full of the language and thought of the Bible. In his time at Cambridge undergraduates had to read the Bible in Latin, Greek, and Hebrew, as well as English; and this reading continued all through the poet's life. Among English versions he certainly knew and used the Geneva Bible of 1576, the favourite translation with the Puritans; but he would seem to have used the King James, or Authorized, Version of 1611 increasingly as he grew older, for his copy, published in 1612, contains his family records. It is therefore from this version that the chapter most important for the events of these two books is here reprinted for convenience of constant reference, viz. Genesis, chapter III:

1 Now the serpent was more subtil than any beast of the field which the LORD GOD had made. And he said unto the woman, Yea, hath God said, Ye shall not eat of every tree of the garden?

2 And the woman said unto the serpent, We may eat of the fruit of the trees of the garden:

3 But of the fruit of the tree which *is* in the midst of the garden, God hath said, Ye shall not eat of it, neither shall ye touch it, lest ye die.

4 And the serpent said unto the woman, Ye shall not surely die:

5 For God doth know that in the day ye eat thereof, then your eyes shall be opened, and ye shall be as gods, knowing good and evil.

6 And when the woman saw that the tree *was* good for food, and that it *was* pleasant to the eyes, and a tree to be desired to make *one* wise, she took of the fruit thereof, and did eat, and gave also unto her husband with her; and he did eat.

7 And the eyes of them both were opened, and they knew that they *were* naked; and they sewed fig leaves together, and made themselves aprons.

8 And they heard the voice of the Lord God walking in the garden in the cool of the day: and Adam and his wife hid themselves from the presence of the Lord God amongst the trees of the garden.

9 And the Lord God called unto Adam, and said unto him, Where *art* thou?

10 And he said, I heard thy voice in the garden, and I was afraid, because I *was* naked; and I hid myself.

11 And he said, Who told thee that thou *wast* naked? Hast thou eaten of the tree, whereof I commanded thee that thou shouldest not eat?

12 And the man said, The woman whom thou gavest *to be* with me, she gave me of the tree, and I did eat.

13 And the Lord God said unto the woman, What *is* this *that* thou hast done? And the woman said, The serpent beguiled me, and I did eat.

14 And the Lord God said unto the serpent, Because thou hast done this, thou *art* cursed above all cattle, and above every beast of the field; upon thy belly shalt thou go, and dust shalt thou eat all the days of thy life:

15 And I will put enmity between thee and the woman, and between thy seed and her seed; it shall bruise thy head, and thou shalt bruise his heel.

16 Unto the woman he said, I will greatly multiply thy sorrow and thy conception; in sorrow thou shalt bring forth children; and thy desire *shall be* to thy husband, and he shall rule over thee.

17 And unto Adam he said, Because thou hast hearkened unto the voice of thy wife, and hast eaten of the tree, of which I commanded thee, saying, Thou shalt not eat of it: cursed *is* the ground for thy sake; in sorrow shalt thou eat *of* it all the days of thy life;

18 Thorns also and thistles shall it bring forth to thee; and thou shalt eat the herb of the field;

19 In the sweat of thy face shalt thou eat bread, till thou return unto the ground; for out of it wast thou taken: for dust thou *art*, and unto dust shalt thou return.

20 And Adam called his wife's name Eve; because she was the mother of all living.

21 Unto Adam also and to his wife did the LORD GOD make coats of skins, and clothed them.

22 And the LORD GOD said, Behold, the man is become as one of us, to know good and evil: and now, lest he put forth his hand, and take also of the tree of life, and eat, and live for ever:

23 Therefore the LORD GOD sent him forth from the garden of Eden, to till the ground from whence he was taken.

24 So he drove out the man; and he placed at the east of the garden of Eden Cherubims, and a flaming sword which turned every way, to keep the way of the tree of life.

It used to be assumed that all additions to the story of the Fall as told in Genesis were due to the invention of Milton. But it is now known that many of these additions could have been found by the poet in Jewish sources of varying dates, mostly 'midrashes' or commentaries on Scripture. (The more interesting of these are mentioned in our

Commentary.) But here, as elsewhere, Milton felt himself free to accept or reject an explanation or a legend as he chose; and the sum of what he may have drawn from these rather obscure sources does not amount to a great deal (see Baldwin: 'Some Extra-Biblical Semitic Influence upon Milton's Story of the Fall of Man' in *J.E.G.P.* for 1929). More interesting and more important are some further expansions and variations on the biblical theme which had made their way into our native literature long before Milton, but have been pretty well ignored from his day until fairly recent times.

Most readers of *Paradise Lost* since its publication would have been able to name two of the three main sources, because these two were familiar to those readers themselves, the Bible and the Classics, more especially the epics of Homer and Virgil. Many of them would also have been able to recognize similarities to Spenser, whom Milton is reported to have called his 'original' (though this should not be taken as referring specially to *Paradise Lost*); and some might have suspected an occasional debt to the Italian Renaissance epics of Tasso, Boiardo and Ariosto. But few after the end of the seventeenth century would have connected *Paradise Lost* with other English poems on Biblical themes, because few of these were of sufficient poetic merit to have survived in general reading. Even the excellent and scholarly edition by Verity at the end of the nineteenth century makes almost no reference to the material dealt with here (apart from the dramas mentioned in the last paragraph). But *Paradise Lost* is in fact the culminating work of a long tradition, much of which must have been known to Milton, but which has only been revealed to us by the work of scholars in this century.

This body of work is entitled 'hexaemeral' or 'hexemeral'

literature, from the Greek words for 'six' (hex) and 'day' (hēmĕra), since it is primarily concerned with the story of the creation of the world in six days, and took its rise in the commentaries on the book of Genesis. But the term has come to be used loosely to include the fall as well as the creation of man and also the rebellion and the war in heaven. The first work of this type seems to be one written in Greek by the Alexandrian Jew Philo in the first century A.D., known by its Latin title *De Opificio Mundi*; and it was followed by many others. England made a comparatively early contribution to hexaemeral poetry in a work ascribed to the Anglo-Saxon Caedmon of the seventh century. This so-called *Later Genesis*, which forms the later part of the Caedmonian poem and is now thought to belong to the ninth century, was long ago dubbed 'a *Paradise Lost* in miniature' (Todd). There are anticipations of *Paradise Lost* in the fall of the rebel angels, who through self-love threw off the love of God, and in the passionate and defiant character of Satan; but, although one of the Anglo-Saxonists in London contemporary with Milton had a manuscript of the poem, there is no proof that Milton knew it. Moreover (as J. M. Evans points out) the trick by which Satan, pretending to bring a message from God, deceived Adam and Eve is very different from the biblical temptation. (There is a convenient translation in the Everyman volume of *Anglo-Saxon Poetry*.)

The sixteenth and seventeenth centuries saw a considerable outburst of hexaemeral poetry, some, like Cowley's *Davideis*, concentrating on the Creation proper, others on Satan's rebellion or the Fall of Man. 'From the varied books which made up this powerful and universally respected tradition Milton drew, consciously or unconsciously the great majority of the ideas, themes and episodes which

gave substance to his epic' (McColley). Of all this literature
the best known was the work of a Frenchman, Du Bartas,
called *La Sepmaine ou Creation du Monde* (1578) with its
sequel *La Seconde Semaine ou Enfance du Monde* (1584),
running into some 200 editions in fifty years. It was trans-
lated into English in 1605–6 by Joshua Sylvester as *The
Divine Weeks and Works*, and became very popular. 'In
the whole range of Jacobean poetry', wrote one of the
most acute of the older critics in 1909, 'the work to which
Milton has most recourse is a second-rate translation of a
second-rate original.' It was not till many years later that
a detailed study, *Milton's Use of Du Bartas*, was made by
an American scholar (1934), who 'ventures to establish
beyond dispute that no other work of the Renaissance had
a more important and definite influence on *Paradise Lost*'.
This influence is at its highest in the entry of Satan into
Paradise, the temptation of Eve, and the diseases that
afflict mankind after the Fall. Sylvester even supplied
Milton with one great line which was to provide a pattern
for others; viz. 'Immutable, Immortal, Infinite' (III, 373);
but otherwise the influence was almost entirely upon subject-
matter and not upon expression. A brief examination
of the work will enable the claims made for it to be more
fairly assessed.

Sylvester (Du Bartas) treats the subject of *Paradise Lost*
IX and X about halfway through his work in a book of
some 650 lines called 'The Deceipt'. He begins with the
contrast of Justice and Mercie, of which

> Th' one from Earth's Eden Adam did dismiss
> Th' other hath raised him to a higher bliss,

which is implicit in Milton. But where Milton gives us a
lively and dramatic story of the temptation we have nothing

but didacticism and endless similes in Du Bartas; nothing of Eve's gardening pleas or her giving the fruit to Adam. Instead we have about a hundred lines on Satan's determination to change his form. He discusses the nature of the change, in six numbered paragraphs, introduced by these lines:

> But now, to censure how this change befell
> Our wits come short, our words suffice not well
> To utter it: much less our feeble Art
> Can imitate this slie malicious part;

and concluding thus:

> But this stands sure, how ever else it went,
> Th' old Serpent serv'd as Sathan's instrument
> To charme in Eden with a strong illusion
> Our silly Grandame to her selfes confusion.

There follow twenty lines of simile, and thirty more of the various ways in which in later times Satan can play the Lion, the Dog, the Swine, the Nightingale and an Angel

> But (without numbering all thy subtle baits,
> And nimble jugging with a thousand sleights)
> Timely returning where I first digrest,
> I'll only heere thy first Deceipt digest.

and so we come to the actual temptation.

The Fall itself is as good as missed, being recorded in one commonplace line, followed by a long simile. At other points Eve is termed Adam's 'wanton fondling', and anyone who dares to question God's treatment of Adam is addressed as 'O dustie wormling'. When God finds Adam hiding himself after his sin he rebukes him in these words:

> Naked (quoth God) why (faithless renegade,
> Apostate Pagan) who hath told thee that?

Such specimens indicate the lack of dignity, or even decorum, in the most famous previous handling in verse of

> Adam's Doome in every sermon common,

and may serve to increase our appreciation of Milton's treatment of the same theme.

When we turn to the original English poets of the seventeenth century we may be fairly certain on general grounds that Milton would have known all those works in which modern scholars have suspected an influence. Chief of these are the Spenserian imitators, Giles and Phineas Fletcher. The former was the author of a work published in 1610 called *Christ's Victory and Triumph in Heaven and Earth*, which forms a link between Spenser and Milton, in form and language more akin to Spenser, in its subject nearer to Milton, particularly to *Paradise Regained*, but containing a conclave in Heaven like that in *Paradise Lost*. Phineas Fletcher published *The Apollyonists* in 1627, a satire on the Jesuits, which represents Satan as majestic and defiant, and gives a portrait of Sin as 'The Porter to th' infernal gate' which anticipates Milton's.

Nearer to Milton in date is the *Davideis* of Cowley, which appeared in 1656, just when Milton was starting to work on *Paradise Lost*. Milton's third wife is reported to have mentioned Cowley with Spenser and Shakespeare as his favourite poets, but, if the report is true, Cowley must have held third place *longo intervallo*! His *Davideis* is an epic in twelve books (the number being 'not for the Tribes sake, but after the Pattern of our Master Virgil') on the life of King David, but manages to include two scenes anticipating *Paradise Lost* in matter, where Satan